PRAISE FOR *AI-POWERED B2B MA*

"This is the book I have been waiting for. It is an essential guide for navigating the evolving B2B marketing landscape providing a clear, concise overview of the theories and practical strategies for integrating AI across all aspects of marketing. It is full of actionable tips, real-world examples and a comprehensive framework to leverage AI to help B2B marketers thrive in this rapidly changing environment."
Richard Robinson, General Manager, Confused.com

"As a marketing leader in the tech industry, I've already used AI in a lot of different ways, but I still found *AI-Powered B2B Marketing* eye-opening. Simon Hall makes complex topics easy to understand and backs them up with practical examples that sparked new ideas I can't wait to try. This is a great read for any B2B marketer who wants to keep learning, adapting and staying ahead in the age of AI."
Jayson Gehri, Vice President, Marketing, Delinea

"I've read all of Simon Hall's B2B Marketing books, and *AI Powered B2B Marketing* is yet another standout. It blends practical wisdom with forward-looking strategy, showing how AI enhances the timeless principles of great marketing. A brilliant, inspiring guide to how technology can empower both creativity and human connection – and a must-read for anyone shaping the future of marketing."
Mariana Pereira da Silva, Meetings and Events Manager, BCG Global

"Uniquely, and in true Simon Hall fashion, this text is a thoroughly researched and practical look across the entire B2B marketing mix through the lens of AI's potential to add demonstrable value. Simon's exhaustive work provides a clear, articulate and non-patronising step-by-step analysis of the landscape of potential tools and, critically, is underpinned by practical, real-world examples."
Paul Collier, CMO, FunnelFuel

"Surely no B2B marketer would deny that AI is the single most disruptive force in B2B – certainly now, and probably ever. But AI is still leaving many marketers confounded, not only in understanding its various forms and implications, but more importantly in how, where and when to deploy it. And this is where Simon Hall's book will be invaluable: it methodically unpacks, explains and demystifies how AI can be used to drive better B2B marketing. It's structured and pitched as an essential reference guide that will help marketers use AI in the right place, the right time and the right way, applying it to the key marketing channels and challenges being faced today. Someone had to write a handbook for B2B in the era of AI, and we must be thankful that Simon has risen to the challenge."
Joel Harrison, Founder, B2B Marketing

"Simon Hall's latest book is an invaluable resource for any B2B marketer. It serves as a practical and grounded guide on how to integrate AI across all aspects of marketing, offering brilliant insights on striking the right balance between human creativity and AI capabilities. The book demystifies a topic that can often feel overwhelming, especially for those of us who are learning and experimenting with AI in our roles. This will be a go-to reference for me in the years to come."
Helen Curtis, Founder, Coterie Marketing

"*AI-Powered B2B Marketing* arrives exactly when we need it most – at the start of what promises to be the most exciting chapter in our field. Simon Hall's AI B2B Marketing Framework gives us what we've been crying out for – a practical way to navigate AI's capabilities across every area of B2B marketing, covering both mainstream and niche tools with clear guidance on applying them for maximum impact.

With AI developing at breakneck speed and B2B marketers facing unique challenges, this book fills a critical gap. For anyone serious about staying ahead in B2B marketing, this is essential reading."
Ceris Burns, Founder, CBAi and Ceris Burns International

"*AI-Powered B2B Marketing* is an incredible guide for any B2B marketer looking to enable AI within their marketing. What sets this book apart is its perfect blend of strategy and practicality, with each chapter packed with proven models, actionable tips and clear ways of working that can be applied immediately. Rather than just talking about the potential of AI, it shows you exactly how to integrate it into your marketing operations to drive measurable impact. This is a must-read for any B2B marketer ready to transform how they work."
Catherine Dutton, Vice-President Global Marketing, Pegasystems

"*AI-Powered B2B Marketing* is a timely and essential guide for marketers navigating today's fast-evolving digital landscape. Simon Hall brings clarity and confidence to a complex topic, offering practical tools and real-world examples that show how AI can be embedded across the marketing mix. From lead generation to customer insight, content creation to campaign optimization, this book empowers marketers to work smarter, not harder.

For those who want to lead with confidence, unlock new levels of creativity, and deliver measurable impact, this is a powerful and practical resource."
Chris Daly, FCIM CMktr, Chief Executive, Chartered Institute of Marketing

AI-Powered B2B Marketing

Develop AI-enabled strategies and practices for maximum impact

Simon Hall

First published in Great Britain and the United States in 2026 by Kogan Page Limited

Kogan Page
Kogan Page Ltd, 2nd Floor, 45 Gee Street, London EC1V 3RS, United Kingdom
Kogan Page Inc, 8 W 38th Street, Suite 902, New York, NY 10018, USA
www.koganpage.com

EU Representative (GPSR)
Authorised Rep Compliance Ltd, Ground Floor, 71 Baggot Street Lower, Dublin D02 P593, Ireland
www.arccompliance.com

Kogan Page books are printed on paper from sustainable forests.

ISBNs
Hardback 978 1 3986 2198 5
Paperback 978 1 3986 2196 1
Ebook 978 1 3986 2197 8

British Library Cataloguing-in-Publication Data
A CIP record for this book is available from the British Library.

Library of Congress Cataloging in Publication Data
A CIP record for this book is available from the Library of Congress.

Typeset by Integra Software Services, Pondicherry
Print production managed by Jellyfish
Printed and bound by CPI Group (UK) Ltd, Croydon CR0 4YY

Laura, your enduring strength and radiant enthusiasm for life have fuelled me in writing this book; I can't thank you enough for being such a powerful source of inspiration.

CONTENTS

LIST OF FIGURES AND TABLES

FIGURES

TABLES

ABOUT THE AUTHOR

Simon Hall is a seasoned marketing innovator with over 30 years of experience in B2B marketing across direct and indirect channels in both EMEA and the UK. He served as UK Chief Marketing Officer at Dell from 2010 to 2016 and has held senior leadership roles at Microsoft, Acer and Toshiba.

Throughout his corporate career, Simon has successfully marketed to businesses of all sizes – from small enterprises to global corporations – across various verticals and distribution models. Notably, during his tenure at Acer, he built a business from the ground up, growing it to over £300 million within just four years.

Simon is passionate about redefining marketing boundaries and pioneered several innovative strategies. He is actively involved in key industry organizations, including the DMA & IDM B2B Council and the Chartered Institute of Marketing. He also shares his expertise as a senior lecturer at Henley Business School and the University of Kent.

In 2016, Simon founded NextGenMarketingSolutions to help businesses of all sizes overcome modern B2B marketing challenges and apply contemporary strategies to drive growth. He also serves as a Course Director for the Chartered Institute of Marketing.

PREFACE

AI-Powered B2B Marketing is a clear and practical guide that demystifies artificial intelligence in the context of B2B marketing. It explores key concepts, introduces innovative ideas and outlines processes for effectively applying AI across the full spectrum of B2B marketing functions.

In today's rapidly evolving digital landscape shaped significantly by advancements in AI over the past four to five years, marketing strategies are undergoing a fundamental transformation. This book aims to break down the major areas where AI is making an impact and demonstrates how it can be practically integrated into B2B marketing efforts.

Ideal for B2B marketers of all experience levels, as well as professionals looking to better understand or enter the B2B space, this guide offers valuable insights into how AI can enhance marketing performance. It's also a helpful resource for non-marketers seeking a practical starting point for using AI in specific B2B marketing tasks.

The book blends actionable tips and hands-on activities with a clear framework for understanding core AI concepts. It also features real-world examples from a variety of B2B sectors to illustrate how AI is being successfully implemented in practice.

Introduction

> What you will gain from this chapter
>
> Understanding of the following:
>
> - overview of AI
> - understanding of the role of AI in B2B marketing
> - key AI B2B marketing trends
> - AI use cases

Introduction

In less than 100 years we've moved through multiple eras of business and industry, from the production age through to the marketing age and recently from the globalization era to the era of digital and applications.

We've also seen a number of changes in business-to-business (B2B) marketing; in fact, from a recent survey it was stated that 68 per cent of B2B marketers feel marketing has changed more in the past three years than the previous 50 years (Howarth, 2024).

Customers are changing how they engage businesses, how they evaluate products and services and how they respond to marketing and sales efforts, and artificial intelligence (AI) has just impacted even further in the past decade.

What is AI?

AI refers to technologies capable of performing tasks that typically require human intelligence. These tasks may include decision-making, learning, understanding and recognizing patterns from data. AI has become increasingly prevalent across industries, providing innovative solutions in fields such as marketing, finance, healthcare and more.

AI can be categorized in several ways. One approach is to classify AI as narrow, general or super. Narrow AI focuses on very specific activities, such as language translation, and is commonly applied in B2B marketing to support speech-to-text transcription, keyword analytics or specialized business functions. General AI refers to systems that can perform any task a human can do, demonstrating versatility and adaptability. Super AI surpasses human intelligence and remains a theoretical concept, with potential implications for society and technology.

Another way to categorize AI tools is by their function. Examples include natural language processing (NLP), predictive analytics, machine learning and conversational AI. These tools address distinct needs, from interpreting human language to forecasting future trends or enabling human-like interactions.

A prime example of NLP and conversational AI is generative pre-trained transformer (GPT) models, which are a subset of large language models (LLMs). LLMs are advanced neural networks trained on vast amounts of text data to understand, generate and manipulate human language. GPT models, such as ChatGPT, leverage deep learning techniques to predict and generate coherent text, enabling applications in content creation, customer support and data analysis. These models can understand context, answer complex questions and even engage in dynamic conversations, making them valuable across various industries.

Machine learning is another critical component of AI, focusing on enabling systems to learn from data and improve performance over time without explicit programming. By identifying patterns and relationships within data, machine learning models can make predictions, automate processes and support decision-making. These models are widely used in fields such as fraud detection, personalized marketing and medical diagnostics, where continuous improvement and adaptability are essential.

History of AI in marketing

AI in marketing dates back to early developments in the 20th century

1950s–1980s: The concept of AI came about in the 1950s; at this point it was all about machines simulating human intelligence. The applications in the period were quite limited; early experiments were more academic in nature. Marketing during this period was still relying on traditional methods such as TV advertising and print marketing.

1990s–early 2000s: Between 1990s and early 2000s we see the increase in data being used in marketing. This was related to the advent of internet

FIGURE 0.1 Evolution over time

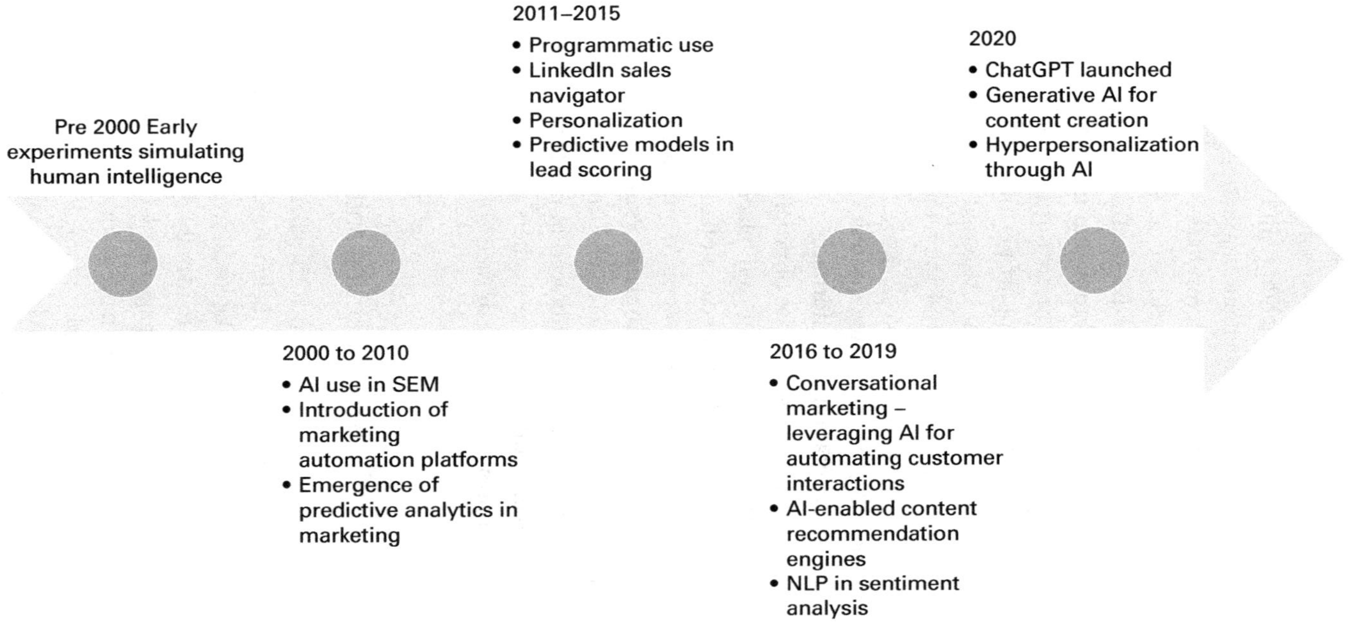

Pre 2000 Early experiments simulating human intelligence

2000 to 2010

- AI use in SEM
- Introduction of marketing automation platforms
- Emergence of predictive analytics in marketing

2011–2015

- Programmatic use
- LinkedIn sales navigator
- Personalization
- Predictive models in lead scoring

2016 to 2019

- Conversational marketing – leveraging AI for automating customer interactions
- AI-enabled content recommendation engines
- NLP in sentiment analysis

2020

- ChatGPT launched
- Generative AI for content creation
- Hyperpersonalization through AI

and digital technologies which allowed marketers to collect more data about customers. Customer relationship management (CRM) systems were introduced as well as marketing automation software. Email automations were introduced; examples were Mailchimp and salesforce.com. Marketing started to use AI also in search engine marketing, e.g. Google introduced AI-based ranking to improve search results.

2010s: During the 2010s we could see AI take automation to the next level as well as a greater degree of personalization facilitated through AI tools. AI has become more integral to digital marketing strategies enabling more personalized experiences. In the area of B2C we've seen Amazon and Netflix increasingly using AI to support personalized recommendations or for suggesting personalized content. AI-based chatbots were also increasingly used in tools such as Drift and Intercom, although this was largely used in the area of customer service.

AI-driven tools began optimizing content creation, predictive analytics and customer segmentation, transforming how businesses targeted and engaged with their audiences. The rise of programmatic advertising allowed companies to automate ad buying and placement using AI algorithms, enhancing the efficiency and effectiveness of ad campaigns.

2020s: In the past years we've seen AI powering other areas such as search optimization, sentiment analysis and supporting hyper personalization. Predictive analytics which have largely been used in operations, finance and other fields is starting to be embraced in marketing. Platforms such as HubSpot, salesforce, Adobe, Canva and others are now including AI features to enhance and improve experience of their solutions.

B2B marketing and AI

AI has had a significant impact on B2B marketing in a number of areas including lead generation, customer behaviour analysis and more.

Though AI technology leads can be identified and scored, AI tools help by analysing data from various sources to identify potential leads and assess their quality. By evaluating factors like engagement levels, company size and type of industry, AI tools can prioritize leads more accurately than traditional methods.

AI tools have also increasingly played a role in providing more accurate customer insights. For example, previous buying patterns can be analysed to support customer segmentation. Tools like Salesforce Einstein help businesses understand their customers better and tailor their strategies accordingly.

Another main area where AI tools work well is through analysing large volumes of data to identify market trends, market changes, market growth and other market research information.

AI tools also help improve marketing productivity and efficiency; marketing teams are seeing benefits from using tools such as speech to text, and team collaboration and project management tools.

In the area of content creation where marketing teams have been struggling to keep up with content creation requirements and personalization, AI can really alleviate some of the workload. AI tools can assist in creating, optimizing and repurposing content. Content can be optimized by analysing successful past content and predicting what will resonate with audiences.

AI tools in the area of predictive analytics can support marketing in different ways, by predicting market trends, predicting customer purchases, customer churn prediction and other areas of B2B marketing. Through predictive analytics markets can forecast customer needs, customer actions and optimize resource allocations. Examples are SAS Analytics which offer predictive analytics capabilities.

These are just some of the areas where AI is impacting and improving B2B marketing; we'll be exploring these areas and more in greater depth in the next chapters.

In Figure 0.2 we can find a selection of AI use cases in marketing aligned to four key areas. Please note this list is not exhaustive, and we will be providing a more extensive view of use cases through this book.

State of AI adoption in B2B marketing

The following are some recent statistics regarding AI in B2B marketing.

- According to a recent report from Gartner, 55 per cent of B2B organizations have adopted AI in some capacity, with many investing in AI to enhance their marketing strategies and operations (Gartner, 2023).
- B2B marketers are prioritizing investments in social media advertising (60 per cent), AI tools (60 per cent), video (53 per cent) and podcast advertising (50 per cent) in 2025 (McKinsey, 2024).

Key benefits of AI in B2B marketing

AI has delivers numerous benefits for B2B marketing. Here are some of the key benefits explained in detail:

ENHANCED PERSONALIZATION

One of the key benefits is enhanced personalization, which allows businesses to create tailored experiences with less effort, lower costs and reduced reliance

FIGURE 0.2 AI main use cases

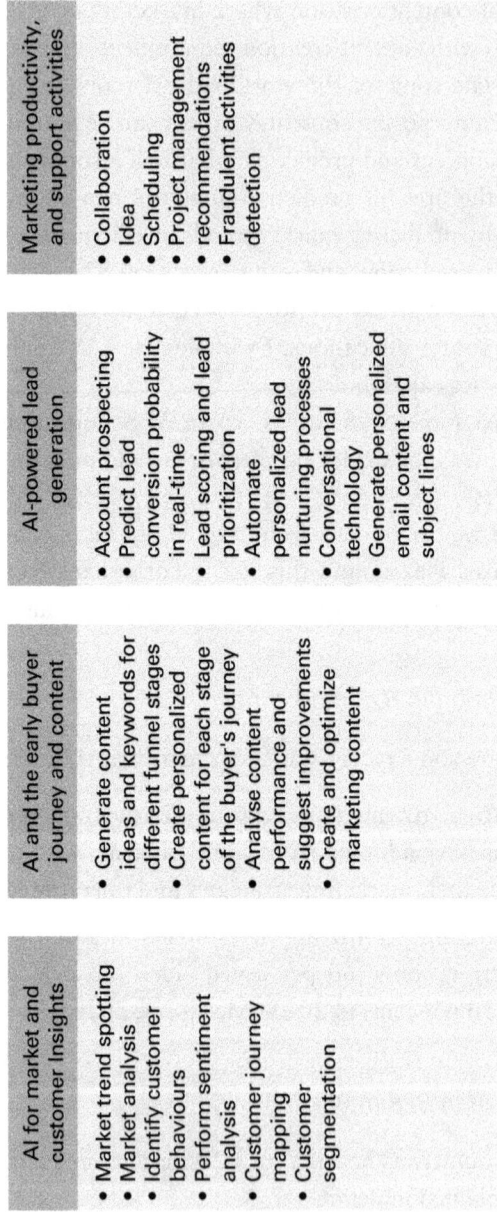

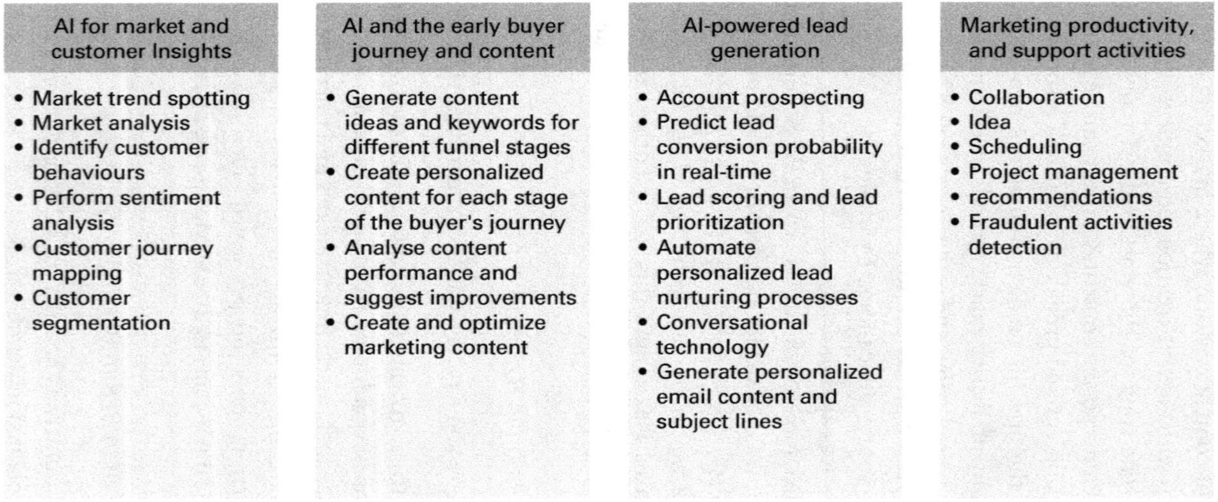

AI for market and customer Insights	AI and the early buyer journey and content	AI-powered lead generation	Marketing productivity, and support activities
• Market trend spotting • Market analysis • Identify customer behaviours • Perform sentiment analysis • Customer journey mapping • Customer segmentation	• Generate content ideas and keywords for different funnel stages • Create personalized content for each stage of the buyer's journey • Analyse content performance and suggest improvements • Create and optimize marketing content	• Account prospecting • Predict lead conversion probability in real-time • Lead scoring and lead prioritization • Automate personalized lead nurturing processes • Conversational technology • Generate personalized email content and subject lines	• Collaboration • Idea • Scheduling • Project management • recommendations • Fraudulent activities detection

on external agencies. AI automates the process of analysing customer data and preferences, making it easier and more affordable to deliver personalized content, offers and recommendations.

IMPROVED LEAD SCORING

AI algorithms assess and prioritize leads based on their likelihood to convert, enabling sales teams to focus on high-value prospects. This results in higher conversion rates, greater efficiency by eliminating manual scoring and better resource allocation, as marketing and sales efforts are directed where they are most likely to generate revenue.

AUTOMATED CAMPAIGN MANAGEMENT

AI also streamlines campaign management by automating tasks such as email scheduling, social media posting and ad optimization. This saves time, ensures campaigns perform consistently by adjusting parameters in real time and allows for scalability, enabling businesses to run larger campaigns with minimal manual input.

OPTIMIZED CONTENT CREATION

When it comes to content creation, generative AI tools enable businesses to produce high-quality, audience-relevant content quickly and cost-effectively. By analysing user preferences and performance data, AI not only speeds up the creative process but also ensures that content resonates with the target audience, driving better engagement and reducing reliance on external agencies.

ENHANCED CUSTOMER INSIGHTS

AI provides enhanced customer insights by processing vast datasets to uncover trends and behaviours that inform more effective strategies. These insights lead to better decision-making, improved targeting and early identification of emerging trends, ensuring marketing efforts are both precise and proactive.

REAL-TIME DATA PROCESSING

AI tools enable the analysis and interpretation of data in real time, allowing businesses to respond immediately to changes in market conditions or customer behaviour. This agility supports timely decision-making, helps businesses adapt quickly to dynamic conditions and provides a competitive edge in fast-paced industries.

ACCURATE ROI MEASUREMENT

Accurate return on investment (ROI) measurement is another area where AI excels. By precisely tracking and evaluating the performance of marketing campaigns, AI offers clear insights into ROI. This transparency ensures resources are allocated to high-performing initiatives, allows for optimization of future strategies and provides accountability by aligning marketing efforts with business objectives.

Common misconceptions about AI in B2B marketing

Over the years there have been some common misconceptions about AI.

AI REPLACES HUMAN JOBS COMPLETELY

One misconception is that AI will fully replace and do away with human beings in marketing. Of course this is not the case; there have been increasing studies showing AI vs humans in ad copy creation which have shown a massive improvement on click-through rate (CTR) and impressions for ad copy created by humans. There is also substantial evidence to show that AI in most fields plays an augmented role and assisting role as opposed to a replacement role.

While AI can automate repetitive tasks and enhance efficiency, it's not meant to replace human creativity and strategic thinking. It serves as a tool to augment human capabilities, allowing marketing professionals to focus on more complex and strategic tasks.

AI IS EXPENSIVE AND ONLY CATERS TO LARGE BUSINESS NEEDS

Another misconception is that AI is only possible to use for large enterprises with substantial budgets; actually, AI tools and technology have become a lot more accessible and affordable also for small businesses. Throughout this book we'll be highlighting low and no-cost AI options as well as more comprehensive AI technologies.

YOU NEED TO BE A TECHNICAL EXPERT TO USE AI

For the majority of AI tools, a technical knowledge or even deep technical knowledge and expertise is not required. Increasingly, AI tools in the past years have been designed to be user-friendly and intuitive. Even in the space of predictive analytics one can find no-code or code-free AI technologies.

AI IS A FAIL-SAFE SUCCESS GUARANTEE

AI systems are only as good as the data behind it and the algorithms; also, the outputs are reflecting the inputs in terms of data and/or queries so AI outputs can have inaccuracies. There are also issues such as data quality, algorithmic bias and incomplete data which can affect AI performance.

AI WILL LEAD TO PRIVACY VIOLATIONS

There is also the misconception that AI will infringe on data privacy and customer privacy. The majority of AI tools and technologies on the market have been operating for many, many years and adhere to data privacy regulations.

Legislation and ethics

Two key areas are currently trending in relation to the use of AI in marketing and B2B marketing: that of data privacy and the ethical use of data.

LEGISLATION, PRIVACY AND DATA

As data about people and behaviours has increased, there has been increasing concern about privacy and protecting individual interests. These two seemingly opposing trends force companies to think differently regarding data and data management. The enforcement of the EU General Data Protection Regulation (GDPR) and, in the UK, the passing of the Data Protection Act on 25 May 2018, was a clear prompt for companies to think more carefully about how they use data if they weren't already.

As well as the GDPR, there are various legal aspects impacting privacy such as the EU ePrivacy Regulation. These mean companies need to think how they secure more permissions from customers and understand how they manage and use data. Privacy impacts direct marketing and digital marketing directed at particular individuals; as B2B marketing is aimed at multiple individuals within organizations, it has particular relevance here.

Some companies are proactively thinking about how to reassure customers regarding data collection, management and use: those companies are also benefiting from using customer insights and data to optimize digital marketing.

ETHICS – TRANSPARENCY AFFECTING COMMUNICATION

B2B brands are becoming more transparent with their customers: their behaviours are publicly discussed or even scrutinized by buyers. As consumers we care about the companies we buy from, so B2B companies need get a balance between company objectives, profit targets and managing marketing and messages to customers.

How companies conduct themselves is therefore becoming increasingly important. Rather than relying solely on marketing, they actually need to ensure that any messages related to ethical and sustainable behaviours is actually backed up by how companies operate. Any lack of coherence between what a company claims and what they actually do can quickly surface through social media and online applications, and could affect public perceptions and consequently, sales.

The recent explosion of AI marketing technology

In the past years we've seen an explosion of AI marketing technology; it is difficult to say how many marketing technologies have been introduced, although there are estimates that between 2020 and 2024 there was an increase of about 2000 AI marketing technologies; when one considers that the entire marketing technology universe in 2020 was around 8000, that is a substantial uptick (Davis, 2024).

So why is this happening 'now' considering AI has been around for the past two decades? Here are some clues that may shed light to the recent explosion.

ABUNDANCE OF DATA FUELS AI ADOPTION

The surge in AI adoption is closely tied to the explosion of data available to businesses. Companies today collect vast amounts of information from sources like social media, website interactions and customer transactions. The sheer volume and complexity of this data pose challenges in management and interpretation, making AI indispensable for extracting actionable insights. According to Forrester, 68 per cent of marketers now use AI to leverage big data for personalized marketing and improved decision-making, underscoring its role in transforming data into value (Petrenko, 2024).

ACCESSIBILITY OF AI PLATFORMS

AI tools have become more intuitive and accessible, particularly since the introduction of user-friendly platforms like ChatGPT and other query-based NLP tools. Historically, AI was confined to specialized solutions for tasks such as programmatic advertising, data integration and sentiment analysis. However, the rise of affordable or even free AI tools has democratized access, allowing more marketers to harness its potential.

BREAKTHROUGHS IN AI TECHNOLOGY

Advancements in machine learning, NLP and embedded AI technologies have significantly enhanced the power and usability of AI tools. For example, AI-driven tools like Google Ads' Smart Bidding and Facebook's ad targeting algorithms use sophisticated machine learning to optimize ad placements and improve targeting accuracy, delivering superior marketing results.

COST REDUCTION AND EFFICIENCY GAINS

AI is highly appealing to B2B marketers because of its ability to reduce costs while improving efficiency. By automating repetitive and time-consuming processes, AI enables teams to do more with fewer resources.

UNPARALLELED PERSONALIZATION OPPORTUNITIES

In the B2B space, customers increasingly expect personalized experiences, and AI makes achieving this at scale much more feasible. AI-powered algorithms analyse customer behaviours and preferences to create tailored content, product recommendations and targeted offers.

AI B2B marketing maturity model

One way to identify steps to developing AI in B2B marketing is through using the maturity model (see Figure 0.3). The maturity model is there to help B2B marketers understand the current status of AI usage within the business as well as understand next stages in development of AI.

There are five main stages in this model: (1) casual interest (not used), (2) light touch, (3) new AI marketing experimentation, (4) cross integration in marketing into a key process and (5) full business process integration.

- Casual interest – not actively used: This is where the current B2B marketing department is not actively using AI or not knowingly using, i.e. AI features may be embedded into software which is being used.
- Light touch: Typically, text-based/prompt-based tools like ChatGPT are being used to create text, e.g. blog of posts.
- Experimentation: This is where marketing is actively and purposely seeing and using an AI software solution to apply to a new area; this may be using a generative AI tool to create images, videos or other content; this may be where marketing is using AI tools to better analyse data and extract data.

FIGURE 0.3 AI marketing maturity model

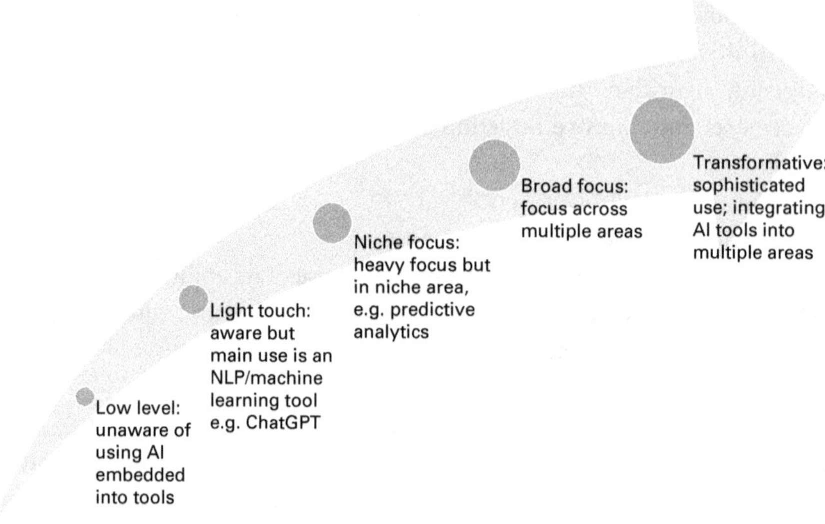
Low level: unaware of using AI embedded into tools
Light touch: aware but main use is an NLP/machine learning tool e.g. ChatGPT
Niche focus: heavy focus but in niche area, e.g. predictive analytics
Broad focus: focus across multiple areas
Transformative: sophisticated use; integrating AI tools into multiple areas

- Cross-marketing integration: This is where AI is not used as a standalone activity and in a standalone software, but the AI tool is also integrated into a process, e.g. this might be where within a lead generation process, AI is used in the first stage to identify new prospects.
- Business integrated: AI is both integrated within marketing processes and also integrated outside of marketing, e.g. between marketing and sales and/or marketing and operations.

Main risks in using AI in B2B marketing

In implementing AI in B2B marketing we'll be outlining in this book all the benefits; to provide a balanced view we'll also be highlighting main risks and challenges and how as B2B marketers we can deal with them. The main risks are summarized here.

PROTECTING DATA PRIVACY AND SECURITY

AI systems often require access to vast amounts of data, including sensitive customer information, which raises serious concerns about privacy and security. Mismanagement or breaches of this data can result in legal penalties, reputational damage and loss of customer trust. For example, under

GDPR regulations, improper handling of customer data could lead to hefty fines. Businesses must prioritize robust data protection measures, such as encryption and access controls, to mitigate these risks and ensure compliance with legal frameworks.

ADDRESSING BIAS AND ENSURING FAIRNESS

AI algorithms can unintentionally perpetuate biases embedded in their training data, leading to unfair outcomes. For instance, if an AI system is trained on historical sales data that disproportionately favours certain geographic regions, it may prioritize outreach to those areas while neglecting others. This can create inequities in customer targeting and decision-making. Regular audits of AI systems, combined with diverse and representative training datasets, are essential to minimize bias and ensure fair outcomes.

BALANCING AI AND HUMAN EXPERTISE

Over-reliance on AI can result in reduced human judgement and creativity, which are critical for crafting effective marketing strategies. For example, if a B2B company relies solely on AI to predict customer churn, data anomalies could lead to flawed predictions and the loss of key clients. Businesses must strike a balance by using AI to complement human decision-making rather than replace it. Combining AI-driven insights with human expertise ensures a holistic approach that incorporates strategic adjustments and innovative solutions.

OVERCOMING INTEGRATION AND IMPLEMENTATION BARRIERS

Integrating AI tools into existing marketing systems and workflows can be a challenging and resource-intensive process. Poor integration can lead to inefficiencies and diminished returns on AI investments. For example, a B2B firm attempting to incorporate AI-driven lead scoring into its CRM system may face compatibility issues that cause delays or errors. To address this, businesses should ensure compatibility, allocate adequate resources and engage cross-functional teams to streamline the implementation process.

ENSURING DATA QUALITY

The accuracy and effectiveness of AI systems are heavily dependent on the quality of the data they process. Inaccurate, incomplete or outdated data can result in misleading insights and suboptimal outcomes. For instance, a marketing campaign based on outdated customer information might send irrelevant offers, damaging the brand's reputation. Regular data cleansing and validation processes are critical to maintaining data integrity and maximizing the benefits of AI-driven insights.

NAVIGATING ETHICAL CONSIDERATIONS

AI introduces ethical dilemmas, particularly regarding transparency and the potential for intrusive marketing practices. Hyper-targeted ads based on detailed behavioural analysis, for example, can feel invasive to customers, leading to dissatisfaction and distrust. Businesses must establish clear ethical guidelines for AI usage, ensuring transparency in how AI is applied and respecting customer privacy. Demonstrating responsible AI practices can foster trust and strengthen customer relationships.

MANAGING COSTS AND RESOURCE ALLOCATION

The financial and resource commitments required to implement AI technologies can be substantial, posing challenges for smaller organizations. For example, a small B2B company investing in AI for campaign automation might struggle to achieve ROI due to limited expertise or data. To address this, businesses should conduct thorough cost-benefit analyses and prioritize high-impact, scalable AI solutions. Starting with cost-effective pilot projects can help manage expenses while demonstrating the value of AI.

BRIDGING SKILL GAPS

AI adoption often requires specialized skills that marketing teams may lack, hindering the successful implementation and operation of these tools. For instance, a B2B firm with an advanced AI analytics platform may underutilize it due to insufficient expertise. To bridge this gap, businesses should invest in employee training and upskilling or hire professionals with relevant knowledge. Partnering with AI vendors that offer training and support can further ease the transition and also maximize the effectiveness of AI investments.

What this book is and isn't

This book is not a book about how to write the best prompts for ChatGPT or a book providing you with a list of prompts. This book is also not about data; it is also not a book discussing the theory of AI. This is not a book about using AI to create great images, content and videos.

So, what is this book about?

What you will find is an overview of key areas of B2B marketing and understand a broad view of AI tools you could use for each area and sub activities. You will see examples of prompts and guidance on how to write prompts for machine learning tools like ChatGPT. We will also look for an extensive range of AI tools according to different focus areas.

HOW TO USE THIS BOOK

There are different ways to use this book; you can read it through from cover to cover to give you a broad and a deep understanding of AI potential tools per B2B marketing area. You could also use this as a reference book and look into a specific section and use that to help you learn about a more specific area.

You could also focus on the practical tips and work it through practical tips and sections to better familiarize yourself with the AI tools. Where possible, I've provided tips and guidance on how to get started with AI tools; in other situations where the AI tool is more enterprise oriented, I've included explanations of what the AI tools do.

The AI B2B marketing framework

OK, so AI B2B marketing covers a lot of areas; to deal with the scope and scale of AI and its uses in B2B marketing, we can break down AI B2B marketing into five main areas. Although in reality there is some overlap between these areas, we'll be treating each separately in the separate sections in the book.

1. AI-based market and customer research.
2. AI awareness and content marketing
3. AI-powered lead generation.
4. AI for optimizing customer relationships where we look into personalization, retention marketing, events marketing and conversational marketing.
5. Responsible AI management where we look into ethics, data privacy, AI for performance management and AI for marketing operations and AI planning.

References

Davis, B (2024) What the 2024 trends decks say about AI, 8 Jan, econsultancy.com/ai-2024-trends-decks/ (archived at https://perma.cc/M49K-CV49)

Gartner (2023) Gartner survey finds 55% of organizations that have deployed AI take an AI-first strategy with new use cases, 27 July, www.gartner.com/en/newsroom/press-releases/2023-07-27-gartner-survey-finds-55-of-organizations-that-have-deployed-ai-take-an-ai-first-strategy-with-new-use-cases (archived at https://perma.cc/EVB3-QCUD)

Howarth, J (2024) 60+ B2B marketing stats, 21 August, explodingtopics.com/blog/b2b-marketing-stats (archived at https://perma.cc/8AQW-N2R4)

McKinsey (2024) The state of AI in early 2024: Gen AI adoption spikes and starts to generate value, 30 May, www.mckinsey.com/capabilities/quantumblack/our-insights/the-state-of-ai-2024 (archived at https://perma.cc/NRL5-2WXL)

Petrenko, V (2024) AI marketing analytics: How to leverage AI to drive personalization and customer engagement, 3 October, litslink.com/blog/ai-marketing-analytics-how-to-leverage-ai-to-drive-personalization (archived at https://perma.cc/QD95-4U69)

Further reading

Brohan, M (2024) B2B marketers will double down on AI and video in the year ahead, 31 December, www.digitalcommerce360.com/2024/12/31/b2b-marketers-survey-ai-video-2025/ (archived at https://perma.cc/8CML-XK5N)

Gartner (2023) Gartner survey finds 63% of marketing leaders plan to invest in Generative AI in the next 24 months, 23 August, www.gartner.com/en/newsroom/press-releases/2023-08-23-gartner-survey-finds-63-percent-of-marketing-leaders-plan-to-invest-in-generative-ai-in-the-next-24-months (archived at https://perma.cc/2QQA-7U9V)

Morgan, B (2022) 50 stats showing the power of personalization, 10 December, www.forbes.com/sites/blakemorgan/2020/02/18/50-stats-showing-the-power-of-personalization/ (archived at https://perma.cc/56U3-KESN)

Rowe, K (2024) How Google Search uses AI, 18 September, searchengineland.com/how-google-search-uses-ai-446639 (archived at https://perma.cc/N2E4-7AMG)

PART ONE

AI-based market and customer research

01

AI-powered market research

What you will gain from this chapter

Understanding of the following:

- understanding qualitative and quantitative research
- how AI plays a role in market research
- how to use AI for creating polls and surveys
- using AI tools for market data analysis

Introduction

Today's B2B marketers are increasingly challenged to keep up with rapidly changing market trends, with traditional market research methods and approaches becoming non-viable. One way which allows market researchers to play catch-up and deal with this is through AI tools.

So, what is market research? Quite simply it is the discipline of collecting information about customers, about market tends, target markets and analysing the resulting data to support business decisions.

During this chapter we're going focus on market research looking at market research methods, market trends, marketing insights and competitor research.

Qualitative and quantitative market research

Let's first define the areas of market research by looking at qualitative and quantitative research.

Qualitative research

Qualitative research involves such methods as focus groups, observations, personal interviews and other methods to capture qualitative information. Qualitative research often provides more context to research and can capture broader aspects such as opinions on topics. The disadvantage of this area of research is that it can be quite time-consuming and expensive, and it is subsequently difficult to review the results from such results.

Quantitative research

Quantitative research involves collecting data; this can be through different methods such as surveys, questionnaires, polls and other methods. Quantitative research provides numerical-based information; the benefit of this research is that it is easier to present information, analyse.

Challenges in market research

Some of the challenges of conducting market research in the B2B space can come down to a number of areas. One area is the competency required to carry out market research; other challenges are resources required, i.e. actually having necessary tools, techniques as well as people. Other challenges are required budget to carry out research as well as the time needed to conduct market research.

When considering quantitative-based market research, challenges might be in finding data, in making sense of data and combining data.

In B2B particularly, data is not always available like it is in B2C; in B2B we typically need to be more targeted in terms of type of industry, the type of target audience being considered. Choosing the right audience can be a challenge in itself, e.g. how does one select the right target audience when, on average, there are four to seven stakeholders involved in the purchase of a B2B product or solutions.

Let's look at the main challenges here as follows:

- Gaining access to the target audience: As the audience can be quite specialized and specific, this can create difficulties in identifying the right audience and then reaching those respondents.
- More complex buying process: Other challenges are the complex buying process which not only involves multiple stakeholders but also multiple different decision points and milestones in the buyer journey.

- Data availability and reliability: We've mentioned already the availability and accessibility of data being challenging considering the niche nature of most B2B businesses.
- Integration of data: The other challenge is that often data to support market research can come from different databases or datasets, and it can be challenging to integrate and merge the data; even if data can be combined then this needs to be in a meaningful way.

AI and market research phases

AI-based market research can allow companies to work with large volumes of data and can help companies dive more deeply into customer behaviours. Through AI tools, companies can crunch data faster and extract more meaningful insights, e.g. to tailor propositions, understand market trends, identify customer segments, etc. AI tools can allow us to keep on top of market trends and changes; they can also help in capturing market research information, in creating surveys, as well as making it easier to find market information. AI can also benefit market researchers by allowing users of AI tools to carry out menial tasks faster and more easily, which in turn frees up time.

AI tools in market research can cover anything from capturing information, identifying trends, summarizing large pools of data, providing recommendations or key take-away from data or extracting themes seen across areas of market research.

We can look at the role of AI in market research for each of the stages in the market research process (see Figure 1.1), i.e.:

1 Design the study.
2 Recruit participants.
3 Collect data.
4 Analyse data.
5 Publish results.

Generating ideas

AI can help B2B marketers come up with themes based on market trends; it can collect and combine large amount of data to recommend key themes; those themes in turn can be used for market campaigns.

FIGURE 1.1 Market research phases and AI's role

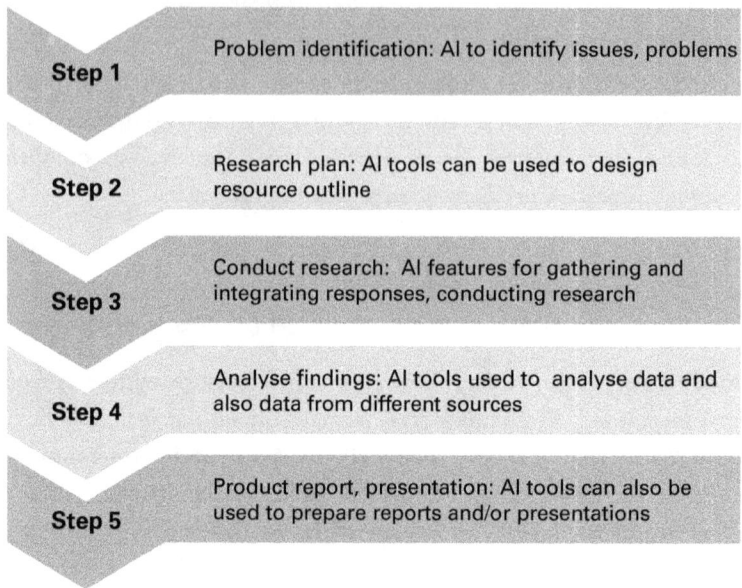

Step 1	Problem identification: AI to identify issues, problems
Step 2	Research plan: AI tools can be used to design resource outline
Step 3	Conduct research: AI features for gathering and integrating responses, conducting research
Step 4	Analyse findings: AI tools used to analyse data and also data from different sources
Step 5	Product report, presentation: AI tools can also be used to prepare reports and/or presentations

Identifying market themes

Sometimes the risk is that having in-house dedicated agencies conducting research may mean that the focus of the market research can become too narrow; through AI tools one can identify potentially broader themes.

Support in writing surveys, polls

AI tools can be used in the selection of appropriate surveys or polls, in structuring surveys and in coming up with questions and many more related to survey and poll creation. Tools such as Pollfish support the creation of surveys and polls, and provide ideas for structuring questions.

The emergence of AI in market research

With natural language processing (NLP) becoming more advanced as well as machine learning being taken to the next level, the latest AI-based market research tools can achieve much better levels of analysis.

Development in AI technology also means that predictive features of tools have become more sophisticated; AI can not only spot current trends but predict emerging trends and market changes with more accuracy. With more accurate predictive possibilities, companies can better change and tailor marketing strategies and faster than competitors. Marketers can support organizations to spot opportunities faster and capitalize on them.

Other benefits of this evolved AI technology are in spotting patterns and correlations in data which can support product development, in identifying customer behaviours and identifying more relevant and specific audience segments.

Types of AI in market research

AI features which can be used for market research comes in three main forms:

Natural language processing (NLP): Through NLP researchers can review and use large amounts of unstructured data then in a matter of seconds provide insights. This is done through prompts and asking specific questions.

Machine learning (ML): Through machine learning, trends and patterns can be identified with high accuracy. In practice, one can upload surveys and then leave it to AI to look through responses to come up with insights.

Deep learning: Deep learning is where the tool learns from updates and changes made, thus allowing for the tool to become better at what it does.

FIGURE 1.2 Types of AI market research analysis

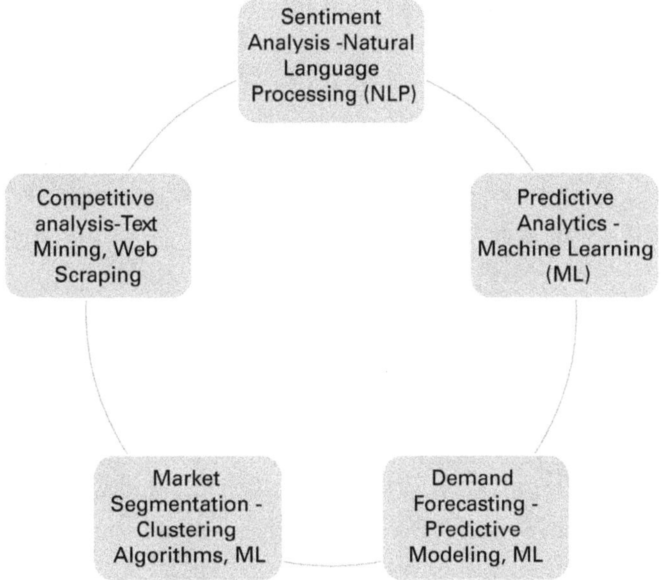

Data analytics and market research

As we've mentioned already, AI can help combine and sort through data; data can be structured as well as unstructured; not only can it combine, but it can identify insights from these large volumes of data in real time.

AI is also less prone to bias and error and therefore can be more consistent.

Areas where AI can be used in market research analytics are as follows:

- sentiment analysis
- predictive analytics
- social media monitoring
- chatbots
- customer journey analysis
- demand forecasting
- consumer segmentation
- image and video analysis

Survey ideation

One of the initial challenges in surveys can be to come up with ideas of surveys, survey questions themselves or the types of questions. AI tools can help with all of these areas (see Figure 1.3).

An AI-based survey involves a set of questions or a process to capture data; AI tools cannot only assist in all the steps of survey development but in optimizing surveys so that one can get more relevant and high-quality responses.

AI tools like ChatGPT can assist in the brainstorming phase by generating different questions for a particular survey topic; this can take away time involved in brainstorming on one's own or within companies. We can also use these tools to generate ideas of questions and types of questions, e.g. multiple choice, open, cloze questions, etc.

With machine learning tools like ChatGPT, we can also simulate the response to questions which can also allow one to understand if the questions are clear enough. These tools can also help us understand how questions might be answered differently depending on different types of buyer personas, e.g. a finance manager may answer a question differently compared to a procurement or HR manager. Through simulation this can also improve efficiency and effectiveness in time used in terms of surveys.

FIGURE 1.3 Types of surveys

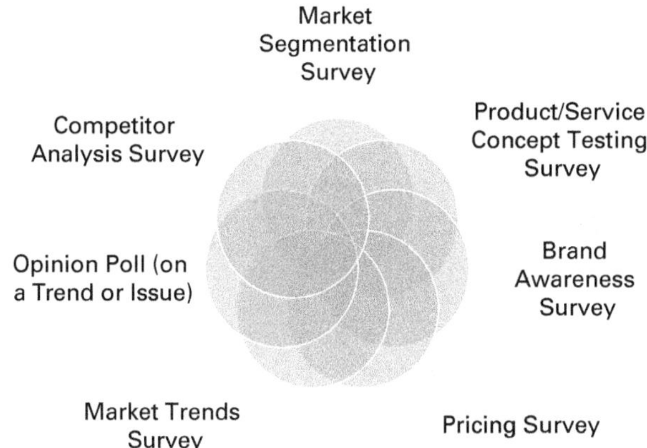

With this technology we can reframe and reword questions according to different seniority levels of respondents, e.g. from a manager to executive to a senior executive.

PUT INTO PRACTICE

Below are some example questions one could use for **a poll**:

How does marketing measure ROMI in terms of digital marketer and senior marketer?

How have digital initiatives improved marketing campaigns? – campaign manager/marcom?

Related prompts one could use in **a machine learning platform** could be as follows:

Please provide four questions for a senior marketer related to how they measure ROMI of digital marketing.

Please provide four questions related to how a campaign manager can review and optimize digital marketing campaigns.

One could also ask prompts to elicit differently structured questions, e.g.:

Please provide four questions for a senior marketer related to how they measure ROMI of digital marketing using different types of questions such as closed questions, multiple choice questions, ranking questions, open questions, Likert scale question, semantic differential scale question, drop-down question (single-choice selection) and other styles of questions.

Industry specialisms

Using such machine learning tools as Gemini and ChatGPT, we can also account for specific industry taxonomy and create questions which incorporate relevant industry language. For example, in the IT sector the words used may relate to computing, storage technology and focus on IT impact whereas in the healthcare space this may relate more to patient care and impact on patient well-being.

PRACTICAL EXAMPLE: POLLFISH

Pollfish is an AI-based online survey technology; it can be used in B2B market research. It has a large global reach and allows research to create and distribute surveys to B2B customer segments across multiple industries.

One of the main advantages of Pollfish is that it has advanced targeting features. Researchers can filter respondents according to different characteristics such as job role, industry, geography and many others.

Pollfish supports real-time data capturing which means researchers can more rapidly analyse results to make better decisions based on data insights.

One of the interesting features in Pollfish is its ability to create surveys and a varied range of questions based on a prompt; prompts might be something like 'How B2B marketers are using AI tools for customer journey mapping'.

The main alternatives to Pollfish are Qualtrics, survey monkey genius, type form, Zonka Feedback, Gravity forms and HubSpot form builder.

PRACTICAL TIP

Here are five examples of questions for the survey ideation phase:

1. What are the top 10 pain points faced by 'x role' in 'the 'x' industry?
2. What are the main influences of the purchase managers in the 'x' industry?
3. What are the main technologies which are impacting (or disrupting) the 'x' industry?
4. What are the main trends in the 'x' industry?
5. What are the main interests of finance managers in evaluating a new vendor of 'x' products?

TABLE 1.1 Type of survey questions

Type of Question	Example	Use Case
Open-Ended - Respondents answer in their own words	'What do you think about our service?'	Detailed feedback, qualitative insights
Closed-Ended - Respondents choose from predefined answers.	'Do you use our product? (Yes/No)'	Specific, quantifiable data
Multiple-Choice - Select one or more options from a list.	'Which of the following do you use? (Select all)'	Preferences, categorical data
Rating Scale (Likert Scale): Respondents rate on a scale (e.g., 1-5).	'How satisfied are you? (1-5 scale)'	Measuring intensity of opinions or feelings
Ranking: Respondents rank options in order of preference.	'Rank these features in order of importance.'	Prioritization of features/ preferences
Cloze (Fill-in-the-Blank) -Respondents complete a sentence with missing words or phrases	'The most important feature is _________.'	Semi-structured open-ended responses

REAL-WORLD EXAMPLE

Living packets

LivingPackets, a French company, operates in the packaging, transportation and logistics industry with its innovative, reusable LivingPackets Box. Living packets products are designed to reduce packaging waste and improve security; its flagship product has gained recognition among large enterprise companies; however, in growing they need to gain a much more detailed understanding of user interactions with their product to understand better pain points and areas of product enhancement.

LivingPackets faced several obstacles in gathering actionable user feedback. For example, they struggled to capture surveys, which hindered their ability to understand user challenges with the product. Additionally, they found difficulty in capturing feedback across multiple channels, including events and digital interactions.

To address these challenges, LivingPackets partnered with Zonka Feedback, adopting a comprehensive feedback strategy. They collected feedback through multiple channels, including online and offline surveys, and automated the process by integrating Zonka Feedback with tools like CRISP and ClickUp via Zapier. The intuitive interface of Zonka Feedback allowed for much easier survey creation and management. Advanced analytics provided valuable insights into user interactions with the physical product and its accompanying app, enabling targeted improvements.[1]

The implementation of Zonka Feedback yielded impressive results. Over 500 responses were gathered across various channels, offering deep insights into user behaviour and identifying areas for product refinement. Zonka Feedback's user-friendly platform allowed the team to maintain focus on continuous improvement. This approach not only enhanced user satisfaction but also reinforced LivingPackets' position as a leader in sustainable packaging innovation.[2]

Market sizing

We can use different AI technology to estimate market sizes of geographies or industries. Consider this, in the field of data capture there are a number of software platforms collecting huge pools of data; other AI platforms will draw on a combination of online, ongoing data as well as company database built over time

Other tools which leverage these large pools of data are Total Availability Market (TAM) calculators from Cognism or Sendinbuzz; through the TAM calculator one can filter by industry, etc. to identify top players by industry and then also at the same time come up with a market size calculation.

One can also use LLM/ML tools like ChatGPT or Perplexity to identify market size information.

PUT INTO PRACTICE

Let's look at another NLP/ML tool, Perplexity.ai, and ask the following: What is the healthcare market size in the UK?

Let's use the prompt: *What is the furniture market size in the UK in £s?*

These are the first few lines in the response to the prompt:

- The furniture market size in the United Kingdom is estimated to be significant and is projected to grow in the coming years. According to multiple sources:
  - The UK Home Furniture Market is expected to reach USD 18.78 billion in 2024 and grow at a CAGR of 3.20 per cent to reach USD 21.98 billion by 2029.
  - The market size of the Furniture, Lighting & Homeware Retailers industry in the UK is projected to be £12.9 billion in 2024.

PUT INTO PRACTICE: USING LONG FORM PROMPTS FOR MARKET RESEARCH

Sometimes it may be more useful to use long form prompts to define better what the output should be and to ensure a more comprehensive output from machine learning tools.

See below an example of a long form version of the above, this time looking at Germany:

Example long-form prompt for market insights on the furniture market in Germany

Provide a comprehensive market analysis of the furniture industry in Germany. The report should be **well-structured and divided into key sections**. Include data-driven insights and relevant trends. The analysis should be formatted as follows:

1 Market overview

- Total **market size** (in revenue) and **growth rate** over the past five years.
- Expected **growth projections** for the next 5 to 10 years.
- Key **economic and demographic factors** influencing demand.

2 Market segmentation

- Breakdown of the furniture market by:
    - o Product type (e.g. home furniture, office furniture, outdoor furniture, custom furniture).
    - o Material type (e.g. wood, metal, plastic, sustainable materials).
    - o Price segments (e.g. luxury, mid-range, budget-friendly).
    - o Distribution channels (e.g. online, retail stores, wholesale, B2B contracts).

3 Consumer insights and buying behaviour

- **Who are the main buyers?** (demographics, income levels, preferences).
- **Key purchasing factors** (e.g. price, quality, sustainability, design trends).
- **Buying habits** (frequency, preferred shopping channels, decision-making factors).
- The impact of **e-commerce vs physical stores** on purchasing behaviour.

4 Competitive landscape and key players

- Major furniture brands and manufacturers in Germany.
- Market share of top companies (if available).
- Strengths, weaknesses and pricing strategies of leading brands.
- Growth of local vs international brands in Germany.

5 Emerging trends and innovation

- Sustainable and eco-friendly furniture demand.
- Smart furniture and technology integration (e.g. Internet of Things, ergonomic solutions).
- Popular design trends shaping consumer preferences.
- Supply chain innovations (local production vs imports).

6 Regulatory and economic factors

- Key **government regulations** affecting the furniture market (e.g. sustainability laws, import/export regulations).
- Impact of **inflation, labour costs and raw material availability** on pricing.
- **EU policies** that influence furniture imports, exports and trade.

7 Future outlook and investment opportunities

- Growth sectors within the industry (e.g. high-end vs budget furniture).
- **Opportunities for new businesses and investors** (e.g. digital-first furniture brands).
- Potential **market risks** (economic downturn, supply chain disruptions).

AI for market trends

AI can also be used to predict market trends; by analysing and sifting through large data sets AI tools can forecast customer demand and needs. It can analyse data such as operational data to also avoid supply chain issues. Through better prediction of customer demands and future purchases, B2B companies can better manage their supply chain, thus improving the overall customer experience.

One example of a tool which can be used is ClickUp Brain, which leverages AI to analysis current market trends; it can decipher current market changes.

PRACTICAL TIP

Type in the following prompt into ClickUp Brain:

> *Analyse the current market trends in the B2B sector. Identify key competitors, market size and emerging opportunities for growth based on recent data and reports.*

Spotting content trends

AI can be used to spot content trends in B2B; AI can identify content which is popular and that resonates with audiences. Examples might be social media discussions or identifying news articles or blog posts which are gaining traction. Through identifying content which is working marketers can focus their efforts more on creating content and content formats which actually work.

AI tools can also be used to identify relevant content and not just content trends; imagine you have a specific niche in terms of market and target audience, AI can be used to find that relevant content; something which normally can take hours. Examples of tools which can be used to spot trends include IBM Watson Analytics and DataRobot.

Detecting weak signals with AI

First, let's explain weak signals; these are vague and early indications of change and often the precursor to major market trends. Up to now these weak signals have been very difficult to identify due to large amounts of data and inability to combine data to see subtle patterns. With AI one can find these weak signals using AI features such as deep learning.

Additionally, AI features like anomaly detection and outlier analysis can be used. In B2B markets, early mentions of a new technology or a minor shift in supplier preferences could be weak signals indicating a significant future trend.

Examples of tools which can be used to detect weak signals include Signal AI, Crimson Hexagon and Quid.

Using AI for market research statistics

AI can also be used to produce and interpret statistics for market research; coming up with statistics or conducting statistical calculations are areas where AI can help.

There are AI-based statistical tools which can be used as well as market research tools which have recently added AI functionality.

Examples of AI use in market research

Microsoft's use of AI for trend detection: Microsoft has used AI-driven tools to identify early trends in cloud computing adoption across industries. By analysing vast datasets from social media, industry reports and customer feedback, AI helped Microsoft spot weak signals of increased demand for cloud-based services in specific sectors like healthcare and finance. This early detection allowed the company to tailor its cloud offerings and marketing strategies to meet future demand, staying ahead of competitors.[3]

Accenture's AI-powered market insights: Accenture applied AI-powered analytics to uncover weak signals in the digital transformation of manufacturing industries. Using AI tools, they detected early adoption of Industry 4.0 technologies (e.g. IoT, AI and robotics) among certain manufacturing segments. These insights enabled Accenture to advise clients on strategic investments and position themselves as leaders in digital manufacturing consulting.

AI and market hypotheses

AI can also be used to test and validate market research hypotheses through data analytics, pattern detection and predictive analytics.

In the first stage of hypothesis identification AI is great for processing large amounts of data from various disparate sources such as market reports, social media, sales data and more. It can help marketers come up with areas to test and check.

In the stage of hypothesis validation AI algorithms can be used to apply statistical models such as regression analysis to determine whether there are relationships between different variables, e.g. between customer experience and repeated purchases.

Machine learning models, such as decision trees or neural networks, can also be used to simulate different scenarios and predict outcomes, helping validate whether the hypothesis holds under various conditions. AI-driven A/B testing can further refine this by comparing two or more strategies based on real-time data, providing concrete evidence on which hypotheses perform better.

Following hypothesis validation, AI can be used to continue to learn and adapt itself as new data is introduced and thus refine the hypothesis over time. This real-time feedback loop allows for a dynamic approach to market research, where hypotheses are not only tested but also evolved as new insights are gained.

Examples of AI tools which can be used in the hypothesis development and validation include Qualtrics XM, MonkeyLearn, DataRobot, H2O.ai and Brandwatch.

AI for competitive research

AI tools can also be great for conducting competitor analysis in different ways; areas where AI can be used is to identify competitors, for example if you're looking to expand to a different geographical region or sector and trying to understand the main competition.

AI can also be used in the following areas:

- conducting a SWOT on competition
- benchmarking competition
- benchmarking specific areas

Identifying competitors – in practice

Let's say I'm in the B2B medical device sector and producing stethoscopes and look to export to Brazil; now I'm interested in the main competitors in Brazil who are providing stethoscopes.

Let's look at the below prompt and type this into ChatGPT.

What are the top 10 providers of stethoscopes in Brazil?

See the initial paragraph and lines in response to the prompt:

> The Brazilian market for stethoscopes includes both international and local brands. Many healthcare professionals in Brazil prefer established brands known for their quality and durability. Here are the top 10 providers of stethoscopes in Brazil, based on popularity, market presence and reputation for quality:
>
> **Littman**
>
> **Overview:** Littman is one of the most renowned stethoscope brands worldwide, and it's also highly popular in Brazil.

Products: Offers a wide range of stethoscopes, including the Classic, Cardiology and Master models.

Reputation: Known for its superior acoustics and durability.

Conducting a competitor SWOT analysis

Often, putting together a competitor SWOT can be a lengthy and time-consuming process due to the need to trawl through websites to identify information; this is where AI can be used as well by trawling through information such as the competitor's website as well as review websites (Figure 1.4).

IN PRACTICE

Let's say we are in the web hosting industry and interested in Germany as a potential market, and we want to quickly evaluate some key German competitors.

We can use machine learning tools and the following command:

Please conduct a SWOT analysis of the top 3 B2B web hosters in the Germany market.

Here's a SWOT analysis for the top three B2B web hosting providers in Germany: Hetzner Online, IONOS by 1&1 and Strato. These companies dominate the German B2B hosting market, offering a range of services including cloud hosting, VPS and dedicated servers. I've just included the response for one of the competitors below and for the strengths.

1. Hetzner Online

Strengths:

- Cost-effective solutions: Hetzner is known for offering competitively priced hosting solutions without compromising on quality.
- Data centers in Germany: Their data centers are located in Germany, ensuring low latency for European clients and compliance with strict EU data protection laws (GDPR).
- High performance: They offer high-performance dedicated servers with excellent uptime and network reliability.
- Custom solutions: Hetzner offers flexible hosting packages that are easily scalable for businesses, from small enterprises to large corporations.

We can expand on the detail of this SWOT by asking for a detailed SWOT or changing the prompt to ask for the top 10 strengths and top 10 weaknesses for that competitor.

FIGURE 1.4 SWOT and next stages

Strengths (S)	Strong global brand recognition and reputation in the pharmaceutical industry Large R&D budget and expertise Robust product portfolio
Weaknesses (W)	Heavy reliance on certain blockbuster drugs High costs of drug development and clinical trial Legal and regulatory challenges (frequent patent expirations, lawsuits)
Opportunities (O)	- Growth in emerging markets (Asia, Latin America) - Rising demand for innovative vaccines, biologics, and personalized medicine - Increased healthcare spending globally - Expansion of telemedicine and digital health solutions
Threats (T)	Intense competition from generics manufacturers Patent expirations Stringent regulations and approvals Political and economic instability

Strategic Type	Description of Strategic Combination
SO Strategies (Strengths + Opportunities)	1. Leverage x's strong R&D capabilities to capitalize on the growing demand for innovative vaccines and biologics(e.g., mRNA technology). 2. Use strategic partnerships (BioNTech) to further penetrate **emerging markets** like Asia and Latin America, focusing on vaccines and treatment solutions. 3. Utilize x's global brand and advanced **digital health** solutions to tap into **telemedicine** and AI-based healthcare services.
WO Strategies (Weaknesses + Opportunities)	1. Reduce reliance on blockbuster drugs by **diversifying the product portfolio**, investing in personalized medicine, and expanding into **digital health**. 2. Mitigate high R&D costs by adopting **AI and machine learning** technologies to streamline drug discovery and development. 3. Address public perception issues by exploring **affordable pricing models**in emerging markets, helping capitalize on global **healthcare spending growth**.

Competition research platforms

Examples of tools which can be used include Crayon, Completely and Qualtrics.

Crayon's platform uses AI to gather intelligence on your competitors. Their AI tool sifts through mass amounts of information on your competition, from publications to websites to reviews and more to create profiles you can look across.

Another great example is ChatGPT; one simply enters the URL of the company you wish to analyse; with ChatGPT you will receive a list of top 10 competitors. Here's an example.

Please provide a list of top 10 competitors for the following company www.nextgenmarketing.co.uk.

What to look for in an AI competitor analysis tool

When choosing an AI tool for competition analysis, one should look at three main factors. First, the AI tool should be accurate and provide precise information. Second, it should be intuitive and easy to use, eliminating time to train for learning how to use it. Finally, it should be easy to integrate into other platforms, e.g. CRM (See Table 1.2).

TABLE 1.2 Types of competitor analysis

Area of Competitor Analysis	Type of AI Tool	Examples of AI Tools
Market Sentiment	Sentiment Analysis / NLP	Brandwatch, MonkeyLearn
Pricing Strategies	Price Monitoring AI / Web Scraping	Prisync, Skuuudle
Product Offerings & Innovations	Machine Learning for Trend Prediction	Brandwatch
Competitor Financial Performance	Financial Analytics / Predictive Analytics	Alteryx, IBM Watson Analytics, Zebra BI
Marketing Strategies & Advertising	Marketing Analytics / Ad Performance Tools	Adbeat, SimilarWeb, SEMrush
Customer Feedback & Reviews	Sentiment Analysis / NLP	Qualtrics XM, Revuze
Website & SEO Performance	SEO Analytics / Web Crawling	Ahrefs, Moz, Screaming Frog

(continued)

TABLE 1.2 (Continued)

Area of Competitor Analysis	Type of AI Tool	Examples of AI Tools
Social Media & Content Strategy	Social Listening / Content Analysis	BuzzSumo, Hootsuite Insights, Sprinklr
Sales Channels & Distribution	Sales Intelligence Tools	InsideView, ZoomInfo
Customer Acquisition & Retention	Churn Prediction / Retention AI	ChurnZero, Salesforce Einstein, Optimove

References

1 Kanika (2024) LivingPackets enhances product experience with Zonka Feedback, Zonkafeedback.com (archived at https://perma.cc/RBT6-XSZ7), www.zonkafeedback.com/customer-stories/livingpackets (archived at https://perma.cc/K5F5-9G7W)

2 Smith, M (2025) LinkedIn post, www.linkedin.com/posts/matt-smith-407743320_customerexperience-productfeedback-smartpackaging-activity-7304914537470652416-QTmC/ (archived at https://perma.cc/777M-WSN3)

3 Pargesoft (2024) Can Microsoft Dynamics 365 AI predict market trends and customer behavior? Pargesoft, https://pargesoft.co.uk/can-microsoft-dynamics-365-ai-predict-market-trends-and-customer- (archived at https://perma.cc/KX2M-TGKT)

Further reading

Turner, R (2020) The future of market research: How AI and machine learning are shaping the industry, Research World, https://researchworld.com/articles/the-future-of-market-research-how-ai-and-machine-learning-are-shaping-the-industry (archived at https://perma.cc/K3WR-8JWC)

02

AI for customer insights

> What you will gain from this chapter
>
> Understanding of the following:
>
> - areas of AI in customer insights research
> - how AI tools are used for buyer persona creation
> - using AI to investigate areas of the buyer persona
> - identifying and researching B2B communities
> - using AI for customer journey maps

Introduction

This chapter builds on the previous chapter, i.e. subsequent to market trend, market research and competitive insights collection, we can then move to the step of looking into customer segments and buyer personas and other customer insights.

Customer insights are interpretations of data; it is about gaining a deeper understanding of customers, their behaviours, feelings, thoughts, and bringing to life customer data and extracting value from customer data.

Insights differ from research in that people can conduct research in all different scales and forms; the research can lead to extracting good insights or not; research sometimes may not lead to anything conclusive in terms of real insights.

Gaining deeper customer insights

In gaining a more in-depth understanding of customers, we can use some of the traditional methods such as customer roundtables, social media listening, conducting in-person surveys or online surveys, customer advisory panels and polls, though in this chapter we will look deeper at non-traditional AI methods.

How we use customer insights

So, we've talked about ways to capture customer insights and gain a deeper understanding of customers, but what can we do with customer insights? Customer insights can give us valuable understanding of different aspects such as identifying pain points, getting an understanding of how brands, products are viewed; we can gain a view on how trends are perceived and which trends will be more impactful; we can understand what customers are experiencing in the industry.

The role of AI in customer research

AI has multiple roles in capturing customer insights which span multiple topics and chapters in this book including sentiment analysis, keyword analytics, understanding purchase behaviours, identifying churn and predicting other purchase behaviours.

Within this chapter we're going to focus on how AI can play a role (1) in buyer persona creation and (2) key areas of the buyer persona, (3) in customer segmentation, (4) in customer journey mapping and (5) in customer data platforms.

Creating a buyer persona

The buyer persona is one of the key tools within the B2B digital marketer's toolbox and is especially important to carry out effective personalization marketing. As it is a semi-fictional representation of your ideal target customer and formulated according to your key target customer segment, many questions relating to personalization marketing and digital marketing more widely can be answered through a comprehensive buyer persona.

What is included in a buyer persona?

Typically, a B2B buyer persona should include stakeholders, attitudes, pain points, motivations, influences and key media used by them.

More comprehensive B2B buyer personas include media and key words, as well as content preferences and key phrases used according to different stages in the buyer journey. This 'a day in the life' of the persona, can help identify why they may buy the respective products and services as well as why they don't buy. (Please see Figure 2.1 for aspects which would ideally be included in a B2B buyer persona.)

> PRACTICAL TIP: USE PROSPECT LANGUAGE
>
> When creating a buyer persona, it's best to create content and messaging based on terms and phrases actually used by the customers. Otherwise, when the information gets translated into content and marketing campaigns, it will resonate well with the intended audience.

Challenges in creating buyer personas for B2B marketers

One challenge in creating buyer personas is in identifying specific individuals which fit the profile of an ideal target audience; if this is a new type of persona then finding individuals upon which to base the buyer persona might be challenging. Once identified, then other challenges might be resource limitations in creating the buyer persona, i.e. people, budget and time resources might be an obstacle.

Other challenges are the number of personas required; when we consider that typically multiple stakeholders are involved in a B2B purchase, then we should ideally be using more than one buyer persona; ideally, we would need three to four buyer personas, something which very few B2B marketers are able to cater for today.

The other main challenges are:

Gathering data: Gathering data can be difficult as B2B markets can fall into specific areas and data may be scarce.

Time: Considering that for any purchase there are two to three or more stakeholders involved, it can be difficult in terms of resourcing to create these two to three buyer personas.

Understanding the decision-making process: Capturing diverse motivations and pain points of each stakeholder can be challenging.

Adapting to market and industry changes: Where industry shifts happen, it can be difficult to resource in terms of people, time and money to create updated buyer personas.

AI and buyer personas

Regarding the aforementioned challenges, AI can play a role to address these; AI tools can get around some of the resource challenges in terms of people budget and time in creating a buyer persona. AI tools can also process vast amounts of information to identify patterns and characteristics that define the ideal customer. This capability is particularly advantageous in the B2B realm, where the buying process is often more complex and involves multiple stakeholders.

As buyer personas may change over time, AI can help in collecting and extracting information related to changing buyer personas. AI tools can help collect different data from various sources including CRM systems, social media sites and websites, and more quickly uncover patterns and insights relating to the buyer persona.

AI tools are also able to also analyse digital behaviours as well as content engagement and combine this with other data to create a more comprehensive buyer persona. Through predictive analytics, AI tools can also predict the most suitable content and products one can propose and use to engage with buyer personas.

AI-powered tools can automate the collection and analysis of survey data, including open-ended responses. Natural language processing (NLP) can help interpret customer feedback, extracting themes and sentiments that inform persona characteristics.

Types of AI tools for creating buyer personas

There are different approaches and methods to using AI to create buyer personas. One can use command-based tools to create the full buyer persona or elements of the buyer persona. One can use dedicated buyer persona technology which leverages social media and websites, etc. to identify buyer personas.

AI tools can track customer interactions and update personas in real time on an ongoing basis; this more dynamic approach means that personas stay market relevant as customer needs and changing market conditions are accommodated.

The easiest way to start with AI for creating buyer personas is through using machine learning AI tools; ChatGPT is a good place to start, although there are alternatives such as Gemini, Perplexity.ai and Copilot.

How to use AI tools for buyer persona creation

There are different approaches in using AI tools:

Approach 1: Use dedicated tools which allow you to build buyer personas from website data and other data from existing traffic; such tools include Delve.ai; etc. One of the limitations is that this will highlight the current best fitting buyer persona but may be limited in helping you craft a future new ideal target buyer persona.

Approach 2: Using text-based tools to build a buyer persona.

Another approach is simply to leverage tools through prompts and request them to create a buyer persona, although there are different ways to ensure higher quality and detailed buyer personas are produced based on the prompt – we'll look into this in the practice section later.

Approach 3: Use AI-based tools to support primary research; these include tools such as AI-based polls, surveys which assist B2B marketing in conducting primary research.

Beyond this one can use AI tools to support the carrying out of primary research.

Please see Figure 2.1 for an outline of the main ways to create a buyer persona in terms of types of tools.

Dedicated AI buyer persona tools

One dedicated tool is Delve.ai, which builds persona profiles from website traffic, social media and customer interactions to automatically generate B2B buyer personas. The personas generated by Delve.ai are regularly updated based on the ongoing collection of new data, which means the buyer personas evolve with changing market trends and buyer behaviours.

The importance of the command

Consider what you're interested in, in terms of the buyer persona; it may be that initially you're just trying to understand more about the role itself, i.e. finance manager, procurement manager. We can start to gather information simply by inputting the following prompts.

- *Prompt: Please provide a buyer persona for 'x'.*

FIGURE 2.1 Building buyer persona through queries

Step 1: General
Ask about general overview of buyer persona for segment
Per segment, think of specific buyer persona role
With queries be as specific as possible, e.g. what products are they looking to buy?
Step 2: Specifics –Part 1
Customer requirements, challenges
Needs
Pain points, challenges
Main interests
Benefits sought
Step 3: Specifics –Part 2
Marketing communications and content
Content preferences
Media preferences
How they share views
Main communication channels used
Queries
Please provide an overview of a purchase manager in the 'x' sector looking to buy…
For a purchase manager in the 'x' sector, looking to buy 'x' please highlight top 10 needs, top 10 pain points and challenges and top 10 benefits sought
For a purchase manager… please highlight main content preferences, media preferences

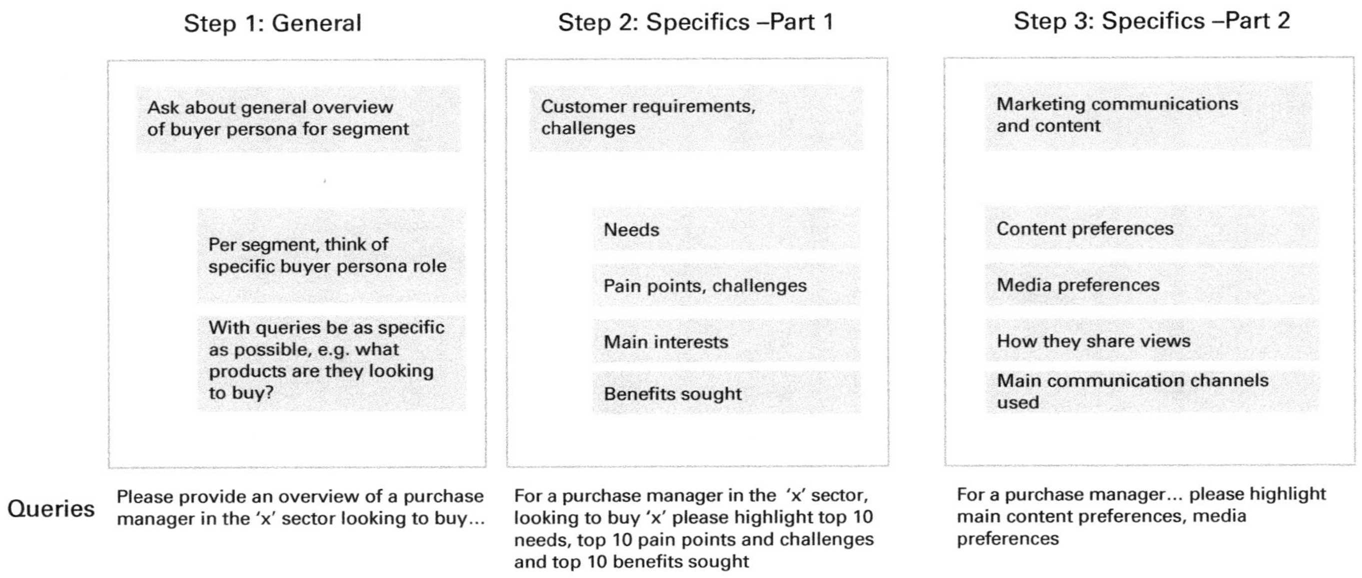

- *Prompt: Please provide a 500-word outline for a purchase manager buyer persona.*

Of course, we probably want to get a more specific and tailored buyer persona. Please see below the differences in the prompts and the difference in the quality of response.

Examples of prompts:

1. Prompt: *Please produce a 500-word outline of a B2B buyer persona of a purchase manager purchasing financial services for the 'sector'.*
2. Prompt: *Please produce comprehensive/detailed buyer persona of a purchase manager.*
3. Prompt: *Please write a detailed 1000-word buyer persona of a purchase manager in the financial sector looking to buy cybersecurity software. Please highlight potential examples for each area of the buyer persona and include aspects such as media preferences, key pain points, key challenges and key stakeholders.*

USING AI MACHINE LEARNING TOOLS AND LONG-FORM PROMPTS

We can also use long form prompts to obtain more comprehensive buyer personas or specific key outputs we're looking for in a buyer persona.

Here is an example:

Create a detailed buyer persona for a **purchasing director in a mid-to-large healthcare organization** responsible for procuring IT equipment. The persona should include the following:

Demographics: Age, years of experience, job titles.

Job role and responsibilities: Key activities related to IT purchasing, budget control, compliance considerations.

Pain points: What challenges do they face when purchasing IT equipment (e.g. budget constraints, security concerns, integration with existing systems, regulatory compliance)?

Decision-making process: Who influences their choices? What factors matter most (e.g. cost, quality, vendor reputation, compliance)?

Buying triggers: What events prompt them to seek new IT solutions (e.g. outdated equipment, security threats, regulatory updates)?

Media preferences: Where do they seek information (e.g. trade publications, industry reports, peer recommendations, vendor websites)?

Objections: What concerns might prevent them from buying (e.g. budget approval, risk aversion, complex implementation)?
Value propositions: What key benefits should be highlighted (e.g. cost-efficiency, security, compliance, long-term reliability)?

Show the persona in a structured format with clear headings and bullet points for clarity.

Filling the gaps

AI tools like ChatGPT and Gemini can also help us fill gaps in buyer personas. Quite often we don't need AI to create the full buyer persona as we may already have created buyer personas in-house; typical gaps which we may want to look into are pain points, media preferences, business communities, stakeholders and typical stages in the buying process, etc.

How to build using machine learning: summary

Approach 1: use machine learning tools to build buyer persona in a stepwise approach; one step wise approach is to first create the framework and key high-level information for a buyer persona.

One example would be to do the following.

1. Submit queries for a buyer personal outline highlight main information.
2. Once created then ask for particular areas to be expanded on.

Approach 2: use machine learning tools to build a buyer persona in a stepwise approach, though this time increase the level of tailoring and specificity.

1. Step 1: Generic buyer person.
2. Step 2: Think of a buyer persona from a type of industry in a type of role.
3. Step 3: Now consider differences by looking at their role and the type of product/solution they're interested in buying.

Media preferences

We can now start to look at more specific areas of the buyer persona using AI tools.

Let's take a look at Table 2.1 and the first few lines. What are the typical media preferences for a purchase manager, a finance manager and a human resource manager?

We can also see differences being picked up by region, e.g. what are the typical media preferences for a purchase manager in Brazil, in the UK and in Germany.

Let's try this out. The following are examples of commands we could use:

- *What are the top typical media preferences for a purchase manager?*
- *What are the top media preferences for a finance manager?*

The commands can also be more specific. The following is a prompt and the response from ChatGPT:

- *Please show in bullet point format in a table the top five media preferences for a purchase manager in the United States and a finance manager in Brazil.*

TABLE 2.1 Media preferences

Role	Top media preferences
Purchase manager (US)	1. Industry-specific trade publications (e.g. *Supply Chain Management Review*, *Procurement Magazine*)
	2. Professional networking platforms (e.g. LinkedIn for industry news and networking)
	3. Webinars and online events (e.g. ISM, Gartner virtual conferences and demos)
	4. Vendor websites and blogs (product specs, case studies, customer testimonials)
	5. Procurement and business news websites (e.g. Procurement Leaders, Spend Matters, Bloomberg)
Finance manager (Brazil)	1. Business and finance news websites (e.g. Exame, Valor Econômico, Reuters)
	2. Professional networking platforms (e.g. LinkedIn for finance-related content and networking)
	3. Research reports and white papers (e.g. Deloitte, PwC reports for financial decision-making)
	4. Webinars and online events (e.g. CFA Society Brazil, FDC webinars)
	5. industry-specific journals (local finance journals for business trends, regulatory updates and investment analysis)

B2B communities

Another area we can investigate through AI tools is which B2B communities are being used in a particular industry.

What are these B2B communities and why is it interesting to identify these? Online B2B communities are online spaces where professionals share knowledge, discuss trends, share views and generally network. One can find different forms of communities online such as role-based communities, such as identifying communities for procurement professionals or for finance professionals, industry communities, e.g. healthcare, biotech, IT or other.

Through AI tools such as ChatGPT one can identify B2B communities which would typically be participated in by that type of buyer persona; depending on the command used this can also be specific to the location.

What to do next?

Once those communities are identified one can use the tool to ask for more information on the particular platform

Example prompt: *Please provide a brief outline for Procurious, its main features and describe how a B2B marketer might be able to use this platform.*

The decision-making unit

One can investigate typical types and number of stakeholders for a decision-making unit. For example, if I asked Perplexity for the number and type of stakeholders for a list of industries, it provides the information in Table 2.2. We'll go more into detail on this space in the account insights chapter later in the book.

See in Table 2.2 the response from Perplexity for the following command. *Please show in a table the top typical stakeholders for the following two scenarios: (1) an agriculture company buying agriculture equipment and (2) a healthcare company buying HR services.*

TABLE 2.2 Top stakeholders by industry

Agriculture company buying equipment	Healthcare company buying HR services
Farmers/employees	Employees
Owners/shareholders	Management
Suppliers (equipment manufacturers)	HR service providers

(continued)

TABLE 2.2 (Continued)

Agriculture company buying equipment	Healthcare company buying HR services
Customers	Patients/customers
Local community	Regulatory bodies
Government/regulatory bodies	Unions (if applicable)
Financial institutions	Board of directors
Dealers/distributors	Investors/shareholders

Limitations

Is it better to create a buyer persona on one's own? Yes, but let's consider how many B2B marketers have B2B buyer personas in place for their marketing and then per segment or campaign how many buyer personas are used.

Ideally, we should all be creating and updating buyer personas on a regular one- to two-year basis and they should be comprehensive; often this doesn't happen. From my own poll/survey of 50–100 B2B marketers, only 50 per cent have buyer personas in place.

Customer segmentation and AI

Defining customer segmentation

Before looking at AI applications in customer segmentation, let's define better customer segments. B2B customer segmentation typically involves grouping customers based on different criteria; these could be any of the following criteria.

Firmographic data: This includes industry, company size, revenue and location.

Behavioural data: This includes digital behaviours such as digital engagement, clicks, bounce rate.

Purchase behaviours: This includes purchase frequency, size of purchases, types of purchased products and services.

Technographic information: This may include the customers' current technology usage and its software preferences.

Business needs: This could include pain points and goals.

AI for customer segmentation

AI tools used for customer segmentation use sophisticated algorithms and machine learning to understand B2B customers. The benefit of using AI-based customer segmentation over traditional methods are as follows.

- **More precise customer segmentation:** AI can identify small micro or nano segments within the larger segment which means niche markets can be more easily identified; often overlooked in traditional methods. Through this more granular segmentation more specific buyer personas can be created which cater to subsets of customers with more specific needs
- **Scalable:** AI tools can scale to include large datasets.
- **Real-time update:** AI tools can update B2B customer segments in real time. This agility ensures that B2B marketing and sales strategies stay relevant to current market conditions.

How AI tools segment customers

1. **Data collection:** AI tools collect data from many sources, including CRM systems, social media, website interactions, purchase histories and external databases.
2. **Data analysis:** Machine learning algorithms analyse the collected data to find patterns and correlations. For example, AI might identify that companies in a particular industry with a specific revenue range are more likely to engage with certain types of content or purchase specific products.
3. **Segment creation:** AI tools can automatically segment the customer base into distinct groups, each with specific attributes and needs. For example, it might create segments for 'high-growth tech companies in the SaaS space' or 'small businesses in the healthcare industry with high engagement'.

Examples of AI tools

- ZoomInfo: ZoomInfo uses AI to create advanced B2B customer segments based on firmographic and technographic data. Segmentation can be based on company size, industry and even organizational changes like new executive hires.
- Salesforce Einstein: Salesforce Einstein leverages AI to analyse CRM data and automatically segment B2B customers based on factors like deal size, purchasing cycle and customer interactions. Einstein identifies ideal B2B customers for cross-selling and upselling using predictive analytics.

PUT INTO PRACTICE

NLP-based: try the following command for NLP-based tools, e.g. ChatGPT.

- *Please highlight top five B2B segments for multimedia sector looking to buy IT equipment.*

Based on the prompt, five segments were described, i.e. (1) media production companies, (2) advertising agencies, (3) broadcasting networks, (4) digital content creating companies and (5) postproduction studios.

Response for **media production companies:**

- **Description**: These include companies involved in creating video content, television, film and animation studios. They require high-performance IT equipment like powerful workstations, rendering servers and storage solutions to handle large multimedia files and complex graphics processing.
- **Key IT needs**: High-end graphic workstations, robust storage solutions (NAS or cloud-based), rendering servers, video editing software and network equipment for fast data transfer.

This information can be further delved into by asking more specifics per segment you're interested in or perhaps if the segmentation was too broad you may ask for sub-segmentation for one of these core segments.

Customer journey maps

What is a journey map?

So, what is a customer journey? It is the sequence of steps a customer goes through to fulfil a particular goal; there can be various journeys which customers conduct throughout their interactions with a vendor. Customer journeys are very much aligned to different needs or activities which customers carry out in the pre-purchase and post purchase phases.

This provides an understanding of the sequence of touchpoints or steps the customer undertakes for a particular task as well as which digital channels and related content are used. (See Figure 2.2.)

By understanding the sequence of the steps this can help to optimize the flow or the touchpoints may be identified. For example, if search or SEO is an initial step followed by prospective customers going to a vendor's website and visiting the vendor's social media pages, organizations can ensure they include necessary website links in SEO content and social media links are on the suitable website pages. A customer journey map proved to be so effective

FIGURE 2.2 Customer journey maps

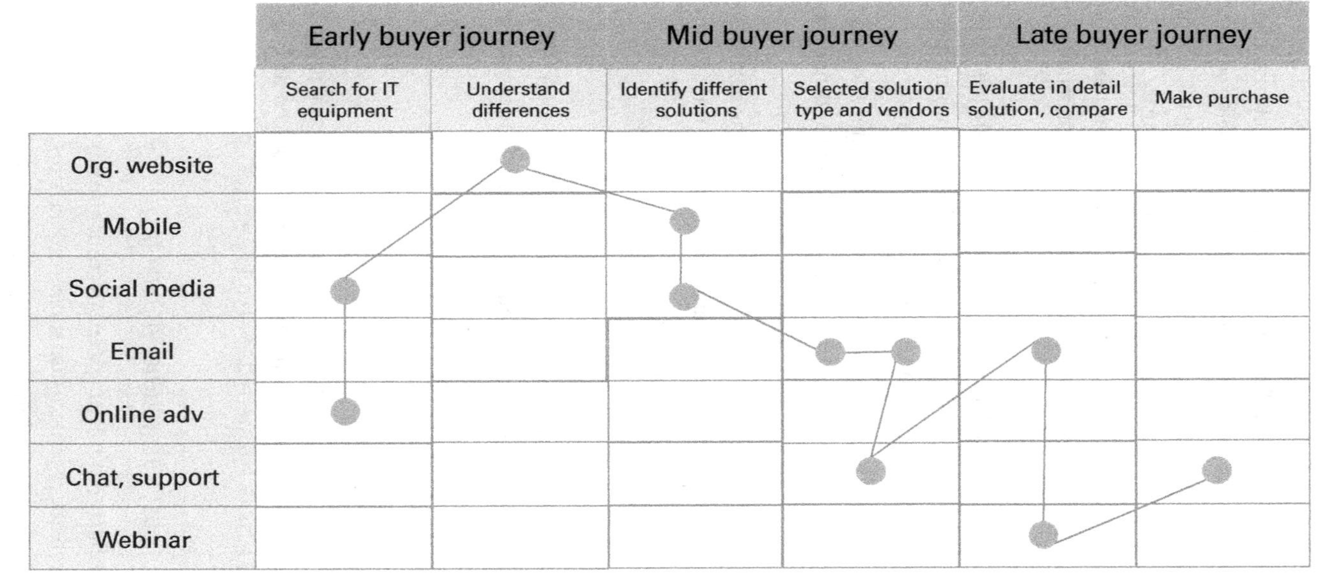

Early buyer journey
Mid buyer journey
Late buyer journey
Search for IT equipment
Understand differences
Identify different solutions
Selected solution type and vendors
Evaluate in detail solution, compare
Make purchase
Org. website
Mobile
Social media
Email
Online adv
Chat, support
Webinar

STEPS IN CREATING A B2B CUSTOMER JOURNEY MAP

Step 1 Define the buyer persona: The first step is to select or define the B2B buyer persona; this should match your ideal target customer profile and then the main stakeholder who is involved in buying your company's products and services. Typically, in B2B marketing this is a purchase manager or finance manager, but it varies by industry.

Step 2 Identify key customer journey touchpoints. The next step is to define the touchpoints, i.e. the points where prospective companies interact with your brand.

Step 3 Gather data and insights: Once touchpoints are identified then data needs to be collected for those touchpoints. Sources include CRM systems, website analytics, customer feedback and sales teams.

Step 4 Create the journey map: Once data is collected the next step is the create the journey map itself; typically, phases are defined for early buyer journey, mid buyer journey and late buyer journey.

Step 5 Once the customer journey map is in place the next steps are to optimize the journey as well and implement and track the changes made to optimize the customer journey.

in companies that the Gartner Group predicted that 60 per cent of large organizations will contain in-house customer journey mapping abilities in 2018.[1]

AI role

When we consider the above steps in the customer journey map, AI tools can be used in all these steps; we've already looked at buyer persona creation so let's focus on steps 2–5 (see Figure 2.3).

AI tools for customer journey mapping

AI can collect data from various touchpoints; examples of touchpoints include website interactions, social media sites, customer service logs and purchase history. Machine learning algorithms can process this data to identify patterns and trends that might be missed by human analysts.

AI-powered tools can create visual representations of customer journeys, making complex data more accessible and actionable.

FIGURE 2.3 Customer journey mapping and AI

Phases	Select buyer persona	Identify touchpoints	Gather data	Optimize
Activities	Segment and role	Identify touchpoint per persona	Gather data from different sources	Optimize touchpoints, customer journey
AI Role	AI tools can help us identify key stakeholders in DMU	AI tools can allow us identify touchpoints	AI tools can amalgamate and integrate data	AI tools can provide recommendations regarding where, how to optimize customer journey
AI tool	Machine learning/NLP tools like ChatGPT	Machine learning/NLP tools like ChatGPT Tools like 6sense	CDP platforms	CDP platforms NLP/machine learning

One example is UXPressia's AI-powered journey mapping tool which can create informative journey maps based on input data. However, it's important to note that while AI can greatly enhance the process, human oversight and interpretation remain crucial to ensure the insights are applied effectively and ethically in business strategies.

HOW TO CREATE A CUSTOMER JOURNEY MAP IN PRACTICE

The first step is to download marketing activity for new customers; remember to use customers which fit your ideal target customer criteria. After that the next logical step is to consider tracking touchpoints by key areas of the customer journey in terms of early buyer journey (pre lead capture) and post lead capture but before sales handover and after sales handover.

Before lead capture one can use non-AI tools as well, but the AI tools here are the main touchpoint areas:

- website via Google analytics
- website experience via website heatmapping software
- social media interactions via social analytics software

Post lead capture, one can use non-AI tools or tools with embedded AI features such as HubSpot marketing automation and CRM tools to track touchpoints.

Integration of touchpoints to support customer journey creation can include tools such as customer data platforms, CRM platforms which integrate marketing automation and other sources of data or dedicated customer journey mapping software.

Examples of AI-based tools which can create customer journey maps include Uxpressia, Miro, TheyDo and JourneyAI.

REAL-WORLD EXAMPLE: UXPRESSIA WITH URSPECTR

In 2016, UrSpectr launched an innovative legal tech product and quickly aimed to enhance user satisfaction by introducing new features. However, prioritizing which features to roll out became a significant challenge. Despite regularly engaging with customers and having a general understanding of their preferences, the team lacked the tools and expertise to derive actionable insights from these conversations. By 2018, it became clear that they needed an increased focus on customer centricity to address these issues. Recognizing the complexity of this transformation requires changes in mindset, culture and processes, UrSpectr sought the expertise of UXPressia's CX team and customer journey mapping (CJM) tools.

UXPressia approached the transformation iteratively, beginning with a series of in-house workshops to introduce UrSpectr to customer journey mapping. These sessions gradually engaged interdisciplinary teams, empowering them with skills to build customer journeys, conduct effective user interviews and analyse research findings. Over time, the teams became increasingly independent, capable of organizing CJM workshops, creating customer personas and interpreting insights using UXPressia's tools. This process also enabled UrSpectr to establish a dedicated customer experience department that streamlined efforts and improved the product based on quality user insights.

The results were impressive. UrSpectr successfully developed in-house CX experts who now act as agents of change, fostering a company-wide culture of customer-centric innovation. With UXPressia's tools and guidance, the teams became adept at creating journey maps and personas, which in turn allowed for better product enhancements and sustainable growth. Reflecting on the experience, Tatiana Skorik, Chief of Customer Experience at UrSpectr, noted, 'UXPressia's journey mapping and persona tools make it so much easier to implement these practices at scale. My team and I especially loved the sharing capabilities.'

Ultimately, UrSpectr overcame its initial hurdles, leveraging AI-powered tools and a customer-first approach to achieve a profound transformation that continues to drive innovation and success.

Voice of customer analysis

Voice of customer (VoC) is basically where customer state feedback and opinions, so voice of customer analysis is vital to understand what customers are saying. Sources of voice of customer include surveys, emails, social media, CRM systems, reviews and call centre transcripts.

The three types of AI tools which can do voice of customer analysis are NLP for sentiment analysis, text-based mining and automated survey and feedback collection.

AI tools can use NLP to process and analyse unstructured customer feedback, identifying sentiments, opinions and themes. An example of a tool is MonkeyLearn, which uses NLP and machine learning to analyse large datasets of customer feedback, reviews and emails, offering sentiment analysis and identifying key themes. Companies like Dell use AI-based NLP to analyse VoC data from customer surveys, chat logs and support tickets to improve its enterprise IT solutions and customer experience. We'll be looking more into sentiment analysis in the following chapter.

Other text-based AI tools can look through large amounts of text data to identify trends and patterns. Text mining helps companies identify recurring topics, challenges or requests that customers have and allows businesses to prioritize product features or improvements. One tools which offers this is IBM Watson, which carries out text mining to extract meaningful insights from unstructured data, such as customer emails, reviews or service tickets.

Automated survey and feedback tools represent the third type of tools. AI tools can design, distribute and analyse customer surveys automatically. By using machine learning algorithms, these tools can adapt survey questions in real time based on customer responses. Qualtrics XM is an AI-powered Voci platform that automates survey distribution, analyses responses and provides actionable insights.

Customer data platforms

Customer data platforms (CDPs) are sophisticated software solutions which consolidate data from different data sources and data based to allow companies to create a unified customer profile. Data which is used can include websites, CRM systems, marketing automation platform, social media, media data bases, ERP systems and others. The main advantage of CDPs is that they can be very comprehensive; the comprehensiveness depends on how much data is being consolidated. CDPs are specifically designed to handle real-time data, making them highly valuable for marketers who need up-to-date insights to drive their campaigns.

CDPs can also carry out functions such as lead scoring and lead prioritization; through analysing customer data, marketers can focus on high-value leads thus improving focus and conversion rates. CDP are often used in conjunction with account-based marketing. Examples of CDP include ZoomInfo and Segment.

AI features and functions in CDP platforms

AI features within CDPs include machine learning algorithms, predictive analytics and NLP.

Predictive analytics enable CDPs to forecast future behaviours, such as the likelihood of a lead progressing through the sales funnel or the potential for churn. This allows B2B marketers to proactively engage with prospects who are showing signs of interest or to re-engage those who might be slipping away. Machine learning algorithms in CDPs also continuously refine customer segments, ensuring that they remain accurate and relevant as more data is collected.

Reference

1 Perez Vega, Dr Rodrigo (2019) How to create a customer journey map, www.rodrigoperezvega.com/blog/how-to-create-a-customer-journey-map/ (archived at https://perma.cc/C88G-X2MT)

Further reading

Clark, S (2024) How AI transforms customer journey mapping, CMSWire, www.cmswire.com/customer-experience/the-benefits-of-combining-customer-journey-mapping-with-ai/ (archived at https://perma.cc/L9XA-K7N2)

Lemlist Blog (2023) 3 steps to create detailed ICPs and buyer personas with AI, www.lemlist.com/blog/ai-buyer-personas (archived at https://perma.cc/286M-5V6U)

Levdikova, T (2024) AI mapping in UXPressia: Visualize your customers' journeys, UXPressia Blog, uxpressia.com/blog/ai-mapping (archived at https://perma.cc/L9CD-4E36)

PART TWO

Awareness and content marketing

03

AI-powered advertising

What you will gain from this chapter

Understanding of the following:

- understanding of AI use cases in B2B advertising
- learn about types of AI tools in advertising
- learn about AI for ad fraud protection
- understand AI in B2B PR

Introduction

This chapter we'll look at the role of AI in supporting the awareness phase, aka the early buyer journey; we'll focus on how AI is used in advertising and in PR, and in general how AI is used in generating awareness.

Turning to advertising and more specifically digital advertising, digital advertising has become increasingly used and more sophisticated in its application in B2B marketing. There are a number of differences compared to traditional advertising; some key differences relate to how aspects can be better controlled and managed in digital advertising such as where the advert is displayed, how it is displayed and who should see the advert.

Types of B2B digital advertising

The main types of digital advertising include digital advertising, native advertising, PPC (pay-per-click) and mobile advertising.

Display advertising is advertising on websites, social media and usually comes in the forms of banners; although other formats such as video, images and GIFs can be used. Native advertising is another form of digital advertising and is so called as the content or information advertised is native to the page and stand out. It comes in different scales of implementation: in its purest form it matches in text, font and the way it is displayed. Native advertising works because when it is done well, it is informative, educative, strongly targeted and isn't interruptive in nature.

B2B mobile advertising has become increasingly used and adopted by B2B marketers. Smartphones and tablets are being used more and more, mobile applications and the technologies have matured and mobile advertising has become more sophisticated to suit.

AI and advertising

AI has already been present in the digital advertising space for a long time now. It is used in the area of programmatic advertising, and it has been used to choose which ads are to be shown based on target audience preferences. Through AI such advertising has just become smarter and more effective.

Ad copy creation and quality

Ai is also used to create advertisement copy (ad copy); it is not only the aspects of creating the copy through AI but the speed at which ad copy can be created. Today, with generative AI technology, one can create ad copy almost instantaneously rather than the hours or days it could take with non-AI-based methods. Other benefits of AI in ad copy creation is not just time and efficiency but also in the ability to tailor and adapt ad copy. Through AI, businesses can better adapt and tailor ad copy and experience to customers. AI in this case analyses account data and can tailor website content to adjust to customers and individual needs, which in turn improves the website experience; here we refer to how AI is used for contextual ads. Technologies and AI tools have come a long way in the last decade such as that visuals are not only more realistic but one can create incredible combinations.

Advertising campaign management

AI is now also used for advertising campaigns. AI is used to improve metrics of ads such as engagement rates and conversion rates; apparently, 26 per cent of companies use technology to improve advertising metrics. Advertising campaigns can be improved through AI; AI plays the role of automating ads, targeting ads and improving bidding as well as forecasting performance for ad campaigns. According to the Marketing Artificial Intelligence Institute, both Google Ads and Meta Ads 'use AI to sell, target, and place ads micro-second by micro-second'.[1]

Ad campaign channel selection

AI can also help in selecting best advertising channels determining best engagement timings using data from past ad campaigns as well as customer data. Through AI, businesses can reduce bounce rates and improve conversion rates

AI and real-time bidding optimization

AI algorithms make on-the-spot decisions on ad bids in real-time auctions to maximize the value of each advert for B2B campaigns.

Other benefits of real-time bidding (RTB) are that it allows marketers to make better decisions and ultimately increase return on ad spend. RTB and machine learning tools can identify patterns in advertising responses; machine learning can allow marketers to understand their target audience better.

Predictive analysis for advertising campaign performance

Advertising can use predictive analysis for customer lifetime value (CLV) to better allocate advertising budgets. Through combining CLV and predictive techniques, advertisers can look at ways to increase lifetime value of particular customer segments. Platforms which support predictive analytics in advertising include DataRobot.

Cons of using AI in advertising

We've heard about the advantages of using AI in advertising such as automating tasks, optimizing advertising, more detailed analytics, etc. But what about the disadvantages? The following are some of the cons of using AI in advertising.

Ethics: Not understanding the AI technology or concerns over ethics regarding the use of AI in advertising; apparently 33 per cent of businesses in a recent survey don't utilize AI in their content marketing due to comprehension of the technology and worries regarding plagiarism, quality and legal implications.[2]

Data quality: If AI is to be used for advertising, the data needs to be up to date, accurate and not have any data integrity issues; this required constant review and checking of data to ensure the data itself is up to scratch.

Too mechanical and missing creativity: AI-based advertising is missing the human interaction and involvement and therefore may be missing out some of the nuances which humans can pick up on; one example might when looking at generative AI and using generative AI to depict people in images; while images are much better in quality than 10 years ago there are still some giveaways to show that the images are not real people. A related argument in this area is that with the increasing use of AI tools in advertising there are concerns that we are reducing or removing valuable stages of creativity which lead to higher quality and more creative advertisements.

Skills required: Using AI in advertising requires people to be skilled up in using AI tools; AI tools and technologies might require investment in training or even in people in using AI tools and technologies.

AI features in social media advertising

Aside of dedicated AI-based advertising tools and technology, one can make use of the latest AI features built into social media platforms which enhance advertising, let's take a look at some of the last AI features in social media.

Facebook and Instagram – Meta

FACEBOOK AI-BASED ADVERTISING FEATURES

Facebook offers a number of AI-based features to help businesses personalize ads and effectively reach their ideal audience. One such feature is Meta's automated ads, which allow advertisers to input specific campaign goals. Based on these inputs, the AI suggests personalized ads tailored to meet the desired objectives. Another feature is the Audience Network, which extends ad reach across multiple platforms, including Facebook and Instagram. According to Meta, displaying ads on multiple platforms increases conversion rates, making this tool essential for businesses aiming to maximize their advertising impact.

INSTAGRAM AI-BASED ADVERTISING FEATURES

Instagram has recently introduced innovative AI tools designed to enhance user engagement and advertising potential. These include AI-generated stickers, which allow users to create unique stickers based on prompts.

These stickers can be used in chats or added to stories, making them a versatile tool for personalized content creation. Additionally, the 'Start a Chat with AI' feature enables users to engage in conversations with AI for advice, suggestions or other interactive activities, creating a dynamic and engaging platform experience. Instagram also offers AI backdrops for stories, allowing users to customize and update story backgrounds with tailored designs using AI technology, adding another layer of personalization to content.

LinkedIn advertising and AI

LinkedIn also has been integrating new AI features over the past years to improve and enhance its advertising. One feature is 'Accelerate', which helps advertising optimize campaigns in Campaign Manager.

Accelerate optimizes ad creations by reducing time and effort in the ad creation phase. More specifically Accelerate uses an AI model to automatically adjust bids and associated budget to better performing ads. Accelerate also integrates multiple AI aspects including predictive audiences, which allows business to improve campaign targeting and supports targeting of higher-value accounts/customers.

AI-enhanced ad targeting: LinkedIn leverages AI to analyse user profile and interest data to create more optimized audience segments thus ensuring ads are targeting very specific and relevant audiences.

In performance and analytics LinkedIn has integrated new AI features; one area is in generated performance summary reports on spend, impressions, clicks, etc. which help advertising understand how to optimize advertising strategies.

Other AI-based advertising tools

Outside of social media we can find AI advertising tools in the following spaces.

AI-based tools in B2B advertising

AI is transforming B2B advertising by providing tools that automate tasks, personalize content, optimize targeting and analyse performance (see Figure 3.1). The main types of AI-based advertising tools include the following:

AI FOR AD COPY GENERATION

AI-powered tools like Jasper, Copy.ai and Persado assist in creating high-converting ad copy, headlines and CTAs tailored to B2B audiences. These tools analyse data and audience preferences to produce personalized, engaging content.

Talking more specifically about Persado, this leverages AI to generate advertising content; this in turn improves conversion rates. This tool can be used across multiple social media advertising platforms including LinkedIn ads and Facebook ads. Persado's solution automatically takes ad copy and tailors it to the language that motivates each user most. Another recent development is Microsoft Copilot, which is an AI-powered tool providing suggestions for product images, headlines and descriptions using AI.

AI FOR PROGRAMMATIC ADVERTISING

Programmatic AI tools like AdRoll, Basis Technologies and The Trade Desk automate the process of buying, placing and optimizing ads. They use real-time bidding and audience data to target specific segments efficiently.

AI FOR ADVERTISING ANALYTICS

AI-driven analytics platforms like Google Analytics 4 (GA4), Pathmatics and Heap Analytics help track and interpret ad performance. These tools provide insights into ROI, audience behaviour and campaign effectiveness to refine strategies. Google Ads also use AI within bidding to optimize bidding as well as provide advertising performance insights to support businesses to improve their advertising strategies.

AI FOR TARGET AUDIENCE IDENTIFICATION

Platforms like Leadfeeder and Demandbase leverage AI to identify high-value prospects, map accounts and target ads to the right decision-makers in a B2B setting.

AI FOR DYNAMIC CREATIVE OPTIMIZATION (DCO)

Tools like Celtra and Google Web Designer enable the creation and real-time optimization of personalized ad creatives, ensuring relevance for each target segment.

Practical insights: Google PMAX

Another area where Google ads use AI is in PMax campaigns.

Google introduced the PMax campaigns that advertise across all of Google's networks. This is a machine learning feature which improves an

FIGURE 3.1 AI features in advertising tools

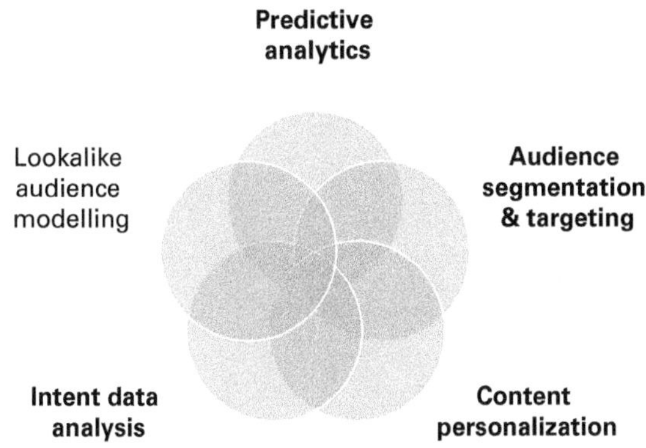

advertiser's presence and conversions Smart bidding is used and ads are shown in the format most likely to perform best for each placement.

In practice – advertising efficiency and optimization

So how does one make sure to use AI features for improving advertising efficiency? In most cases it is aware of the new AI features which are now embedded into popular software solution.

If we consider Google Ads; this platform leverages AI in different ways; one way is through its smart bidding AI feature which Google's leverages machine learning to optimize bids in real time based on campaign goals and other data.

If we look another platform, Adobe Advertising Cloud, one can leverage AI through its predictive analysis to predict ad performance, to optimize targeting. The platform also uses AI for bidding which monitors ad performance and adjusts ads on an ongoing basis to ensure ROI is maximized.

Ad fraud detection

AI systems are able to detect and prevent fraudulent advertising activity. So, what is fraudulent advertising activity? One fraudulent ad activity is the practice of illegally and artificially inflating the number of clicks or impressions on an online advertisement in order to generate revenue from advertisers. Other types of ad fraud are domain spoofing where fraudsters misrepresent low-quality sites as premium, high-value domains to attract higher-paying ads, pixel stuffing.

To counter this AI can distinguish between genuine human engagement and bot-type behaviours which itself may indicate fraudulent activities; AI tools can also identify abnormal patterns which indicate bots being used; or where fake interactions are taking place.

PR and AI

AI is also being increasingly used in the area of PR. Let's first define what PR is about.

PR DEFINED

PR is about building relations, which is largely the same for B2B and B2C marketing. However, there are a number of other roles for B2B PR; these include content creation, messaging and positioning, reputation management, supporting product/service launches, market research, storytelling, social media and thought leadership. Some of these latter aspects differ very much between B2B and B2C PR. PR has gone through a transition over the past 10 years to involve new things such as storytelling, blogging, social-based PR and sustainability initiatives.

AREAS OF AI USAGE IN PR

The main areas of B2B PR today include strategic planning, media relations management, thought leadership, executive profiling, partner communications, reputation management and crises management (Figure 3.2).

Thought leadership

Thought leadership is very much an area of B2B marketing, and it involves becoming a trusted go-to authority on topics. To successfully establish thought leadership involves ensuring articles are placed correctly offline and online, promoting to the right audience, arranging speaking engagements and monitoring quality of the content.

AI tools like ChatGPT, Jasper or Writesonic can help generate ideas, write first drafts of blog posts, white papers or social media content, and assist with content optimization for SEO. Automated research uses AI to gather industry trends, data and insights quickly for reports and articles, reducing the time spent on manual research.

FIGURE 3.2 Areas of AI usage in PR

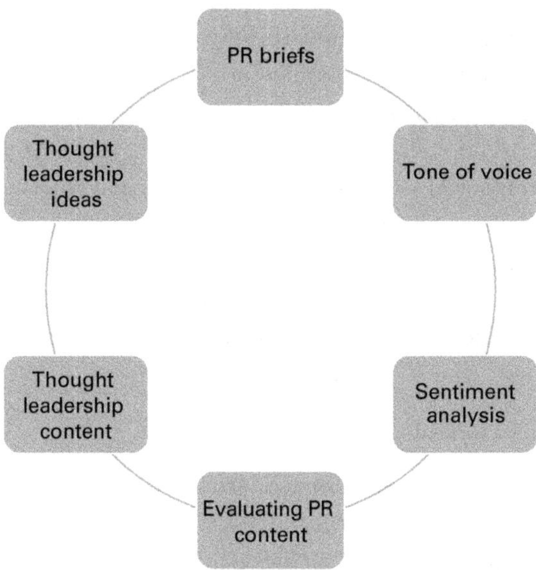

> PRACTICAL TIP: PR RESEARCH USING AI
>
> Why not get your PR agency or go-to person to conduct some initial research to help you with your marketing. You could use the following questions for the PR person or even as commands in your NLP/ML tool like Gemini or ChatGPT:
>
> - What social networks does 'the buyer persona (here you would specify the type of role/industry)' use?
> - What trade shows do they frequent?
> - Which trade publications do they read?
> - What influencers are most likely to reach my prospects?
> - What blogs, news media sites and other websites do prospects frequent?
> - What groups, networks and forums do they use?

Media relations and AI

AI has become an invaluable resource in supporting media relations, offering advanced tools and features that streamline monitoring and outreach efforts. For instance, platforms like Meltwater and Cision utilize AI to track mentions of a brand, its competitors or key industry topics across various media outlets, including news websites, social media and blogs. Users can set up keyword-based alerts, enabling real-time updates whenever their brand is mentioned or relevant stories surface. This capability not only provides insight into media coverage but also helps in identifying emerging trends and potential PR opportunities. Additionally, tools such as Prowly take media relations a step further by leveraging AI to recommend journalists and media outlets that are best suited to cover specific press releases. By analysing the content of a release and matching it with a journalist's area of expertise or prior work, PR professionals can use Prowly to ensure targeted and effective outreach, reducing the time and effort involved in identifying the right contacts.

PR measurement and analytics

Measuring the impact of PR efforts is crucial for understanding the effectiveness of campaigns, and AI tools have revolutionized this process. Platforms like Muck Rack and Onclusive offer robust media impact analysis features that assess the performance of media coverage. These tools use AI to evaluate metrics such as reach, engagement, sentiment and even return on investment (ROI). For example, Onclusive's AI capabilities can determine how a specific article or media placement drives audience engagement or contributes to business outcomes, such as website traffic or lead generation. Muck Rack provides intuitive dashboards that display detailed analytics, allowing users to track trends, compare performance over time and adjust their strategies accordingly. By leveraging these features, PR teams can not only report on campaign success but also make data-driven decisions to optimize future efforts.

Creating PR narratives using AI

AI tools also play a valuable role in crafting compelling PR narratives, supporting both the ideation and writing phases. During the brainstorming stage, AI can generate ideas for campaign themes or story angles by analysing industry trends, historical data or audience preferences. For example, tools like ChatGPT or Jasper can be prompted to provide creative concepts for a product launch campaign by inputting details about the target audience, industry and key messages. In the narrative development phase, AI can assist in drafting press releases, blog posts or media pitches. For instance, users can provide a basic outline or key points, and AI tools can generate polished, professional content that serves as a starting point. However, it's important to use AI as a complement to human creativity rather than a replacement, as the human touch ensures the narrative aligns with brand tone and resonates authentically with the target audience.

Tone of voice in PR

One surprising area where AI can help is in the tone of voice; not only can AI tools be used to help input into the writing process, but once the PR article or PR piece has been written we can use certain AI text-based tools to produce different tones of the content

So, what do we mean in terms of tone? Tone can be referred to as joking, authoritative, scientific, data-driven or other.

Applications such as Grammarly and Jasper can help us convert text and present it in a different light; one can use such tools to test out the tone of voice of article to different audiences particular if the PR piece is regarded as more strategic.

In other areas of reputation management or crises management, tone of voice becomes even more critical and so AI tools can be used to hit the right balance between dealing with the crises in an authoritative manner and not coming across overly corporate.

Creating press reports and releases

AI tools can be used to detect patterns, uncover trends and evaluate the effectiveness of PR campaigns based on historical data. Platforms such as Onclusive include predictive analytics features which are able to forecast the potential reach and engagement of future PR efforts. This is done by identifying what types of content or media strategies have worked best in the past, which in turn allows PR to make better informed decisions and adjust their tactics to achieve better results.

Another key benefit of using AI in B2B PR reporting is the ability to generate visually compelling and customized reports automatically. AI tools like DashThis or Google Looker Studio leverage data visualization techniques to turn raw data into clear, easy-to-understand charts, graphs and infographics.

AI can both accelerate the reporting process as well as improve the quality of PR by providing deeper insights and enabling more proactive, data-driven PR strategies.

Identifying media lists

AI tools can support PR practitioners in building customized media lists and identifying media coverage. For example, these tools can analyse large volumes of content quickly, pulling out relevant keywords, names and themes related to a specific topic or industry.

Let's take the example of someone targeting a company or audiences in the construction industry. A PR professional could use an AI-driven media monitoring tool (like Meltwater or Cision) to analyse news articles, press releases and social media for topics such as 'sustainable construction', 'construction technology' or 'smart cities'. This enables them to identify journalists frequently covering these topics and add them to their media list. AI tools (e.g. Muck Rack) can suggest journalists who are most likely to respond to pitches about construction topics by analysing the frequency of responses or coverage success from previous interactions.

In practice: evaluating PR effectiveness through queries

We can use the commands in Table 3.1 to help us evaluate PR effectiveness; while these prompts via applications such as ChatGPT 3.5 may not replace dedicated PR AI tools, they can already start to shed some light on key questions we may have.

Influencer identification

The fierce competition in the B2B digital marketing domain has led to a drastic increase in the cost of paid advertising. Consequently, several B2B marketers are looking to influencer marketing to enrich their brand image and generate leads.

TABLE 3.1 Queries to evaluate PR effectiveness

Query type	Example query
1. Sentiment analysis	'Analyse the sentiment of media mentions of our company in the past month.'
2. Key message analysis	'Identify the most frequently mentioned key messages in media coverage of our recent product launch.'

(continued)

TABLE 3.1 (Continued)

Query type	Example query
3. Competitor analysis	'Compare our media coverage to that of our main competitors in the past quarter.'
4. Audience reach	'Estimate the total audience reached by our press releases in the last year.'
5. Share of voice	'Calculate our share of voice in the industry compared to our competitors.'
6. Influencer engagement	'Identify the top influencers who have mentioned our company on social media.'
7. Website traffic	'Analyse the impact of our PR efforts on website traffic to our product pages.'
8. Brand reputation	'Assess changes in our brand reputation over time based on media coverage.'

Influencer marketing identifies individuals who have influence over potential buyers and orients marketing activities around such them and their platforms in order to leverage their influence.

The concept of using influencers to market a product or service is not new. In fact, most consumer advertisements feature influencers such as professional athletes or movie stars. However, B2B marketing budgets often cannot accommodate the high costs associated with these high-profile figures. Fortunately, such mainstream influencers may not be the most effective in influencing business customers' purchasing decisions.

In the B2B space, there are influencers with a smaller audience but significant sway over a highly targeted customer base. These niche influencers can have a profound impact on purchasing decisions, making them valuable assets in B2B marketing strategies.

Influencer marketing and AI

AI tools can be used in influencer marketing in areas of influencer identification, predicting influencer performance, content optimization, detecting fraud and automated influencer outreach.

INFLUENCER IDENTIFICATION

One of the primary challenges in influencer marketing is identifying the right influencer for one's business (Figure 3.3). This fit can refer to the influencer's target audience, although there are other factors to consider in terms of influencer fit. According to a study by Influencity, AI-based influencer identification can increase campaign efficiency by 30 per cent compared to traditional methods.[3]

Tools like Traackr or Upfluence use AI to assess an influencer's reach, relevance and engagement levels within specific industry niches, allowing marketers find the right influencers who align with a brand and target audience.

AI can identify experts in specific niches like cloud computing, enterprise software or supply chain management, ensuring the influencers you collaborate with are relevant to your audience. For example, a company offering cybersecurity solutions can use AI to find influencers who frequently write or speak about data security issues in the B2B space.

INFLUENCER EVALUATION

AI assesses the depth of expertise by evaluating how often an influencer shares thought leadership content, white papers or research reports. For example, if you're targeting decision-makers in manufacturing, AI can help identify influencers who are publishing data-driven insights and thought leadership on smart manufacturing and automation trends.

PUT INTO PRACTICE: USING MACHINE LEARNING TO EVALUATE INFLUENCERS

Let's first select criteria of trustworthiness, expertise, and social media presence and usage and ask ChatGPT or Perplexity.

Command: *Please conduct an evaluation of 'a named influencer in Healthcare technology' based on the criteria of trustworthiness, expertise, and social media presence and usage. On a score of 1–10 where 1 is low and 10 is high please rate influencer including any evidence, facts of data to support the score.*

See a summary of the output in Table 3.2.

TABLE 3.2 Summary table of scores for John Nosta

Criteria	Score (1–10)	Supporting Evidence
Trustworthiness	8/10	Affiliation with Google Health; known for transparent, reliable insights.
Expertise	9/10	30+ years in healthcare, contributor to Forbes, speaker at major health tech events.
Social media presence	8/10	Strong Twitter and LinkedIn presence; high engagement with healthcare tech audience.

FIGURE 3.3 AI for influencer identification

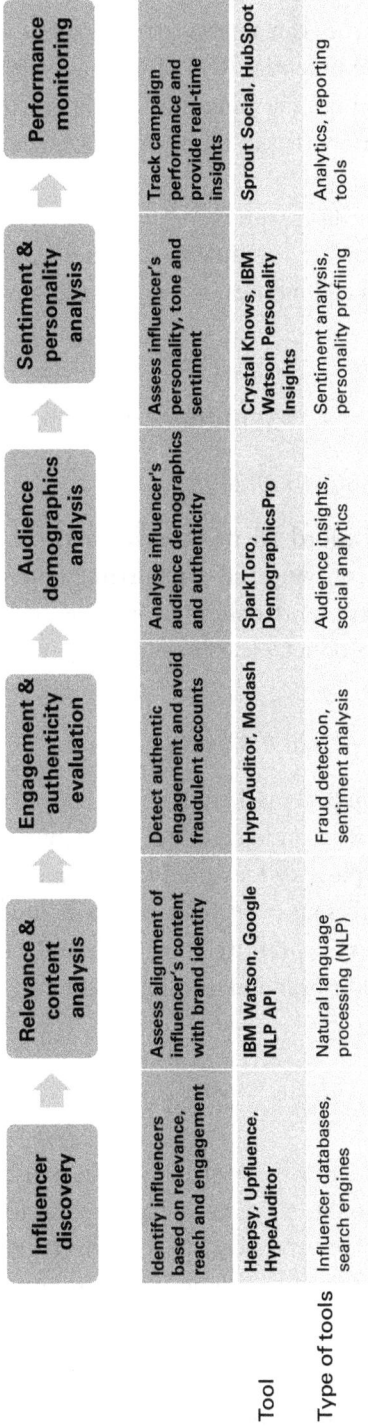

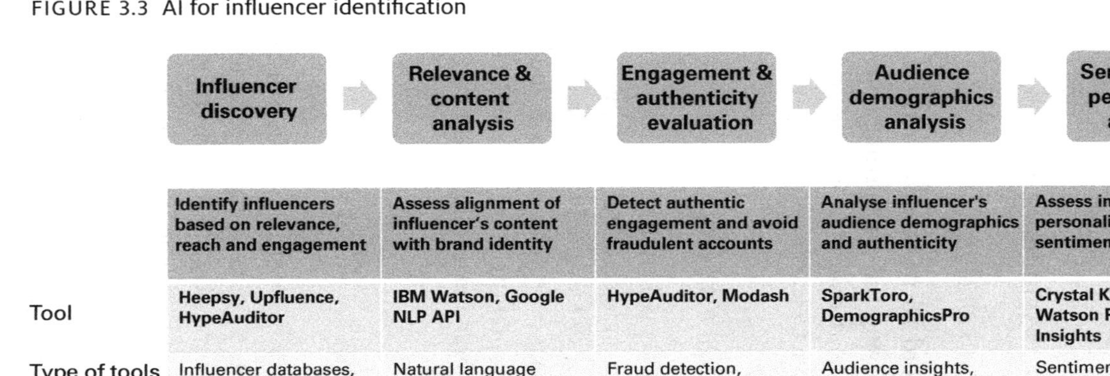

Influencer discovery
Relevance & content analysis
Engagement & authenticity evaluation
Audience demographics analysis
Sentiment & personality analysis
Performance monitoring
Identify influencers based on relevance, reach and engagement
Assess alignment of influencer's content with brand identity
Detect authentic engagement and avoid fraudulent accounts
Analyse influencer's audience demographics and authenticity
Assess influencer's personality, tone and sentiment
Track campaign performance and provide real-time insights
Tool
Heepsy, Upfluence, HypeAuditor
IBM Watson, Google NLP API
HypeAuditor, Modash
SparkToro, DemographicsPro
Crystal Knows, IBM Watson Personality Insights
Sprout Social, HubSpot
Type of tools
Influencer databases, search engines
Natural language processing (NLP)
Fraud detection, sentiment analysis
Audience insights, social analytics
Sentiment analysis, personality profiling
Analytics, reporting tools

PREDICTING INFLUENCER PERFORMANCE

AI's predictive analytics can assess past campaigns and influencer collaborations to forecast the potential ROI of working with a particular influencer. Tools like Onalytica use machine learning algorithms to predict the performance of influencer content in terms of engagement, reach and conversion.

INFLUENCER FRAUD DETECTION

AI tools can also detect fraudulent activities such as false followers, bot engagements or inflated metrics in an influencer's profile.

Sentiment analysis

Introduction to sentiment analysis

According to the Oxford Dictionary, sentiment analysis is the process of computationally identifying and categorizing opinions expressed in a piece of text, especially in order to determine whether the writer's attitude towards a particular topic, product, etc. is positive, negative or neutral.

Sentiment analysis in B2B marketing

Sentiment analysis in B2B marketing can be used in many different contexts; it can be used by PR in understanding reactions to PR posts and in understanding tone of a piece of text for PR. Outside of PR, sentiment analysis can be used to track sentiment related to a brand and support marketing improve and address aspects relating to brand building; other areas are related to a product or brand in picking up comments relating to product or customer experience.

AI and sentiment analysis

AI is a fundamental part of sentiment analysis tools; AI can help process and deal with large amounts of data to identify the tone of texts as negative, positive or neutral. It can be used also to identify nuances in text by looking at more subtle aspects of text language in terms of cultural nuances and language nuances.

Improving customer experience

Through sentiment analysis, businesses can analyse a client's feedback and identify product-based strengths and weaknesses; it can also be used to look at broader aspects of customer experience relating to engagement and support from the business. Using this information business can prevent customer attrition as well as improve overall offering and experience the customer has.

In PR, sentiment analysis can be used to track crises and respond quicker. Sentiment analysis allows issues to be caught faster and corrected more quickly. One area for building better customer loyalty is in the reaction time to customers' crises.

TOOL

IBM incorporates sentiment analysis within its Watson suite of services. Business can make use of this for specific industry needs. For example, sentiment analysis in finance or financial institutions is used to analyse trends related to economic indicators. This enables them to make informed investment decisions that optimize profitability while minimizing potential losses.

HOW TO GO ABOUT CONDUCTING SENTIMENT ANALYSIS

The main tools today for carrying out sentiment analysis typically fall under the umbrella of social listening tools. Social listening is all about listening to conversations between customers or prospects and their peers on social media platforms in order to gain insights about your brand and industry. Of course, this can be done manually but the interpretation of the conversation will vary by who is listening, and sometimes the mood they are in – hence the use of social listening tools.

Social listening involves tracking keywords and hashtags related to your brand and industry.

Other alternatives to social listening tools involve surveys and automated sentiment analysis.

PUT INTO PRACTICE

It is probably easier to view sentiment analysis in terms of levels of sophistication by looking at the area of social listening.

Level 1 – simple: One can ask NLP-based tools to evaluate in text form a piece of text and provide a commentary on the positive, negative and neutral tone of the text.

Level 2 – intermediate: One can use social listening tools that are free or low cost. Examples of tools include text2data and Hootsuite.

Level 3 – advanced: Using mid- to high-end tools to conduct a more detailed analysis of sentiment.

Endnotes

1. Yemets, A (2021) Artificial intelligence on Facebook and Google Ads: How does it work?, 16 August, adwisely.com/blog/how-ai-for-advertising-works-facebook-google-ads/ (archived at https://perma.cc/6VPC-39Y3)
2. Kelly, B (2024) AI in advertising: A game plan and tools to get started, 4 November, www.semrush.com/blog/ai-advertising/?kw=&cmp=UK_SRCH_DSA_Blog_EN&label=dsa_pagefeed&Network=g&Device=c&utm_content=683809892104&kwid=dsa-2263819780319&cmpid=18352326857&agpid=153751697662&BU=Core&extid=129921785331&adpos=&gad_source=1&gclid=CjwKCAjw5Ky1BhAgEiwA5jGujtMvo2nSKkG67Q0QKK3cJ2P_lz5ANylH94zWKANHlJliYAkm6TcGOBoCcVEQAvD_BwE] (archived at https://perma.cc/5338-6A3D)
3. Ventures, S (2024) How AI is transforming influencer marketing strategies, 23 May, www.linkedin.com/pulse/how-ai-transforming-influencer-marketing-strategies-stanventures-jl2sc/ (archived at https://perma.cc/KR2C-DMRZ)

Reference

Ventures, S (2024) How AI is transforming influencer marketing strategies, 23 May, www.linkedin.com/pulse/how-ai-transforming-influencer-marketing-strategies-stanventures-jl2sc/ (archived at https://perma.cc/VA7H-9CTB)

Further reading

DataFeedWatch (n.d.) 11 Best AI advertising examples of 2025, www.datafeedwatch.com/blog/best-ai-advertising-examples (archived at https://perma.cc/T3JM-G4VJ)

Kaput, M (2024) AI in advertising: What it is, how to use it and companies to demo. Marketing AI Institute, www.marketingaiinstitute.com/blog/ai-in-advertising (archived at https://perma.cc/QC9T-YSAR)

04

AI and SEO

> What you will gain from this chapter
>
> Understanding of the following:
>
> - how to use AI for keyword identification
> - using AI machine learning to identify long-tail keywords
> - learn about dedicated SEM AI tools.
> - use of AI to improve link building

What is SEO?

Search engine optimization (SEO) is about optimizing your website and activities outside of your website to support the search activities of prospects and customers. The official umbrella term relating to SEO and paid search is search engine marketing (SEM). Essentially, there are three core pillars to SEM, and they operate a little differently: paid search (or PPC advertising), on-page SEO and off-page SEO.

In this chapter our focus will be on- and off-page SEO and overall B2B search engine marketing aspects.

SEO offline, online and key areas

Many factors contribute to successful off-page SEO; this includes link building, social media SEO-based strategy and blogging.

Social media can be a good starting point for creating off-page SEO activities. Using likes, followers and shares on Twitter, LinkedIn or even Instagram can start to build awareness and credibility of the brand.

B2B on-page SEO

On-page SEO is about optimizing websites and individual web pages to support search queries. On-page SEO mainly includes the following:

- Title tags are HTML aspects that highlight what the page is about and appear in the SERP (search engine results page).
- Meta descriptions are a brief description of the web page and are displayed underneath the title tag in the search engine results page. They convey what users will find on the page, so search engines read Meta descriptions to determine the page's topic.
- H1 tags are the heading of the web page itself; the H1 tag should be the same as the title tag so as to avoid confusion; H1 tags are not displayed in the SERP but are shown in the webpage itself.
- Image alt text describes briefly an image which helps a search engine understand the context of the name; this also helps those who use images to search on search engines.

SEO data and AI

Data plays a critical role in the area of SEO and as a result AI can also play an important role. Through analysing search data, businesses can make better decisions regarding products, brands as well as capture a wealth of customer insights. Data from SEO can be used to better understand customer preferences and subsequently help businesses adapt content strategies and other areas of marketing.

Understanding which web page or search terms attract lower vs higher conversions can help business change and improve content, as well as help them understand trending terms. Search data can help business better build their customer journey and customer journey maps. Data related to search traffic can also help business understand user interaction and identify which content drives higher engagement and thus improve customer experiences.

Role of AI

In the area of SEO, AI can assist by reducing repetitive tasks and reduce workloads related to keyword research and keyword identification; it can help with search performance. AI tools can also provide more specific and personalized search results relating to user preferences.

AI search engine marketing tools are able to crunch large volumes of data and information at great speeds; not only this but trends, preferences and keywords can be identified on the basis of this analysis. Examples of AI-enabled search engine marketing tools include SEMrush and Ahrefs. Additionally, AI technology can automate tasks, refine those search ranking aspects and provide more valuable insights.

Personalization role of AI

Search engine applications leverage browsing history, such as location and device so in conjunction with AI algorithms can personalize search results; an example might be if someone googles 'Fintech Company'. If they share their location and previous search history with Google, they'll most likely see more local results as opposed to general, global ones.

With the improvement of search engines, we can see more personalized search results based on users' needs and interests. Algorithms which increasingly use AI consider a wider range of factors such as location, search history and device when providing responses to search queries.

In the area of SEO, we also focus on providing more tailored and localized content; localized content can mean content based on languages, locations, business and industry. For example, hreflang tags can help indicate the language and regional targeting of a webpage, ensuring that users receive content in their preferred language and dialect.

Other aspects where data analysis and AI play a role is in leveraging individual digital behaviours such as time on site, bounce rates and other metrics which allow business to better adapt and update content.

Types of analysis which can be carried out through these tools include the following (see Figure 4.1):

- keyword rankings
- keyword identification
- keyword clusters
- backlink profiles
- competitor keyword insights
- intent

Google Search and AI

Google Search employs a suite of advanced AI-driven technologies that enhance the interpretation, understanding and accessibility of information, particularly for businesses engaging in B2B marketing. RankBrain, a key feature of Google's

FIGURE 4.1 Search AI areas

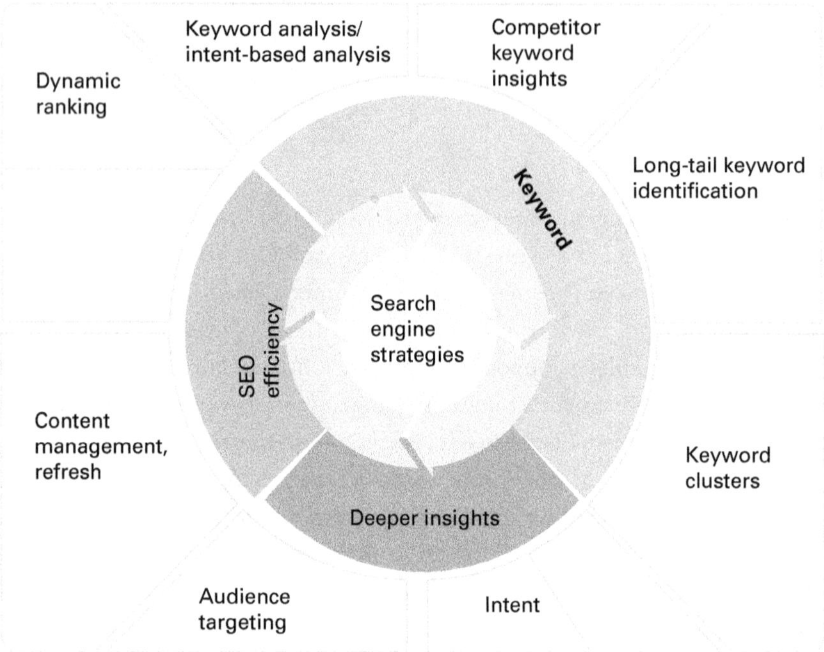

search algorithms, uses machine learning to comprehend and interpret search queries more effectively. It identifies the intent and context behind search terms, helping businesses target their audience more accurately by aligning their content with user intent. Similarly, BERT (Bidirectional Encoder Representations from Transformers) analyses how words relate to one another in a sentence, offering a nuanced understanding of sentence meaning. This enables Google to better interpret complex or conversational queries, which is essential for B2B marketers crafting content tailored to niche audiences.

Google Translate employs neural machine translation (NMT) to translate sentences holistically rather than word by word. This approach ensures greater accuracy, fluency and context-aware translations. By training deep learning models on extensive multilingual datasets, Google Translate can interpret idioms, cultural nuances and context-specific phrases, which is particularly valuable in global B2B communications. This capability allows businesses to break down language barriers, ensuring their marketing and communication efforts resonate with diverse international audiences.

Does Google penalize AI-based content?

Google does not inherently penalize AI-generated content. Instead, it evaluates all content, whether created by humans or AI, using its EEAT framework, which stands for Experience, Expertise, Authority and Trustworthiness. This framework is designed to ensure that the content serves user needs and provides value. AI-based content that meets these criteria is treated no differently from human-written content. However, if AI is used to generate low-quality content that fails to demonstrate EEAT, such as being inaccurate, irrelevant or misleading, it will be penalized. This principle applies universally to all types of content, regardless of its source.

In the context of B2B marketing, the EEAT framework is particularly important because businesses often rely on high-quality content to build trust and authority in their niche. For example, a B2B technology firm might use AI tools to create detailed white papers or blog posts explaining complex technical concepts. If these pieces highlight the company's expertise (such as sharing case studies or proprietary insights), demonstrate authority (e.g. citing credible sources or industry standards) and establish trustworthiness (e.g. ensuring data accuracy and transparency), they align with Google's EEAT standards. On the other hand, if AI-generated content for the same purpose is vague, lacks industry-specific insights or appears generic, it could harm the company's credibility and ranking in search results.

Moreover, Google's emphasis on Experience means that content should reflect practical knowledge or real-world use cases. For instance, a B2B logistics company using AI to create content might include examples of how their solutions have been successfully implemented for clients, thus showcasing first-hand experience. By adhering to the EEAT principles, businesses can ensure their AI-generated content not only complies with Google's standards but also resonates with their target audience, enhancing visibility and engagement.[1]

Keyword identification

Keyword identification is about finding relevant keywords which target audiences use as part of their search activity on search engines. The root to success is to understand in a detailed manner the needs of buyer personas and what they are using as keywords at different stages in the buyer journey.

Keywords can be categorized into generic keywords (known as fat head keywords) or long-tail keywords. The long tail describes the relationship between the costs or competition for certain search terms against the frequency with which they are used. In Figure 4.2, there are three main sections to the shape of the curve: the fat head, the chunky middle and the long tail. Fat head keywords are those with a high volume of traffic and, hence, bidding. This is where you'll find the most popular keywords which are paid for most. The chunky middle and the long tail of the curve are where there are, respectively,

FIGURE 4.2 The long tail

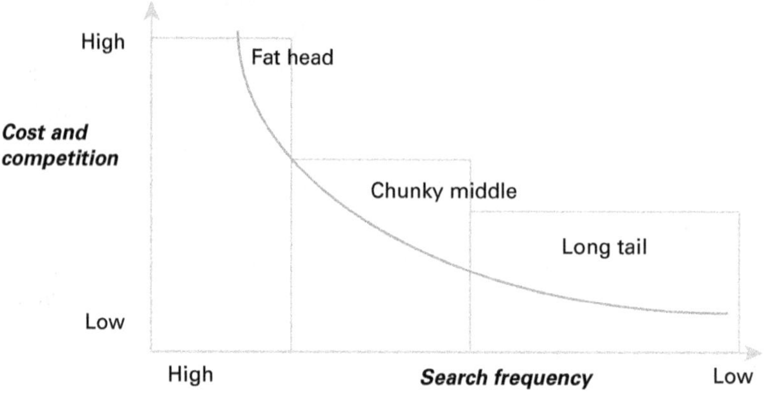

less bidding and less volume in traffic. Long-tail keywords are particularly valuable in B2B because of their high specificity and relevance to an industry; typically, there is not 'one' keyword but they are phrases of are three to five words in length.

Traditional methods or approaches

Traditionally we can find keywords and long-tail keywords using any of the following manual or non-AI methods:

- Look at your internal site search history.
- Review blog posts from customers/prospects who fit your ideal target audience.
- Look at your buyer persona.
- Research competitors.

So how can AI tools help? There are two main approaches in terms of technologies:

1. Text-based AI tools such as ChatGPT, Perplexity and other similar tools
2. Dedicated keyword analytics tools which leverage AI

NLP and machine learning long-tail keyword identification

There are different AI-based approaches to identifying keywords, the first one is to use prompt-based tools and through different ways in formulating queries we can receive different types of commands. With NLP tools such as ChatGPT, Gemini or others we can look at the commands we use to elicit higher quality outputs (see example below).

NLP-based tools can also be used in the following ways outside of just keyword research:

- Content generation: Creating SEO optimized articles, blog posts and web copy that are tailored to target keywords and user intent.
- Meta description creation: Used to automatically generate Meta titles and descriptions that improve click-through rates on SERPs.
- SEO content management and planning: Support planning and scheduling of content related to SEO.
- Competitive keyword analysis: Analysing competition keywords and identify opportunities in the area of keywords usage.

PUT INTO PRACTICE

Let's take an example using tools like ChatGPT or Gemini; here are some examples of commands one could use.

Example comments:

- *Please provide 10 keywords relating to the healthcare industry.*
- *Please provide 10 keywords used by a purchase manager in the healthcare industry looking to buy IT equipment.*
- *Please provide 10 long-tail keywords used by a healthcare industry purchase manager in the early stages of the buyer journey interested in a cybersecurity IT solution.*

See below the first responses according to the different prompts.

Let's now make an even more detailed prompt: *Please provide 10 long-tail keywords used by a purchase manager in the healthcare industry looking to buy IT equipment.*

- Best HIPAA-compliant computers for healthcare organizations
- Affordable medical-grade servers for hospital use
- Top-rated electronic health record (EHR) systems for small clinics
- IT hardware solutions for healthcare data security and compliance
- Cloud storage solutions for secure patient data management
- Telemedicine video conferencing systems for hospitals
- Healthcare IT infrastructure solutions for large medical centres
- Wireless patient monitoring devices with real-time data integration
- Medical device integration platforms for hospital networks
- High-performance computers for medical imaging and diagnostics

Long-tail keyword identification with SEM tools

The second AI approach is to use dedicated search engine analysis tools and their AI features. For example, Arefs offers a range of tools to help find long-tail keywords, including the Keywords Explorer and Site Explorer. With Keywords Explorer one can enter a keyword, which is usually a short-tail keyword, and Ahrefs will recommend related long-tail keywords. You can filter the results by search volume, traffic potential and more.

With Site Explorer one can enter a URL and go to the Organic keywords report to find long-tail keywords from your competitors.

Keyword analytics and AI tools

Now we move on from keyword identification to keyword analytics. With the growing complexity of search algorithms and audience behaviour, traditional methods of keyword research are no longer sufficient to maintain a competitive edge. AI-driven tools have transformed keyword analytics, offering advanced capabilities like predictive analysis, contextual relevance and audience-specific insights. These tools empower B2B marketers to uncover high-impact keywords, optimize their content and stay ahead of competitors in their niche.

AI plays a crucial role in keyword analytics by processing vast datasets, identifying patterns and predicting trends with speed and precision. For B2B marketers, AI tools help address unique challenges such as targeting niche audiences, understanding industry-specific jargon and analysing the performance of highly competitive keywords. By leveraging AI-powered keyword tools, marketers can extract actionable insights, fine-tune their strategies and drive greater ROI from their marketing campaigns.

PUT INTO PRACTICE: USING NLP AND MACHINE LEARNING TOOLS

Assuming I'm in marketing targeting a B2B HR department and interested in keywords relating to the use of AI in HR, I could use ChatGPT to create a table highlighting affinity, volume and cost per click (CPC). I can use the following prompt: *Please provide a table of keywords for the topic of AI used by a B2B HR department; please show columns for affinity, volume and CPC.*

One can also use ChatGPT to conduct further analysis and provide more detailed information by asking it to compare two different search engine marketing tools using the prompt: *Please provide a table of keywords for the topic of AI used by a B2B HR department; please show columns for affinity, volume and CPC and compare results for different search engine tools.* (See Table 4.1.)

TABLE 4.1 Keyword analytics – NLP based

Keyword	Affinity (1–10)	Search volume (monthly)	CPC (Cost per click in $)	Affinity (SEMrush)	Volume (SEMrush)	CPC (SEMrush)	Affinity (Ahrefs)	Volume (Ahrefs)	CPC (Ahrefs)
AI in HR analytics	8	1,200	2.5	8	1,200	$2.5	7	1,100	$2.4
AI-powered recruitment tools	9	1,500	3.2	9	1,500	$3.2	8	1,300	$3.1
Employee engagement AI	7	800	1.8	7	800	$1.8	6	750	$1.7
AI for workforce planning	8	1,000	2.1	8	1,000	$2.1	7	950	$2.0
HR chatbots	9	1,800	2.8	9	1,800	$2.8	8	1,750	$2.7
AI-driven performance reviews	7	700	1.7	7	700	$1.7	6	650	$1.6
Diversity-hiring AI tools	6	600	3.5	6	600	$3.5	5	580	$3.4

(continued)

TABLE 4.1 (Continued)

Keyword	Affinity (1–10)	Search volume (monthly)	CPC (Cost per click in $)	Affinity (SEMrush)	Volume (SEMrush)	CPC (SEMrush)	Affinity (Ahrefs)	Volume (Ahrefs)	CPC (Ahrefs)
Predictive analytics for HR	8	1,100	2.3	8	1,100	$2.3	7	1,050	$2.2
AI in employee retention	7	900	1.9	7	900	$1.9	6	850	$1.8
HR automation with AI	9	1,600	2.6	9	1,600	$2.6	8	1,550	$2.5

Dedicated AI tools such as SEMrush and SparkToro exemplify how businesses can harness the power of AI for keyword analytics. These platforms provide sophisticated features tailored for B2B marketing, from identifying valuable keywords to understanding audience behaviour and monitoring market trends. By integrating these tools into their strategy, B2B marketers can achieve more precise targeting, develop relevant content and gain a competitive edge.

SEMrush and keyword analytics

SEMrush is a comprehensive digital marketing platform that integrates AI-driven insights to empower B2B marketers with advanced keyword analytics and more. Its extensive database includes over 25 billion keywords across 130 countries making it a great resource for identifying high-performing search terms in global and local markets.[2] One of its standout features, the Keyword Magic Tool, is particularly effective for B2B keyword research. This tool simplifies the process of discovering relevant keywords by categorizing them into topics, analysing search intent and providing long-tail keyword suggestions. B2B marketers can use this feature to uncover niche-specific keywords that resonate with their target audience and align with their industry.

Beyond keyword research, SEMrush offers tools like Site Audit and Market Explorer to enhance a B2B website's performance. The Site Audit tool uses AI to evaluate critical factors that affect search engine performance, such as duplicate Meta descriptions, broken links and slow load speeds. For B2B companies, optimizing these elements can significantly improve website rankings and user experience, both of which are crucial for attracting and retaining business clients.

The Market Explorer feature provides insights into market trends, audience demographics and competitor strategies. For instance, a B2B company specializing in software solutions can use this tool to identify emerging trends in technology adoption, analyse competitors' keyword strategies and refine their own approach. By combining these features, SEMrush enables B2B marketers to craft data-driven strategies that drive visibility, engagement and conversions.

Using SparkToro for B2B marketing keyword analytics

SparkToro is another AI-powered platform designed to provide audience intelligence and keyword insights, making it a valuable tool for B2B marketers. Unlike traditional keyword tools, SparkToro focuses on audience behaviour, demographics and interests to help businesses create highly relevant content. By analysing where specific audiences spend their time online, SparkToro enables B2B marketers to discover the social media platforms, websites and other digital spaces frequented by their target audience.

One of SparkToro's key features is its ability to identify real user behaviour by leveraging data from social media, keyword rankings and clickstream panels. For instance, a B2B manufacturing company can use SparkToro to uncover which YouTube channels or industry blogs are popular among its audience. This information helps marketers prioritize the platforms and content types that are most likely to resonate with their target demographic.

Additionally, SparkToro offers six types of platform results – websites, social accounts, apps and networks, YouTube channels, Reddit and podcasts – allowing marketers to tailor their outreach efforts to audience preferences. For example, a B2B marketing agency targeting tech start-ups could use SparkToro to find niche podcasts or Reddit communities where their audience engages. By aligning their keyword strategy with audience behaviour, B2B marketers can create more impactful campaigns and enhance their brand's visibility in relevant spaces.

Through its deep audience insights and AI-driven analytics, SparkToro enables B2B marketers to go beyond traditional keyword research. By understanding not just what their audience is searching for but also where and how they consume information, marketers can build more targeted, effective and engaging campaigns. This combination of data and context makes SparkToro an indispensable tool for B2B keyword analytics.

Dynamic ranking

Dynamic ranking is an advanced process where AI algorithms evaluate and rank search results by considering a wide range of factors beyond traditional keyword matching. Unlike static ranking methods that rely heavily on keyword density or Meta tags, dynamic ranking analyses nuanced characteristics like user engagement, content quality and contextual relevance. This allows search engines to deliver results that better match the user's intent and preferences.

AI plays a central role in dynamic ranking by leveraging machine learning models to continuously adapt and improve the ranking process. For instance, AI can analyse user engagement metrics such as click-through rates, time spent on a page and bounce rates to determine which results provide the most value to users. If users consistently engage more with a specific type of content, the algorithm adjusts rankings to prioritize similar results in the future. AI enables a more in-depth interpretation of content by understanding context, semantics and relationships between words. AI also considers other dynamic factors, such as location, device type and search history, to personalize rankings. This ensures that results are tailored to the specific needs of the user at that moment. In a B2B context, dynamic ranking helps businesses connect with their audience more effectively by ensuring that their high-quality, relevant content ranks well for the right searches, enhancing visibility and engagement. An example of a tool including dynamic ranking is CanIRank.

Voice-based search and AI in B2B

AI is also being used to support voice-based search; voice-based search is supported by virtual assistants such as Siri and Alexa which are AI-based technologies that understand more conversational comments and conversational queries.

So, what is a conversational query and how does it differ from traditional queries?

Conversational queries are queries phrased in a more natural, human-like way; they often resembling more of a dialogue with the search engine and are typically longer and include more context than traditional keyword-based queries.

See here an example of a conversational query vs a traditional more concise query:

Conversational query: 'Can you recommend some marketing automation tools for a small B2B business with a limited budget?'

Traditional query: 'Affordable B2B marketing automation tools.'

One example of where voice search optimization (VSO) is being integrated into B2B tools is Salesforce's Einstein Voice: Salesforce's Einstein Voice focuses on data collection and management through verbal requests. Other examples include the following.

- Honeywell Voice: Honeywell uses voice-enabled search in its warehousing operations. It allows employees to perform tasks hands-free, reducing errors and enhancing productivity.

- Google Duplex: Google Duplex uses AI to handle voice interactions for booking and scheduling.
- Alexa for Business: This tool uses voice commands to schedule meetings and access information; it also integrates with other applications like Salesforce.

Link building

Introduction

Link building involves forming links from another website to yours. Link building in B2B is about attracting the attention of a target audience or a link 'facilitator'. Facilitators include thought leaders, owners of websites or editors of online magazines.

Search backlinks

What are backlinks and why are they important?

Search backlinks often simply referred to as backlinks act as a signal to search engines that a website has quality content worth linking to. Backlinks are considered a 'stamp of approval' from one site to another, helping search engines determine the credibility and authority of the site being linked to.

Backlinks are important for B2B marketing as they help improve search engine rankings; websites with a large number of high-quality backlinks tend to rank higher in search results. Quality backlinks which come from reputable, authoritative websites can drive more targeted traffic to one's own website. For example, industry relevant publications or business partner websites which direct traffic to one's website would be more likely to convert as they are already within that niche industry space.

In B2B backlinks are also important as they help build authority and trust; through more reputable websites directing traffic to a business, as a result that business earns a greater degree of trust. Backlinks from reputable sources act as third-party endorsements that can influence potential clients. Backlinks also boost brand awareness as well as enhancing referral traffic. When users click on a backlink that leads to your site, it brings in visitors who are already interested in your business or services, improving the likelihood of conversions.

What are the main AI features for search backlinks?

AI tools can identify most valuable backlinks for a website or a particular industry. By also analysing the backlinks of competitors these tools can also allow marketers to prioritize which links to use to improve search rankings. Examples of tools which incorporate this feature include Rankster; another example is SEMrush's Copilot AI which automatically reviews the health of your backlink and provides suggestions for improvements.

AI-based tools review the quality and relevance of backlinks by analysing the reputation of the source as well as related content. This, in turn, ensures the backlinks are drawn from reputable sources.

AI tools are able to recognize patterns in backlink profiles such as spammy sites or differentiate low from high domain authority websites thus supporting and improving backlink strategies.

Identifying desirable backlinks

AI can automate the discovery of new linking opportunities; through automation, marketers can uncover possible link collaborations.

AI tools assess the risk associated with potential backlinks by scanning for blacklisted sites and verifying the authenticity of the content. This helps businesses avoid dubious associations that could harm their SEO efforts.

PUT INTO PRACTICE

Ahrefs uses advanced AI models to evaluate backlinks, offering metrics like domain rating (DR), URL rating (UR) and comprehensive anchor text analysis. Ahrefs includes a Backlink Profile tool which provides insights on the quality and relevance of backlinks, helping B2B marketers identify valuable opportunities for link-building.[3]

SEMrush: SEMrush includes AI-enhanced features like Backlink Analytics and Backlink Audit, providing insights into the quality, toxicity and impact of backlinks. SEMrush's Toxicity Score is driven by AI and helps B2B marketers avoid backlinks that could harm their site's SEO. It flags low-quality or spammy links based on patterns from millions of data points. SEMrush also offers Link Building recommendations using AI to identify potential backlinks based on competitor analysis and content relevance.[4]

Keyword intent and AI

How to align keywords with search intent: the first step in developing an SEO strategy is to establish the search intent. By search intent we are trying to understand what prospective customers are trying to do when they search, i.e. what issue or problem they are trying to solve for?

Intent and queries typically can be very broad in nature for a particular search query; in which case we may call these informational queries; other forms of search intent might be to figure out how to do something, so we could label these as 'how to' queries.

The next stage queries might involve searching and navigating a company's website for something more specific to the company and a product; we can call this navigational intent.

Finally, after navigational intent the search intent might be related to doing something or taking an action online. In B2B, actions online could simply be a prospect sharing their email address in return for downloading a lead magnet. We can call this engagement intent where there is a willingness to engage further.

So, we have main areas of intent that align to the early buyer journey and the first steps in the consideration stage of the buyer journey. Now we know different areas of intent we can also start to think of phrases and keywords which would align to these stages.

AI and keyword intent

AI tools use NLP in order to analyse search queries and to understand the keyword intent (the intent behind the keyword); intent can be categories such as informational, commercial or transactional.

By categorizing intent, B2B marketers can better align content to those needs, i.e. a person search in the informational phase will be using content formats aligned to earlier on in the buyer journey as opposed to those people in the commercial or transactional phases

AI tools can group keywords into intent-based categories automatically which in turn simplifies keyword research; this also allows businesses to see which keywords are more likely to convert or drive informational searches. AI can quickly cluster hundreds or thousands of keywords into relevant groups, saving time on manual sorting.

For example, for a B2B cybersecurity firm, AI can categorize keywords like 'cybersecurity strategies for SMBs' (informational) and 'top cybersecurity vendors' (transactional). This helps them optimize campaigns for both awareness and lead generation. See Table 4.2 for an example of keywords sorted by customer journey stage using an NLP/machine learning tool.

TABLE 4.2 Search intent

Customer journey stage	Keyword intent	Example keywords	Search intent category
Awareness	Understanding the importance of employee development and the potential benefits of training.	'importance of employee training', 'benefits of employee education', 'how to improve employee skills', 'why invest in employee training'	Informational
Consideration	Exploring different training types, comparing providers, and understanding formats and costs.	'online vs in-person training for employees', 'top corporate training providers', 'employee training programmes cost comparison', 'self-paced vs instructor-led training'	Commercial
Decision	Ready to make a purchase or register for a specific training programme.	'corporate training services near me', 'purchase leadership training programme', 'register for employee skill development workshop', 'contact employee training provider'	Transactional
Retention/ advocacy	Evaluating the training effectiveness, considering renewal or seeking recommendations.	'best practices for employee training evaluation', 'renew corporate training programme subscription', 'feedback on [provider name] training services', 'case studies of effective employee training'	Informational / commercial

References

1 Ellis, M (2024) Google E-E-A-T, 18 November, moz.com/learn/seo/google-eat (archived at https://perma.cc/RER5-FG46)
2 SEMrush (2025) What data can SEMrush provide? www.semrush.com/kb/999-semrush-data (archived at https://perma.cc/3NF3-ZZQN)
3 SEMrush (n.d.) What is backlink analytics?, www.semrush.com/kb/21-backlinks (archived at https://perma.cc/W37X-26ME)
4 Yunus Emre Özcan (2024) How AI improves backlink analysis and strategy – Screpy, Screpy, screpy.com/how-ai-improves-backlink-analysis-and-strategy/ (archived at https://perma.cc/JL7J-M3QU)

Further reading

BrightEdge (n.d.) What exactly is AI in SEO?, www.brightedge.com/glossary/how-has-ai-changed-search-marketing (archived at https://perma.cc/ZA48-JV3N)

Loktionova, M (2024) 8 Best AI SEO tools for 2025 (tested firsthand), SEMrush, www.semrush.com/contentshake/content-marketing-blog/ai-seo-tools/ (archived at https://perma.cc/X6MY-9YFD)

Salesforce (2025) Salesforce, www.salesforce.com/marketing/ai/seo-guide/ (archived at https://perma.cc/W3CU-DJGE)

05

Content marketing

> What you will gain from this chapter
>
> Understanding of the following:
>
> - roles of AI in content marketing
> - where AI is used beyond just creating content
> - how AI can optimize content
> - how AI can be used to repurpose content

Introduction

We can define content as information which comes in different formats. Content marketing is the art of understanding what your customers need to know and delivering it to them in a relevant and compelling way.

The role of the content, as a result, is different; content in B2B has many roles from making prospects aware of something such as a product or service, through to educating them and supporting them through their evaluation of something.

Generative AI

The area of AI best suited to B2B content marketing is generative artificial intelligence (Gen AI). Gen AI is the use of AI for creating text, images and videos based on learned patterns from existing data.

Gen AI uses sophisticated machine learning techniques such as GANs (generative adversarial networks) and LLM (large language models) to produce outputs.[1] With recent improvements in transformer architectures, this has meant that Gen AI models have become more sophisticated.

There are a large number of Gen AI uses in B2B marketing; there are, of course, uses outside of marketing in software development product design. Examples of Gen AI include tools like ChatGPT and DALL-E that allow users to generate human-like text or create images from textual descriptions, respectively.

Evolution of AI in content marketing

Traditional AI was occupied largely with data-driven insights and leveraging those insights for optimizing things and tasks, etc. in the field of sentiment analysis, programmatic advertising, keyword analytics; with the addition and inclusion of Gen AI powered by models such as OpenAI's GPT-3.5 this has meant the capabilities have been largely broadened to encompass creation of text, images, video content and other areas.

Accompanied with this shift and addition of Gen AI marketers can automate content generation which means less time or resources are needed for this as well as meaning marketers can devote time/resources to other areas. Gen AI also improves personalization as businesses can tailor content to specific industries and buyer personas. (See Figure 5.1.)

Role of AI

There are different roles for AI in B2B content marketing. AI can be used in the stages of content planning and creation; for example, in the ideation stage it can be used to come up with different versions or views of content such as generating ideas for themes and generating ideas for descriptions of webinars in terms of headlines.

Other areas of content creation in B2B include content brief creation, content creation itself, content optimization, content personalization and content repurposing; all of which we'll be covering in this chapter. Other areas of content marketing are creating the content itself as well as editing and rewriting.

In addition to facilitating and improving each of the areas of content creation, AI tools can also increase the speed of the stage and the speed of creating content.

FIGURE 5.1 Content creation process and AI

Phases	Select buyer persona	Identify touchpoints	Gather data	Optimize
Activities	Segment and role	Identify touchpoint per persona	Gather data from different sources	Optimize touchpoints, customer journey
AI Role	AI tools can help us identify key stakeholders in DMU	AI tools can allow us identify touchpoints	AI tools can amalgamate and integrate data	AI tools can provide recommendations regarding where, how to optimize customer journey
AI tool	Machine learning/NLP tools like ChatGPT	Machine learning/NLP tools like ChatGPT Tools like 6sense	CDP platforms	CDP platforms NLP/machine learning

Creating content briefs

AI tools have become increasingly useful for creating content briefs, which are essential documents used to guide marketing agencies or departments in producing the desired content. By leveraging AI, the process of creating a content brief becomes more streamlined and efficient. A content brief typically includes key details such as objectives, target audience, keyword suggestions and meta descriptions, ensuring alignment between the creators and the strategic goals. (See Table 5.1.)

Several AI platforms specialize in supporting content brief creation such as Taskade, Hyperwrite and Scripted. Beyond these specific tools, there are more comprehensive platforms such as Narrato Workspace, which supports a wide range of brief creation processes. Narrato allows users to generate various types of briefs, including content briefs and SEO-focused briefs, while considering all aspects of the creation process.

Another notable example is Copy.ai, which simplifies the process by generating content brief outlines and even sample content. By inputting a target keyword, content goals and additional relevant details, the platform produces a concise, yet detailed content brief tailored to specific needs.

These AI-driven solutions are transforming how content briefs are created, enabling marketers to save time while maintaining a high level of precision and effectiveness.

TABLE 5.1 Content brief creation

Section	Details	Notes/Guidance
1. Campaign title	Building a sustainable future in construction	Should be compelling, industry-relevant and action-oriented
2. Campaign objective	Educate and inspire construction professionals to adopt sustainable practices	Focus on awareness, engagement and action-driven content
3. Target audience	Developers, architects, engineers	Segment content by audience type and level of expertise
4. Key messages	- Sustainability enhances efficiency and cost savings - Green buildings improve long-term profitability - Innovation in materials and energy use is key	Consistent, clear and easy to integrate across content formats

(continued)

TABLE 5.1 (Continued)

Section	Details	Notes/Guidance
5. Core content pillars	1. Sustainable materials, 2. Energy efficiency, 3. Green construction technologies, 4. Regulatory trends, 5. Case studies & best practices	Organize content under clear themes for coherence
6. Content types	Blog articles, white papers, infographics, social media posts, video explainers, webinars	Ensure a mix of formats to cater to different audience preferences
7. Tone & style	Professional, informative, yet engaging and accessible	Avoid overly technical jargon, focus on actionable insights
8. Content calendar	3-month schedule with weekly content releases	Include key industry events, report releases, and sustainability weeks
9. Distribution channels	- LinkedIn (industry insights) - Twitter (real-time updates) - YouTube (explainer videos) - Industry blogs - Email newsletters	Each channel should have tailored content formats
10. Call to action (CTA)	Encourage adoption of sustainable construction methods	Direct readers to further resources, webinars or partnerships

Content planning and ideation

Content ideation is the process of identifying and planning relevant topics for a B2B audience. Content ideation can cover area such as image ideas and video ideas, but here we'll focus on coming up with ideas for content campaign themes. Please see Figure 5.2, which highlights main ideas in a content ideation for campaign themes.

FIGURE 5.2 Content ideation

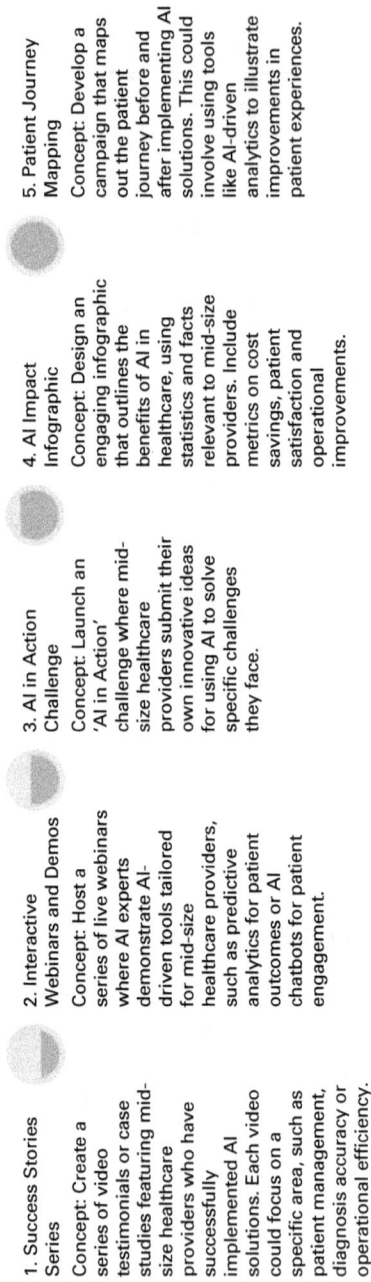

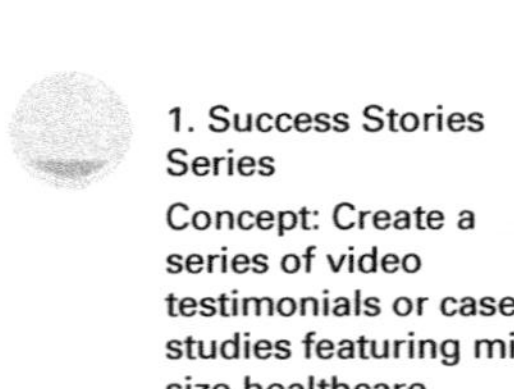

1. Success Stories Series

Concept: Create a series of video testimonials or case studies featuring mid-size healthcare providers who have successfully implemented AI solutions. Each video could focus on a specific area, such as patient management, diagnosis accuracy or operational efficiency.

2. Interactive Webinars and Demos

Concept: Host a series of live webinars where AI experts demonstrate AI-driven tools tailored for mid-size healthcare providers, such as predictive analytics for patient outcomes or AI chatbots for patient engagement.

3. AI in Action Challenge

Concept: Launch an 'AI in Action' challenge where mid-size healthcare providers submit their own innovative ideas for using AI to solve specific challenges they face.

4. AI Impact Infographic

Concept: Design an engaging infographic that outlines the benefits of AI in healthcare, using statistics and facts relevant to mid-size providers. Include metrics on cost savings, patient satisfaction and operational improvements.

5. Patient Journey Mapping

Concept: Develop a campaign that maps out the patient journey before and after implementing AI solutions. This could involve using tools like AI-driven analytics to illustrate improvements in patient experiences.

PUT INTO PRACTICE

Let's take the example of coming up with the ideas for a blog topic. Through machine learning tools such as ChatGPT one can come up with ideas for blog topics and blog outlines.

Considering we're trying to come up with themes regarding B2B healthcare and medical devices, the following might be some prompts we could use for generating campaign themes.

- *What are some innovative campaign themes for a B2B healthcare company looking to sell medical devices to hospitals in 2024?*
- *Give me five campaign ideas that can highlight the value of AI-driven healthcare solutions for mid-size healthcare providers.*
- *Create a content marketing theme targeting healthcare administrators focused on improving patient outcomes through new technologies.*
- *What are some effective marketing angles to attract pharmaceutical companies interested in supply chain optimization solutions?*

We can go further and use machine learning to come up with blog topics related to a buyer persona; there might be some prompts to ensure the blog is catering to a specific persona – in this case a procurement manager in a B2B healthcare company.

- *What are key pain points of healthcare procurement managers when choosing new medical software solutions? Suggest content ideas to address these.*
- *List some content ideas that would resonate with healthcare CIOs interested in adopting cloud-based data management solutions.*
- *What types of blog posts or white papers would attract hospital CFOs when considering investment in new healthcare technologies?*

Content creation and AI

AI tools can help create the following types of content and more: webinar scripts, video scripts, emails, blogs, videos, podcasts, slides, infographics and more.

Like any AI tools this comes down to inputs and intelligent outputs through machine learning, but there are different approaches to doing this

In the coming chapters we'll look at generative AI tools in the context of lead capture, lead nurture and customer retention more specifically, but let's look at some examples of content creation.

Copywriting AI tools

Copywriting tools leverage AI tools to product text-based content; key content one can create are emails, blogs, subject lines for posts, social media posts, articles and advertorials.

> PUT INTO PRACTICE
>
> Let's look at an example of how AI tools can be used to create a comprehensive blog.
>
> Let's consider we've come up with ideas for a blog, the next step would be to write this out; we can use the following prompts to flesh out and have the blog written.
>
> - *Write a blog.*
> - *Write a detailed blog.*
> - *Write a 1000-, 1500- or 2000-word blog on...*
>
> The more specific one is, the better this is, for example, on a particular industry. Following the writing out of the blog we now want to ensure the content is backed up with facts, citations so the work is more comprehensive; the following are commands we can use to do that.
>
> - For the previous prompt please also include citations, references, sources of references, facts and statistics.
> - If one wanted more facts, statistics one can write for each area please include two facts per paragraph to support the statements.

Structures and processes in using machine learning, tools

So, we've seen from the previous example there are different ways to use NLP/machine learning tools; we can describe these main methods as follows.

Method 1: Outline first then flesh out. With this model we ask a machine learning tool to provide an outline, a skeleton structure to what we're looking for; following from the outline we need to start fleshing out the content further.

Method 2: Selective gap filling. Selective gap filling is where there are only parts of the content, we want to use AI tools for; we saw this partially in the buyer persona exercise in Chapter 3, e.g. by focusing on media preferences and/or B2B communities.

Method 3: Stepwise build model. With this model we are creating text-based content through steps

Method 4: Long form prompt. This model is about creating a long form prompt (which can also be done with the help of machine learning AI tools) and using one long form prompt to create our desired output in one go.

We can view these models side-by-side in Figure 5.3.

Video AI tools

AI has become also important in video content creation; there are various AI tools for video creation including avatar–AI tools and generative video.

Avatar-based AI Tools use AI to create digital avatars that can be used in videos to deliver scripts and perform actions. Platforms like Synthesia and DeepBrain AI offer realistic AI avatars that can be customized in terms of appearance and voice. These avatars are particularly useful in B2B marketing for creating training videos, product demonstrations, and corporate communications without the need for live actors. The avatars can be programmed to speak in multiple languages; for example, Synthesia offers over 30 avatars with English accents but overall overs over 150 different

FIGURE 5.3 Models for creating text-based content

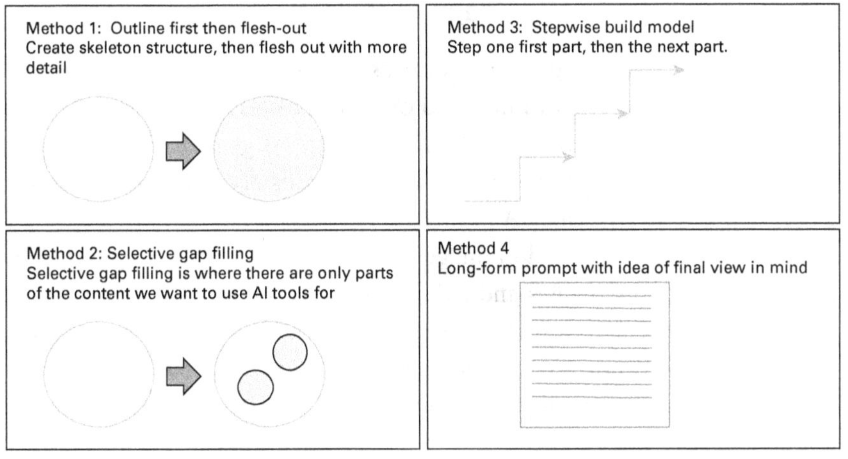
Method 1: Outline first then flesh-out
Create skeleton structure, then flesh out with more detail
Method 3: Stepwise build model
Step one first part, then the next part.
Method 2: Selective gap filling
Selective gap filling is where there are only parts of the content we want to use AI tools for
Method 4
Long-form prompt with idea of final view in mind

avatars which can speak French, German etc. These avatars can perform specific gestures, making them versatile tools for global businesses.

There are also AI-powered video generation platforms like InVideo and Steve AI which allow users to create videos from text inputs. These platforms automatically generate scripts and can select relevant stock footage, and add background music and transitions, according to queries. This significantly reduces the time and effort required to produce videos.

AI-driven editing software tools like Descript and Runway use AI to simplify and make the video editing process more manageable; these tools include features such as script-based editing, where users can edit videos by modifying the text script.

Through easier and more intuitive editing, these mean businesses can improve video turnaround time in video creation; this allows for more real-time adjustments as well.

USING INVIDEO

In using Invideo we can create video content from a simple command. Examples of simple commands might be:

- Persona/situation specific: Show me a day in the life of 'an operations manager in a warehouse'; or 'show me a day in the life of a senior leader travelling by plane to a meeting'.
- Industry specific: create a video of an engineer working on a solar farm.

Image AI tools

Of course, one can't forget tools such as Dall-e and their latest versions; there are different levels of input and output in terms of image-based tools such Adobe Firefly. In the area of text to image AI generator tools we are also seeing other interesting developments in terms of tools such as the tool from Meta (Meta AI), Open AI's Sora tool and others.

AI tools can also be used in image generation in different ways by using text inputs to create images and to optimize and improve images. Some of these image generation tools create higher quality images than others; but generally, these AI-powered image generation tools use advanced AI algorithms to change text prompts into images and offering typically a range of options.

Types of AI image generation tools

Let's look at the following types of AI image generation tools (see Table 5.2).

Text-to-image generation: Text-to-image generators such as DALL-E and Midjourney support text prompts from users to generate images. The AI technology then interprets the text and outputs visuals that match the description. Typically the images can be offered in different styles from drawing to photorealistic images. This type of tool is particularly useful for marketers and content creators who need custom visuals without the need for traditional design skills.

Stock image integration: Some AI tools, like Generative AI by Getty Images, combine AI-generated content with existing stock image libraries. The downside is that the images may not be fully new, but the images tend to be commercially safe as these can be used for business purposes.

Image editing and enhancement: Tools like Picsart's AI image generator both create images from text as well as offer editing capabilities; through editing users can enhance images, change backgrounds, and apply various filters and effects, allowing for greater control over the final output.

TABLE 5.2 Types of AI image generation

Tool name	Type	Key features	Use cases
DALL-E	Text-to-image generator	Generates detailed images from text prompts	Art creation, advertising, concept visualization
Midjourney	Text-to-image generator	Specializes in artistic and stylized images	Graphic design, digital art, creative projects
Stable Diffusion	Text-to-image/image modification	Text-to-image and image-to-image capabilities	Customizing existing images, generating artwork
Canva	Integrated design platform	Combines design tools with AI features	Social media content, marketing materials
Generative AI by Getty Images	Specialized generator	Creates licensed images for commercial use	Stock photography, advertising, creative projects
Colossus Lightning	Multi-style generator	Generates various styles, including realistic and artistic	Product images, character design, marketing content

Key considerations in AI-based image generation

When using AI for image generation, several factors need to be considered to ensure the best results. As with almost all AI-based tools, it is about the quality of the input; here the quality of the text prompt influences the quality of the outputted image. When using AI image generation tools, providing specific and accurate prompts is essential for achieving the intended results. The precision and detail in a prompt directly influence the accuracy and visual appeal of the generated image. For instance, entering a vague request like 'show me a picture of a passenger on a plane' could result in unexpected and impractical outcomes, such as an image of a person sitting literally on top of an airplane or on a plane wing, instead of a passenger seated inside the cabin of a plane.

One consideration regarding use of AI-generated images is that of copyright. Some of these tools are leveraging vast datasets, and some of these tools may include copyrighted material; of course, if the image is 100 per cent freshly generated then this would probably avoid copyright issues as long as logos and copyrighted designs are not used.

Is AI image generation always 'generating'?

It is always worth noting that AI image generation doesn't always mean that images are created from scratch but can leverage stock images and integrate these into the process of image generation. With this hybrid approach it means that users can benefit from a wider range of images.

B2B marketing examples for image and video creation

In B2B marketing one can use these tools in different ways; a company might use Synthesia's avatar-based tools to produce training videos with digital presenters, saving time and resources compared to traditional video production. Marketing teams can use DALL-E to generate unique visuals for campaigns, ensuring that their content stands out in a crowded digital landscape. One can also use Invideo to create video ideas into a video briefing or for internal communication videos.

Content optimization

AI tools are highly effective for optimizing content, offering the ability to automate and enhance various aspects of the content creation and refinement process. However, it's important to explore what 'optimization' truly means, particularly in the context of B2B content, where the goals and strategies can vary widely based on audience, purpose and industry requirements.

In B2B scenarios, content optimization can encompass a range of objectives, depending on what the content needs to achieve (see Table 5.3). Here are some examples of content optimization:

- Enhancing authority: Optimization may involve refining content to make it more credible and authoritative. This could include integrating data-driven insights, referencing reputable sources or incorporating expert opinions to establish the content as a trusted resource within the industry.
- Increasing engagement: AI can help make content more personable or relatable, tailoring tone, language and style to connect with the intended audience. Whether it's simplifying complex ideas for broader accessibility or adopting a conversational tone, personalization helps foster stronger relationships with readers.
- Injecting personality: In some cases, especially for marketing or branding materials, optimization might focus on making content more entertaining or memorable. AI tools can tweak the content to add humour, creative storytelling, or a unique voice that aligns with the brand's identity, making it stand out in competitive markets.
- Aligning with goals: Beyond individual elements, optimization involves ensuring the content aligns with the broader strategic objectives of the business. This might include adapting the tone for specific buyer personas, highlighting solutions to pain points, or addressing common objections effectively.

By leveraging AI tools, businesses can achieve these forms of optimization more efficiently. These tools can analyse existing content, suggest areas for improvement and even generate tailored updates that align with specific goals. This ensures that the final output not only resonates with the target audience but also fulfils the intended purpose, whether it's

TABLE 5.3 Content optimization

Original	Version: Facts and statistics	Version: Industry examples	Version: Humour
The construction industry faces significant sustainability challenges that need to be addressed. The high levels of waste generated during construction, along with the industry's substantial carbon footprint, raise concerns about environmental impacts. Many companies are now seeking innovative solutions to reduce waste and enhance sustainable practices, but these efforts often clash with budget constraints and regulatory requirements. Finding a balance between sustainability and cost-effectiveness is critical for the industry's future.	The construction industry faces significant sustainability challenges, with approximately 39% of global carbon emissions attributed to it (UN Environment Programme, 2021). Furthermore, it is estimated that by 2030, construction waste could reach 2.2 billion tons annually if current trends continue (World Economic Forum, 2020). Interestingly, the use of sustainable materials could reduce emissions by 40%, showcasing the potential impact of greener practices in the sector (McKinsey & Company, 2022). Addressing these issues not only benefits the environment but also leads to long-term cost savings and enhanced public perception.	In the construction industry, major companies like Skanska and Turner Construction are taking strides toward sustainability by adopting eco-friendly practices. For instance, Skanska has committed to becoming carbon neutral by 2045, while Turner Construction actively employs sustainable materials in its projects, reducing waste and emissions. Another noteworthy example is the construction of the Bosco Verticale (Vertical Forest) in Milan, which incorporates trees into the building design, significantly enhancing biodiversity and air quality in urban settings. These examples illustrate that sustainability is not just a trend but a vital aspect of modern construction practices.	Have you ever seen a construction worker passionately hug a tree? It happened last week at a site when the crew realized that sustainable practices were becoming a big deal in construction! 'Who knew saving the planet could be so hands-on?' one worker joked as they switched to eco-friendly materials. The construction industry is like that friend who promises to go on a diet but keeps ordering extra cheese on their pizza. But here's the scoop: if we don't shape up, we might find ourselves buried under 2.2 billion tons of construction waste by 2030! So, let's take a cue from the eco-warriors out there – after all, a greener future is the kind of foundation we all want to build on!

driving conversions, building brand trust or nurturing leads. Below are some examples of AI tools and examples of content optimization.

- ChatGPT: Can be used to create detailed content drafts.
- ContentShake AI: This tool generates SEO-optimized blog posts complete with keywords, images and information on competing content, streamlining the content creation process.
- Clearscope: Includes features for producing highly relevant content by suggesting related keywords and improving readability.
- MarketMuse: Provides a topic-driven approach to content optimization, helping marketers create content that resonates with their target audience.

Content repurposing

AI also plays a role to repurpose content. Repurposing content can mean different things, but for this chapter we'll define repurpose as changing the format of the content where content formats include blogs, webinars, video, and podcasts or other (see Figure 5.4).

AI tools can allow content creations to transform existing materials into new formats. This aspect is particularly useful considering limited resources and budgets which some B2B marketing have to deal with. Through adapting, content marketers can maximize the use of their resources.

The goal of repurposing is to make content more flexible and appeal to different audiences without investing the people and time resource in creating each content from scratch.

AI tools facilitate this by analysing the original content, identifying key themes and suggesting or creating new formats that maintain the core message while adapting it to a new context.

PUT INTO PRACTICE

Let's look at a few examples of content repurposing and the AI features.

- Repurposing blogs to eBooks: AI tools such as Canva or Designr can allow creators to transform a long-form blog into a guide or ebook in a matter of minutes – in fact, real-time – there are videos demonstrating this transformation in as little as three minutes.

- Image-to-text: AI tools can repurpose images into social media posts, summaries, newsletters or even blog articles. The feature can understand the contents of an image and turn it into text-based content that is relevant and accurate.
- Video transcription and subtitling: One can leverage AI to create transcriptions for videos.
- Transform webcasts into podcast: Descript is an example of an AI tool that can extract audio from video content, allowing you to edit it as a podcast. Other tools which can support repurposing of webcasts to podcast include Adobe Premier Pro and Otter.ai.
- Transform podcasts into social media snippets: Repurposing podcasts into social media snippets improves the reach of the content and engages a broader audience. When creating snippets from podcasts, one should identify the most engaging parts of the episode, add visual elements that resonate with the target platform and ensure high audio quality. Headliner is a popular tool for this purpose, as it specializes in converting audio content into social media-ready videos. It offers customizable backgrounds, waveforms and text captions, making it an ideal choice for platforms like Instagram, Twitter and LinkedIn, where short, visually dynamic clips perform well.
- Transform white papers into infographics: Tools which support white paper repurposing into infographics include Canva with AI Integration; Visme is another tool which via its infographic templates and AI design suggestions can speed up the repurposing process.

FIGURE 5.4 Content repurposing and AI tools

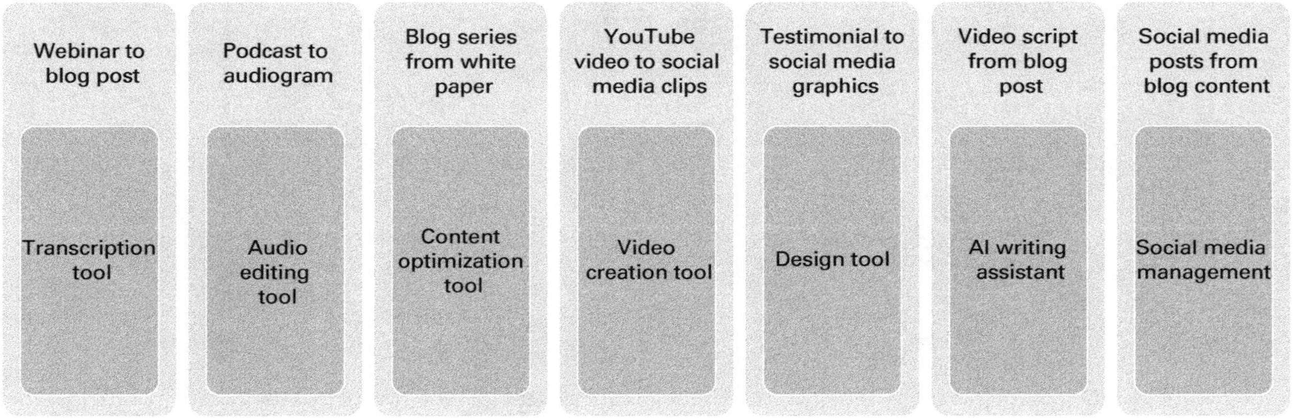

Other examples of software one can use for content repurposing are as follows:

- Wave: wave can repurpose audio types into short video clips, e.g. for use on social media platforms. This tool is used a lot by podcasts as it is an intuitive/easy to use tool.
- Repurpose.io: This platform automates distribution of content across multiple platforms. It can take one piece of content, such as a YouTube video, and change it into various formats like social media posts, blog articles or email newsletters.
- Pictory.ai: Pictory allows users to convert text into videos quickly. By inputting an article, users can generate a video complete with visuals and voiceovers.

Key considerations in AI-based content repurposing

In using AI for content repurposing, one should consider the following:

- Identification of valuable and good quality content assets is the starting point so one needs to be able to evaluate and understand what makes good quality, e.g. by using content metrics.
- AI analytics also play a key role by providing insights into audience preferences and engagement metrics.

Is AI content repurposing always 'generating'?

AI content repurposing is not always about creating entirely new content from scratch. Instead, it often involves transforming existing content into new formats while maintaining the original message and intent. This process can include enhancing content with AI-generated elements, such as visual enhancements or personalized messaging, to better suit the target audience and platform.

Key benefits of AI content repurposing

Key benefits of AI content repurposing are as follows.

- **More efficient** : By identifying content which can be repurposed, this can save time as well as people.

- **Tailoring:** Through using data, content repurposing can also cater to different audiences.
- **Cost efficiencies:** Repurposing content into different formats can save money.

Content localization and translation

If you're working in international marketing or working with businesses in other countries, chances are you've had to deal with differences in languages or different languages. Even between American English, Australian English and UK English there can be some differences, which in certain instances can be quite impactful and trip up marketing.

Here is where localization and translation software come in; and more recently with AI features and AI power localization/translation tools the ability to localize and translate content have been increased.

AI translation refers to automatic content creation. It involves leveraging AI algorithms to understand the input source language and generate a corresponding translation in the target language.

AI content localization and translation has become recently a lot more efficient and accessible for businesses who are trying to reach international audiences. By leveraging AI functions such as NLP AI tools can change content to suit the linguistic, cultural and even regional preferences of key target markets.

B2B examples of AI features in localization and translation

- LinkedIn: LinkedIn uses AI to translate posts and articles, allowing users to engage with content in their native language.
- Airbnb: The platform uses AI to localize its listings and user interface, supporting users worldwide to access information in their preferred language.

AI's role in content localization and translation is not just about generating content from scratch or translating the content but during translation AI can also enhance existing content by adapting it to different cultural contexts. As AI technology continues to evolve, it will further streamline the localization process, offering even more sophisticated solutions for businesses looking to expand their global reach.

B2B use cases for localization and translation

The following are examples of B2B use cases for localization and translation.

LOCALIZING CASE STUDIES FOR SPECIFIC MARKETS

In the B2B sector, AI can significantly enhance localization by tailoring industry-specific materials. For example, a construction equipment manufacturer can use AI to translate case studies into Portuguese and Chinese. The AI-driven system not only translates the text but also adjusts examples, metrics and construction standards to resonate with regional practices. This localization makes the case study more relatable and impactful to stakeholders in different markets.

WEBSITE LOCALIZATION AND MULTILINGUAL SEO

A B2B company expanding into multiple regions needs more than just translation; it requires a culturally adapted website with localized SEO. For instance, a global manufacturing company can use AI to translate its website into Arabic, Korean and Italian. The AI system can identify region-specific keywords, optimizing content to rank higher in local search engines. This ensures the company's content is not only understood but is also easily discoverable in each target market, increasing reach and engagement.

E-LEARNING PLATFORM ADAPTATION FOR EDUCATIONAL SERVICES

In the education industry, e-learning platforms can leverage AI localization to expand into non-native speaking markets. A US-based online education company offering courses on software development might use AI tools to localize their platform into Spanish, German and Mandarin. The AI could translate the course content, adjust for culturally relevant examples and even localize technical jargon to align with regional educational standards. This enables the platform to deliver an accessible, culturally relevant learning experience, making it more appealing to diverse learners.

TRANSLATING PRODUCT DESCRIPTIONS FOR GLOBAL MARKETS

A B2B software company wants to launch its product in multiple regions (e.g. Europe, Asia and Latin America). AI-based translation tools like Google Translate, DeepL or specialized translation models can automatically translate product descriptions into multiple languages while ensuring technical terminology remains accurate. A software as a service (SaaS) company offering cloud security solutions uses AI to translate its detailed product descriptions from English into Spanish, German, French and Mandarin, ensuring that each version conveys the same technical specifications and value proposition in a culturally relevant way.

Content distribution

Content distribution is the act of promoting content across different communication channels. Content distribution is an important element to consider for B2B marketers as carefully organizing content distribution can allow for content to reach relevant and specific audiences in the right time and right way.

Importance of content distribution

In B2B marketing, content distribution is essential for several reasons:

- Increased visibility: It helps get content in front of the right audience, boosting brand awareness and establishing a strong online presence.
- Lead generation: Effective distribution can attract and engage potential customers, generating leads and driving sales.
- Thought leadership: By consistently distributing valuable content, B2B companies can position themselves as industry experts.

Examples of AI used in content distribution

AI plays a role in support and enhancing the content distribution activity; AI tools like Buffer and Hootsuite use machine learning algorithms to identify best timings for posting content on social media platforms. It does this by analysing past data such as engagement data and then uses that to time posts and sending of posts to reach audience and maximize visibility of the post.

Other platforms for content distribution include salesforce Marketing Cloud, which provides AI-powered multi-channel content distribution, and Adobe Experience Cloud, which utilizes AI for personalized content delivery across various channels.

Should generative AI be stand alone?

One might think from some of the writing in this chapter that I'm advocating using AI 100 per cent to produce content, which is not the case; I'm merely showing you the possibilities and the extent to which you can take AI.

If we look at the content creation process in terms of ideation, creation, optimization, editing, etc., AI can be used in all these situations, though one should also consider that skilled and competent staff would still be needed, in particular in the editing and optimizing stages of content creation.

Limitations in generative AI

AI-generated content and images have become powerful tools in B2B marketing; however, despite their advantages, these tools are not without limitations. From challenges in achieving realism and originality to issues with context, accuracy and copyright, understanding the potential pitfalls of AI is essential for leveraging its capabilities effectively.

Image reality and realism

AI-generated images, especially those depicting people, sometimes lack the true-to-life realism of traditional photography. While these images can be visually appealing, they may fail to accurately represent the subtleties of human features, expressions or diversity.

Limitations in deep creativity

While AI excels in pattern recognition and recombining existing data to generate new content, it often struggles with deep originality. AI algorithms are inherently dependent on the datasets they are trained on, which means they tend to replicate or adapt existing ideas rather than create groundbreaking concepts. In B2B marketing, this limitation becomes evident when trying to craft unique value propositions or thought leadership pieces that require original perspectives. For instance, a company producing white papers on emerging technologies may find AI-generated content to be derivative or lacking the innovative insights needed to resonate with a specialized audience.

Content errors and misinterpretation

AI-generated content can sometimes misinterpret the context, leading to inappropriate or inaccurate outcomes. This is particularly problematic in B2B marketing, where content often involves industry-specific jargon, technical details or nuanced messaging. For example, an AI tool creating a blog post for a cybersecurity firm might misrepresent key concepts like encryption protocols, resulting in misleading information. Additionally, AI often struggles with subtleties such as humour, cultural references or sector-specific nuances, which are critical for engaging specialized audiences and avoiding potential missteps.

Copyright concerns and ethical risks

AI tools can inadvertently produce content that closely resembles copyrighted material, raising legal and ethical concerns. Since AI often lacks the ability to properly attribute sources, businesses risk unintentionally plagiarizing existing works. In B2B marketing, where trust and professionalism are paramount, such issues could harm a company's reputation. For example, an AI-generated infographic on market trends might unknowingly replicate visuals or data from a proprietary report, leading to potential disputes.

Challenges in specialized fields and accuracy

In B2B contexts, particularly in specialized industries like healthcare, finance or engineering, the accuracy of AI-generated content can be inconsistent. These sectors require precise terminology and an in-depth understanding of complex topics. AI may produce outputs that oversimplify or misrepresent critical details, which could mislead clients or stakeholders. For instance, a white paper intended for a pharmaceutical audience might include errors in drug nomenclature or regulatory references, undermining its credibility.

The importance of prompt quality

AI's output is only as effective as the quality of the input prompt. Poorly constructed prompts can lead to unexpected or irrelevant results. For example, when using a text-to-image AI tool and requesting 'a person sitting on a plane', the tool might generate an image of someone sitting on the plane's exterior, such as the wing, rather than inside the cabin. In B2B marketing, such misinterpretations can derail creative campaigns or lead to outputs that fail to align with the intended messaging. Crafting precise and detailed prompts is crucial to guiding the AI in delivering accurate and usable content.

By understanding these limitations and applying careful oversight, businesses can harness AI's potential while mitigating its shortcomings. This approach ensures that AI serves as a valuable tool rather than a liability in the B2B marketing toolkit.

Reference

1 Howarth, J (2024) Generative AI vs large language models (LLMs): Key differences, 8 May, explodingtopics.com/blog/llms-vs-generative-ai (archived at https://perma.cc/G28T-4S8Q)

Further reading

Guinness, H (2025) The best AI image generators in 2025, Zapier, zapier.com/blog/best-ai-image-generator/ (archived at https://perma.cc/K8RH-YHBU)

McKinsey & Company (2024) What Is Generative AI?, McKinsey, www.mckinsey.com/featured-insights/mckinsey-explainers/what-is-generative-ai (archived at https://perma.cc/L8JD-2N87)

Wheatley, D (2023) AI generated design vs stock images: Which is better, 29 December, wheatleydigital.medium.com/ai-generated-design-vs-stock-images-which-is-better-8ae7372396df (archived at https://perma.cc/F533-F8WS)

Zewe, A (2023) Explained: Generative AI, MIT News. news.mit.edu/2023/explained-generative-ai-1109 (archived at https://perma.cc/7M7B-DP2P)

PART THREE

AI lead generation and lead nurturing

06

AI and account prospecting

What you will gain from this chapter

Understanding of the following:

- learn about conducting account research
- different AI tools for research organizations
- learn about website visitor identification
- how to use AI to identify lookalike accounts
- practical tips in using AI tools

Introduction

This chapter focuses on finding suitable new acquisition customers or prospects. When talking about prospects we are referring to potential customers and business who do not yet buy from us. During this phase we're interested in identifying and engaging potential business customers who could be interested in our products and services. To expand on that point further in B2B we're interested not only in the businesses but also the stakeholders who would be involved in the decision-making process in buying our offerings.

For a long time now B2B marketers have been using traditional (non-AI) methods and sources for researching accounts; such methods might be as basic as using the online Yellow Pages; other methods might involve trawling through CRM records for dormant accounts; or manually searching through LinkedIn; such methods can be time-consuming and don't always produce the desired results. If budget allows, we can reach out to companies to ask for lists of suitable business and contact names, but again this may be time-consuming and costly when compared to the use of AI features and tools.

Account prospecting and AI

Artificial intelligence (AI) has transformed account research and prospecting by automating complex processes, providing deeper insights and enabling more strategic decision-making. By leveraging AI, organizations can not only identify the right accounts but also personalize outreach, understand organizational structures and predict customer needs with greater precision.

The following are the ways AI can be used in account research and prospecting:

- Website visitor identification: AI tools can analyse website traffic to identify which accounts are visiting your site, providing insights into their interests and engagement levels.
- Lookalike account identification: AI algorithms can identify accounts that resemble your best customers, helping expand your pipeline with high-potential leads.
- Contact discovery: AI can locate key contacts and decision-makers within target companies, ensuring you reach the right people with your outreach efforts.
- Organizational structure analysis: AI tools can map out organizational hierarchies, helping sales teams understand reporting lines and key influencers.
- Financial reviews: AI can analyse financial data to assess the health and stability of target accounts, ensuring alignment with your company's risk tolerance.
- Predictive lead scoring: AI models can evaluate potential leads based on historical data and prioritize them according to their likelihood of conversion.

Website visitor identification

Website visitor identification is about understanding which accounts are engaging with our website; without AI tools it is possible to identify organizations and accounts visiting our company website, but this can be quite manual and more time-consuming; typically via tools such as landing page tools one can see internet protocol (IP) data for visitors. Landing page tools also typically show activities related to IP addresses such as form submission or email opt-ins.

How AI tools identify website visitors

With AI tools one can de-anonymize website visitors in one go; examples are Factor.ai and Happierleads, which allow one to see a list of website visitors as well as additional information. AI tools can detect and analyse the IP addresses of website visitors. By cross-referencing these IP addresses with databases, they identify the organization associated with the traffic.

Data enrichment: Once the organization is identified, AI tools enrich the data with additional details about the company, such as industry, size, location and key products or services.

AI tools can also help in different ways to understand frequency of visits in a given time period but also in assimilating information at the same time so we have in one go a view of key company insights (see Figure 6.1).

Information provided by AI website visitor identification tools

- **Company identification:** AI tools reveal the name of the company associated with the website visit.
- **Frequency and recency:** They track how often and when the company visits, helping prioritize accounts showing consistent interest.
- **Company demographics:** Detailed information such as company size, industry, revenue and headquarters location is displayed.

FIGURE 6.1 Website visitor identification

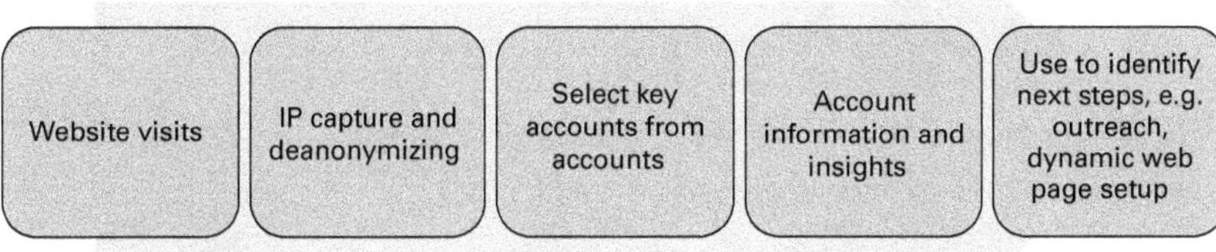

- **Products and services:** AI can identify the products or services the company offers, giving insights into their operational focus.
- **Key contacts:** Tools like Factor.ai and Happierleads can provide contact details or connect to social profiles, such as LinkedIn, to identify decision-makers and influencers.
- **Engagement metrics:** They show specific pages visited, time spent on the site and actions taken, helping understand the visitor's intent.
- **Account insights in one view:** These tools consolidate all the above information into a single dashboard, allowing quick assimilation of data for strategic follow-up.

Finding account information

One core success factor for acount-based marketing (ABM) is correctly targeted accounts based on analysis and insights, and this can be drawn from different areas:

- **Past purchase and portfolio gaps:** These can be drawn from previous purchase history and can highlight purchase gaps, e.g. where only a few of the products/services are being purchased from a larger product portfolio.
- **Account propensity modelling:** A more sophisticated approach is to take multiple criteria such as sector, size of company and past purchase history, and use them to create a more accurate set of accounts based on richer detail. The idea is that a vendor can identify accounts with a higher propensity for purchasing its products or services.
- **Account plans:** Account manager input can help with customer insights and highlight likely prospects for targeting with additional products or services.
- Other sources of information include external telemarketing and data research companies.

PUT INTO PRACTICE: COMMANDS FOR ACCOUNT RESEARCH

Here are some useful prompts to get you started researching accounts when using an AI NLP/machine learning tool like ChatGPT.

Prompt 1: *Do a search for information about www.cim.com. Summarize your findings and include recent news and noteworthy events. Only include information from the last 12 months.*

Prompt 2: One can do a follow-on prompt to the above.

Based on the above information, provide the following information: Who are CIM's ideal customers? What are CIM's main product offerings? What pain points does CIM address? What benefits do they deliver?

Prompt 3: *Compare the marketing strategies of [Company A], [Company B] and [Company C] in the [specific B2B sector]. Highlight unique approaches and areas for potential improvement.*

Prompt 4: *Identify the key factors influencing B2B buying decisions in the [industry] sector. Provide examples of how top companies are addressing these factors in their marketing.*

Lookalike accounts

Lookalike account modelling is a technique for finding accounts which match an ideal organization; lookalike modelling in itself is not necessarily AI, although we're going to discuss the role and benefits of AI in this section.

As we can see from Figure 6.2, this is about looking for similar accounts in a set of data. Note the numbers refer to level of similarity of these looks alike accounts.

Benefits of lookalike account usage

- **Scaling search:** B2B lookalike accounts can more quickly scale audience searches based on matching data.

FIGURE 6.2 Look-alike accounts

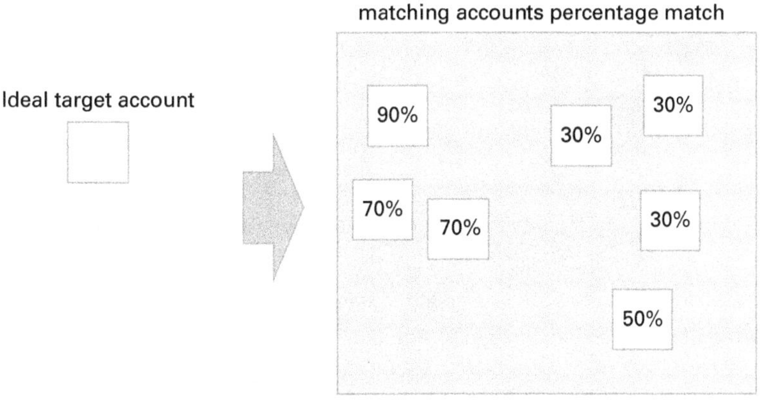

- **Hyper-segmentation:** B2B lookalike accounts can create hyper-segmentation based on matching audiences.
- **ROI:** By using lookalike accounts B2B businesses can maximize campaign ROI with effective targeting.
- **Sales cycle:** B2B lookalike accounts can help scale campaigns quickly and reduce the overall sales cycle.
- **Finding potential clients:** B2B lookalike accounts can help find high potential clients with ready business.
- **Marketing costs:** B2B lookalike accounts can help reduce marketing TCO.

AI role and tool

AI can now play a role in identifying lookalike accounts; AI does this by looking for accounts with similar characteristics as the accounts proposed or the ideal account profile.

Examples of AI functionalities and features for look-alike account identification:

- Tools that automatically segment companies based on firmographic, behavioural and transactional data.
- Data enrichment: Integrating with external data providers to gather more granular details about companies.
- NLP for intent detection: Analysing website content, product descriptions and company profiles to extract key business insights.
- Graph learning: Uncovering hidden connections and relationships between businesses.
- Automated reporting and suggestions: Providing real-time insights into new potential lookalike accounts, including automatic campaign suggestions.

PUT INTO PRACTICE: OPPWISER

Oppwiser is an AI-powered platform which helps B2B businesses identify high-potential B2B accounts that resemble a company's best clients. This technology also includes capabilities like the AI Opportunity Scanner to find new sales opportunities and the ability to track buyer signals, such as hiring trends and management changes, which indicate potential readiness to purchase. It integrates data enrichment and CRM support, helping businesses stay updated with fresh, actionable insights.

One of the key interesting features of Oppwiser is their AI Lookalike Company Finder which allows businesses to focus efforts on accounts that are most likely to be interested in their products and services. To get started one can do this simply by inputting one's ideal named account and Oppwiser then returns a list of companies which match the account. Oppwiser also highlights the level of similarity by showing a similarity score; for example, where there is a high similarity, the score would be between 80 and 100 per cent or low similarity would be less than 30 per cent.

AI Lookalike Company Finder supports users to identify the top players in any industry or industry niche; it does this by processing large amounts of public company data.

Other AI tools which support lookalike account searching include 6sense and Ocean.io.

LinkedIn sales navigator

LinkedIn sales navigator works by connecting employees own LinkedIn accounts to leverage the collective network of multiple employees; through this combined aggregate network this allows for a richer set of data one can use for free. LinkedIn sales navigator includes the following AI features (note these are features at time the book went to print).

AI-assisted search

AI-assisted search in LinkedIn offers personalized lead recommendations based on your search history, preferences and past interactions. It generates a tailored list of potential leads who are more likely to be interested in your products or services.

PUT INTO PRACTICE

Navigate to the Sales Navigator section of LinkedIn (accessible via the 'Work' drop-down menu in the top right corner of the LinkedIn homepage).

Steps:

1 Use the search bar within Sales Navigator and enter your criteria (e.g. job title, industry, location).

2. LinkedIn will display a list of prospects, with AI-powered recommendations shown under 'Recommended Leads' or 'Similar Leads'.
3. Refine results using advanced filters such as company size, years of experience and engagement level.

Pro tip: Use the 'Save Lead' feature to track prospects and receive updates on their activity or profile changes.

PUT INTO PRACTICE – HOW TO USE

Available in LinkedIn Sales Navigator under the Account Insights tab.

Steps:

1. Open Sales Navigator and select a target company.
2. Navigate to the 'Insights' section of the company's profile to view aggregated data on news, financials and organizational updates.
3. Use the AI-generated suggestions, such as ideal times to contact the company or potential areas of interest, to plan your outreach.

Pro tip: Set up alerts for key account updates (e.g. leadership changes, funding announcements) to stay informed and time your outreach effectively.

Relationship explorer: This feature prioritizes potential allies within an account who are most likely to champion a product and engage with salespeople. Using this feature B2B businesses can focus their attention on those individuals to where they have a better chance of building connections and initiating conversations.

The DMU

DMU introduction

In organizations buying is usually undertaken by two or more individuals and as such they are often referred to as the buying group; this can also be referred to as a buying unit or decision-making unit (DMU). A typical decision-making unit comprises about five types of stakeholders' users, influences, buyers, deciders and gatekeepers; these stakeholders in larger organizations can be entire departments with more than one person involved per department (see Figure 6.3).[1]

DMU stakeholders – understanding dynamics

The other aspect to note is the level of influence stakeholders have in the buying unit as not all stakeholders have the same level of influence; of course, not all influence will be even therefore it is up to marketing and sales to consider the top two or three stakeholders with the most influence and to focus on those. Figure 6.3 shows an example of the main types of stakeholders in the DMU as well as the degree of influences where level of influence is reflected by the size of the circles, i.e. in this diagram, we can see that the Influencers and the buyers have the most influence.

We can use AI tools to identify typical stakeholders involved in a buying decision; in this case we're more interested in which stakeholders are involved in the buying decision for our products/services.

Let's look at the output from ChatGPT and ask it to create a table for four different scenarios; we'll ask it to list the top five stakeholders considering that in some cases there can be over 10 stakeholders (see Figure 6.4).

FIGURE 6.3 The DMU

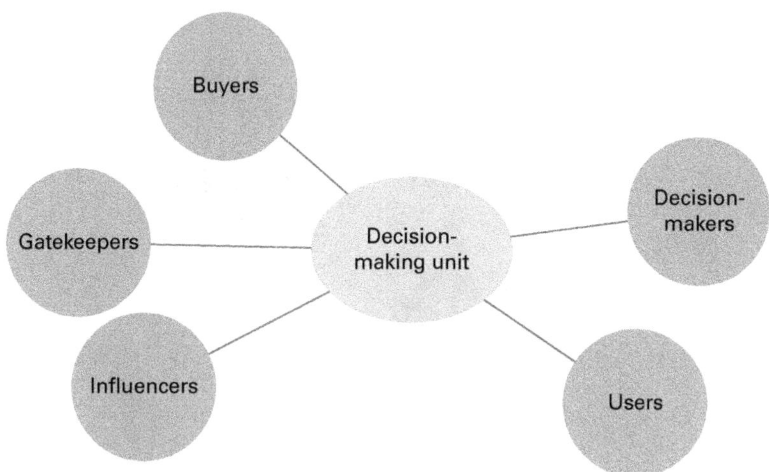

FIGURE 6.4 Types of DMU

Stakeholder role	Healthcare buying IT equipment	IT company buying marketing services	Financial company buying office space	Agricultural company buying farm equipment
1. Decision-maker	Chief information officer (CIO)	Chief marketing officer (CMO)	Chief operations officer (COO)	Chief operations officer (COO)
2. Influencer	Medical directors/ department heads	Sales and business development team	Real estate consultants	Lead agronomists
3. Buyer	Procurement officer	Procurement officer	Procurement manager	Procurement officer
4. User	Healthcare staff (doctors, nurses)	Marketing and creative teams	Employees and Office Managers	Farm operators
5. Gatekeeper	IT manager	Finance manager	Real Estate/Facilities Manager	Financial controller

PUT INTO PRACTICE: IDENTIFYING STAKEHOLDERS

Here are some prompts to use for identifying stakeholders.
Prompt:

- *What are the key stakeholders involved in buying IT equipment for a healthcare business?*
- *What are key stakeholders involved in choosing cybersecurity software for a company in the finance sector?*

More detailed prompts:

- *Please highlight key stakeholders involved in buying IT equipment for a healthcare business highlighting key roles of the stakeholders; where possible highlight if some stakeholders are a higher degree of influence than others and whether different stakeholders may have higher importance at different stages in the buying process.*

The response for one of the stakeholders:

Procurement and supply chain managers

- **Role**: These individuals manage the sourcing, vendor negotiation and contract management aspects of the purchase. They ensure compliance with internal procurement policies, negotiate the best prices and manage supplier relationships.
- **Influence**: High during the **negotiation and procurement phase**. They play a crucial role in ensuring cost-effectiveness and timely acquisition of the equipment.
- **Involvement**:
  - Supplier selection and negotiation: Their expertise is key when negotiating terms, evaluating vendor proposals and ensuring compliance with purchasing policies.
  - Contract finalization: They finalize contracts, ensuring that warranties, support and service level agreements are included.

More detailed prompts:

We can even go further to understand more about the roles, activities of the stakeholders by stage of the buying process; here is an example of a prompt.

For a financial company buying IT equipment and considering different stages of the buying process in terms of budget approval, identifying options, evaluating alternatives and the purchase phase which stakeholders in the DMU are involved more, less and what activities do they typically carry out.

Buyer triggers

A trigger in buyer terms is an event which causes a customer to have a clear need and recognize it; it usually moves a buyer from a state of curiosity or consideration to a more urgent need state.

Identifying and exploiting buyer triggers

Organizations can be effective in sales and marketing by identifying and exploiting customer triggers. Identification can come from monitoring and listening activities that help to not only identify triggers but anticipate them.

Traditional routes

Some possible traditional routes to buyer trigger identification are:

- Taking part in a social forum where customers participate.
- Undertaking needs assessment research with existing/new customers.
- Monitoring market trends through the web or research firms.
- Monitoring technology trends.
- Engaging industry associations that represent the target customer segment.

Organizations can capitalize on the triggers by some of the following:

- Creating customer persona(s) for the trigger event identified.
- Looking at potential reactions the trigger event may initiate.
- Including messaging and content that tap into trigger event reactions.
- Ensuring messaging includes a solution your business can offer for the trigger event.

PUT INTO PRACTICE

- Look at your own business and industry and try to identify trigger events.
- As a customer yourself, can you notice any trigger events that have caused you to buy something?
- Think about purchase influences for customers you're marketing to and identify at least three internal and external influences.

PUT INTO PRACTICE: HOW TO USE AI TO IDENTIFY POTENTIAL TRIGGERS

Prompt: *Please suggest 10 buyer triggers (a buyer trigger is something which would trigger someone or a company to purchase something) for the following two situations: (1) higher education company looking to buy new notebooks for its teaching staff and (2) an HR department in a healthcare company looking to provide training to its senior managers. Please show in a table.*

Table 6.1 is a summarized view of the response to the prompt, by showing 5 out of the 10 buyer triggers.

TABLE 6.1 Buyer triggers

Scenario	Trigger	Scenario	Trigger
1. Higher education company buying notebooks		2. HR department in a healthcare company providing training	
1. Budget approval or new funding	The institution receives a new budget allocation or a grant specifically for technological upgrades.	1. Regulatory changes	New laws or healthcare regulations requiring enhanced management training.
2. Curriculum overhaul	Implementation of new teaching methods or subjects requiring updated technology.	2. Leadership gaps	Identification of weaknesses in senior management skills through performance reviews.
3. Faculty expansion	Hiring of new teaching staff necessitating additional notebooks.	3. Organizational restructuring	Recent mergers, acquisitions or restructuring necessitating new leadership training.

(continued)

TABLE 6.1 (Continued)

Scenario	Trigger	Scenario	Trigger
1. Higher education company buying notebooks		2. HR department in a healthcare company providing training	
4. Outdated equipment	Current notebooks are no longer meeting performance requirements or are incompatible with modern software.	4. Employee feedback	Requests from managers or surveys highlighting the need for training programmes.
5. Accreditation requirements	Compliance with new educational standards that require modernized teaching tools.	5. New technology implementation	Introduction of new tools or systems requiring senior managers to upskill.

Some AI tools one can use to identify stakeholders include reply.io, Seamless.ai and Oneshot.ai; here are some of the key features which are shared by most of these platforms.

1. SOCIAL MEDIA AND DIGITAL PROFILE ANALYSIS

Sales tools like Reply.io utilize AI to analyse social media profiles, email databases and company websites. By gathering insights from these sources, AI can generate contact lists of potential stakeholders. The tool identifies individuals based on their job titles, roles and online activities, ensuring that sales teams can connect with the most relevant decision-makers. This feature helps sales teams focus their efforts on engaging the right people, increasing the likelihood of a successful connection.

2. REAL-TIME SEARCH CAPABILITIES

Another valuable AI feature is real-time search, used by tools like Seamless.ai. This capability enables sales professionals to quickly find, verify and deliver accurate contact information. Using real-time data, AI can continuously scan the web and databases to provide up-to-date information on potential leads. This feature ensures that sales teams can access the most current and accurate contact details, enhancing their outreach strategies and improving the chances of establishing meaningful connections with potential customers.

3. LEAD ENRICHMENT AND STAKEHOLDER IDENTIFICATION

AI-powered tools such as Oneshot.ai enhance lead generation by automating the identification of decision-makers and stakeholders. These tools crawl public and proprietary databases to enrich lead data and identify relevant stakeholders based on their roles, activities and online engagement. Oneshot.ai can even build organizational charts, visually mapping out decision-makers, influencers and blockers within target companies. This helps sales teams understand the organizational structure and identify the most critical individuals to target, making prospecting efforts more strategic and focused.

Account prospecting and intent

We already discussed intent in Chapter 4 when discussing customer journey maps as a reminder intent data is where we use data signals to help us understand where a prospect is in their buying process.

In this section we'll have a closer look at intent data.

Types of intent data

Different types of intent data can help businesses identify and prioritize accounts for acquisition efforts (Table 6.2). Here are the main types of intent data that are particularly valuable in identifying B2B accounts for acquisition.

- **Content consumption:** Accounts that download ebooks, white papers or reports related to your industry or product.
- **Website visits:** Repeated visits to your website, especially to high-intent pages like product demos, pricing or contact forms.
- **Engagement with ads:** Interaction with your ads, such as clicking on display ads or engaging with social media campaigns.
- **Event participation:** Registering for or attending webinars, industry events or virtual conferences that are relevant to your solutions.

TABLE 6.2 Types of intent data

Customer journey stage	Intent data types	Examples
1. Early buyer journey	Website visits & content consumption	– Visits to general industry blogs, white papers, or informational articles
	Search intent	– Searches for broad terms like 'marketing automation' or 'data analytics'
	Social engagement	– Engaging with relevant industry topics, trends or influencers
	Ad engagement	– Clicks on ads related to industry terms or top-of-funnel resources
	3rd-party intent data	– Intent signals from platforms like Bombora on specific topics
2. Mid buyer journey	Website behaviour on competitors	– Visits to competitor websites and product comparison pages
	Content download (e.g., case studies)	– Downloads of case studies, product brochures and buyer's guides
	Event participation	– Attending industry webinars, conferences or panels
	Review platform activity	– Reading reviews on platforms like G2, TrustRadius
	Comparison searches	– Searches like 'top data analytics software', vs 'compare [product]'
3. Late buyer journey	Pricing page visits	– Repeated visits to pricing or package options on the website
	Free trial / demo requests	– Requests for product demos or trials
	Intent from email clicks	– Engaging with emails on pricing, ROI calculators, implementation details
	Direct engagement with sales	– Repeated back-and-forth communication with sales representatives
	Evaluation of solutions on forums	– Activity on forums (e.g. Reddit, LinkedIn) asking for specific tool recommendations

AI tools and types of tools

AI tools which collect intent data include Demandbase, Bombora, 6sense, zoominfo, triblio, leadfeeder; these tools fall into different categories of ABM software or abx (account-based experience tools), or CDP.

Demandbase is an AI-driven ABM tool that offers real-time intent data as well as supporting many other features for account-based marketing. This AI tool helps B2B marketers track account activity, identify buying signals and prioritize leads. Using real-time data, Demandbase analyses web behaviour, company interactions and engagement across digital channels to understand intent and optimize marketing strategies. By integrating intent data with account profiles, Demandbase helps marketers focus on high-potential accounts that are actively researching products or services similar to theirs.

Bombora and 6sense are more specialized in providing intent data; Bombora is known for consent-based intent data. As a result, it can provide insights into the buying behaviour of prospects and customers. Bombora tracks the online behaviour of companies through content consumption patterns, revealing when an organization is researching a solution. Marketers can use this information to trigger timely, personalized outreach and prioritize accounts that are showing buying intent based on their digital activity. 6sense is similar to Bombora in terms of providing intent data and insights.

Lusha is an AI prospecting tool which provides B2B contact information along with intent data, identifying companies searching for solutions you offer. It features data enrichment, CRM integration and a Chrome plugin for easy access to contact details. By combining intent data with direct contact details, Lusha helps marketers quickly connect with decision-makers at companies that are in-market for a specific product or service.

Predicting CLV with AI

AI tools can be used calculate or predict customer lifetime value (CLV) in B2B by leveraging historical data, machine learning models and predictive analytics.

First let's explain CLV; it is a metric that represents the total revenue a business can expect from a customer over the entire duration of their relationship with the company. It takes into account factors such as purchase frequency, average order value and customer retention rate. CLV helps businesses understand the long-term value of retaining a customer versus acquiring a new one, and it can guide marketing, sales and customer service strategies by prioritizing efforts that enhance customer loyalty and lifetime engagement.

AI tools can significantly enhance the ability to calculate and optimize CLV by providing advanced data analytics and predictive modelling. For instance, AI can analyse historical purchasing behaviour, browsing activity and demographic data to predict future spending patterns and customer churn. Machine learning algorithms can also identify key factors that contribute to high-value customers and recommend personalized engagement strategies that increase retention and spending.

How AI tools predict CLV

1 **Step 1:** AI tools first collect and segment data related to an account's transaction history, engagement metrics and demographic/firmographic characteristics. This includes revenue data, customer engagement, industry data, usage metrics and other.
2 **Step 2:** AI uses machine learning algorithms to identify patterns in historical customer data to forecast future purchasing behaviour. These models take into account purchase frequency, churn prediction, upsell and cross sell opportunities.
3 **Step 3:** AI models use data and insights from steps 1 and 2 to segment customers.

AI tools for CLV calculation

Some AI tools which can be used to identify CLV include the following.

- Zeta Global offers an AI-powered platform for predictive analytics, including CLV prediction.
- Optimove is an AI-driven marketing platform that provides robust predictive analytics, including CLV forecasting.
- Gainsight is a customer success platform that focuses on customer health scoring and CLV prediction for B2B SaaS companies.

PUT INTO PRACTICE

To calculate CLV in its basic form we need to identify average time a customer stays with a business or assume an average customer lifetime; the second most important information is the average spend per year from a customer. For such a calculation we can look at our CRM system data to calculate this. When we need to consider multiple types of customer and multiple average order values and then include aspects such as discount rates, we then make use of AI tools.

We can also use machine learning/NLP tools like ChatGPT to help us understand CLV; to get a better understanding of different areas of CLV I used the below commands.

Command 1: *Please provide typical average order values of B2B customers from 10 different industry sectors. See Table 6.3 for the response to this command.*

Command 2: *Please provide average customer lifetimes for B2B customers from 10 different industry sectors.*

Response: Here is a general overview of average customer lifetimes across different B2B sectors:

1 **Healthcare**: Lifetimes range from **8 to 12 years** due to regulatory barriers and high switching costs.

TABLE 6.3 Typical customer lifetimes

B2B industry	Typical customer lifetime length
SaaS (Software as a Service)	2–5 years
Telecommunications	3–7 years
Financial services	5–10 years
Manufacturing	7–15 years
Consulting services	3–8 years
Healthcare technology	5–10 years
Legal services	3–6 years
Construction	5–10 years
Logistics & transportation	5–12 years
Marketing & advertising	2–4 years

2 **Information Technology (IT)**: B2B tech and software solutions often have customer lifetimes of **3–5 years**, though SaaS subscriptions can renew more frequently based on customer success management and integration with workflows.
3 **Manufacturing**: With significant investment in equipment, manufacturing clients tend to stay for **6–10 years**, benefiting from long-term service contracts and maintenance needs.
4 **Financial services**: B2B customers in financial consulting, insurance and similar services generally maintain relationships for **5–7 years**, given high client trust requirements and tailored services.
5 **Retail and E-commerce**: For companies supplying products to retail or e-commerce businesses, lifetimes range from **3 to 5 years**, although this can vary depending on product relevance and service support.

AI tools for financial analysis of accounts

Another area of account research is understanding the financial statements of organizations; financial analysis can include reviewing income statements, balance sheets and cash flows to surface insights about an organization's performance. AI tools which conduct financial analysis of accounts include Alteryx, **IBM Watson** and **Kabbage**, although these tend to be focused more on conducting an internal financial review of 'our' accounts rather than conducting a financial analysis of another company's financial health.

Using machine learning and NLP tools

Using machine learning tools through well-structured commands can save as a lot of time in understanding financial health as well as share valuable insights and interpretation. Through NLP tools we can ask for all possible financial statements to be reviewed and analysed, i.e. income statements, cash flows and more; we can ask for horizontal and vertical analysis, i.e. an in-depth view of the financials for a given year or a horizontal analysis where we ask for comparisons to previous years.

Tip: note that the response may not always be accurate depending on how the information is uploaded when inputting a prompt. It is always better to include a table than an image when asking ChatGPT 3.5 to review and analyse numbers.

PUT INTO PRACTICE

Let's say we want to analyse financials and financial ratio for company 'x'; there are different ways we can ask for financial information to be analysed. One way might be to identify a URL where the financial information or statement is shown, another way might be to upload a table.

Here is a prompt we could use once we've identified a URL (or have a table) where the financial account statement is found.

Please conduct a financial analysis of this financial statement in the (a) URL or (b) table attached using the current ratio, debt-to-equity ratio and inventory turnover ratio.

Here's what the ML/NLP tool provided me:

1. Key financial ratios

To assess company 'xs' financial health, we'll calculate several key ratios:

- **Current ratio:** Measures short-term liquidity
  - 2024: 24,709 / 33,627 = 0.73
  - 2023: 22,648 / 35,756 = 0.63
- **Debt-to-equity ratio:** Measures financial leverage
  - 2024: (71,811 + 25,269) / 50,559 = 1.95
  - d. 2023: (73,764 + 24,378) / 47,065 = 2.02
- **Inventory turnover:** Measures how efficiently inventory is managed.
  - 2024: 7,016 / ((1,617 + 1,863 + 7,073) / 2) = 1.74
  - 2023: 7,073 / ((1,863 + 956 + 4,254) / 2) = 1.85

2. Analysis

Liquidity: The current ratio has improved slightly from 0.63 in 2023 to 0.73 in 2024. However, it's still below 1, indicating that x might have some difficulty meeting short-term obligations.

Leverage: The debt-to-equity ratio has decreased from 2.02 in 2023 to 1.95 in 2024. This suggests that x is using less debt to finance its assets, which can be seen as a positive sign.

Efficiency: Inventory turnover has decreased from 1.85 in 2023 to 1.74 in 2024. This means that x is taking slightly longer to sell its inventory, which could indicate slower sales or less efficient inventory management.

In addition to the interpretation of the ratios; the AI tool provided me with an overall assessment and shared additional considerations. This was of the balance sheet but already I was able to understand some useful things for B2B marketing and to support sales with their future activities, e.g. growth of company, challenges with moving stock and company is managing its debt efficiently.

Please conduct a financial analysis of the income statement of the organization in the copied image highlighting any useful insights for marketing and sales which can be subsequently used for communicating and engaging the organization.

Account mapping

AI technologies can automate the account mapping process via more efficient data collection, analysis and other tasks. AI uses machine learning algorithms to analyse large datasets and identify patterns that may not be immediately obvious to human analysts. This capability allows for a more accurate segmentation of accounts based on various criteria such as industry, size or potential value.

AI systems can also make updates and changes on a continuous basis; this ensures that account information remains current and relevant, allowing businesses to respond swiftly to market changes or new opportunities.

Social media for account analysis

NLP-based AI tools allow businesses to make sense of the context and tone of social media posts. The area where AI is used is social media monitoring, which allows B2B marketers to conduct analysis of potential customers in term of their organizations. Here are some ways how social media monitoring can be used; most of the below features are supported by tools such as Brandwatch and Sprinklr.

Identifying key decision-makers

AI-based social media monitoring tools are increasingly valuable for identifying key stakeholders in the DMU for B2B purchases. These tools can track and analyse social media conversations, company profiles and individual posts to pinpoint the influencers and decision-makers involved in purchasing decisions. By leveraging advanced AI features such as social listening, sentiment analysis and network analysis, these tools can uncover critical insights into the key players within an organization.

One prominent AI tool in this space is Brandwatch, which uses AI to monitor online conversations, identify trending topics and detect key individuals or departments within target organizations. By analysing discussions, Brandwatch can uncover individuals who are actively involved in shaping opinions or making purchasing decisions, helping marketers understand the structure of the decision-making process within a company. Another widely used AI tool is Sprinklr, which employs sentiment analysis and network analysis features to track interactions on social media platforms, identifying which employees or executives are voicing opinions or engaging in discussions about industry-specific products or services. These insights help marketers target the right people in their outreach efforts.

AI features such as social listening allow tools like Hootsuite Insights to monitor public social media channels, track mentions of relevant industry topics and identify key stakeholders who are sharing information, commenting on trends or engaging in conversations around a company's buying process. Sentiment analysis can further refine this by assessing the tone of interactions. For example, if an individual or group within an organization expresses positive sentiment about a competitor's product, it could signal them as a potential key decision-maker or influencer.

Additionally, network analysis tools like BuzzSumo or Followerwonk use AI to evaluate the social networks of individuals and their influence within an organization. By mapping out relationships and interactions, these tools can identify central figures who play a role in purchasing decisions, providing marketers with a clearer understanding of the DMU.

Sentiment analysis

AI tools can assess the sentiment of social media posts related to a target account, providing insights into the company's current challenges or pain points. This allows marketers to tailor their messaging to address these specific issues, making their approach more relevant.

Real-time engagement

Social media monitoring enables real-time tracking of mentions or discussions involving target accounts. This allows marketers to engage immediately, whether it's responding to a query, offering solutions or simply acknowledging a mention, thereby building relationships with potential clients.

Technographic profiling

Technographic profiling of target accounts is the process of gathering, analysing and utilizing data about the technology stack that potential business clients use. This process allows companies to tailor their marketing strategies more effectively by understanding the technological environment of their target accounts.

AI can improve these activities through data collection; in this case AI uses web scraping and data mining features to automatically scrape websites and mine data to collect information on the technologies used by target accounts. This includes software, hardware and applications, as well as details like purchase dates and usage patterns. AI tools can also integrate with existing CRM systems and other data platforms to enrich technographic profiles with additional insights.

AI can analyse the effectiveness of technographic profiling and provide feedback for continuous improvement. This feedback loop helps refine data collection methods and analytical models, enhancing the overall accuracy and utility of technographic data.

Reference

1 De Backer, G (2024) Decision making unit (DMU): B2B & B2C buying center [+ example], 28 June. gustdebacker.com/decision-making-unit/ (archived at https://perma.cc/A5CB-YY67)

Further reading

Barron, J (2025) AI for sales prospecting: The ultimate guide, Cognism, www.cognism.com/blog/ai-sales-prospecting (archived at https://perma.cc/W98Q-548N)

Sharma, M and Nowoslawski, E (2023) AI for sales prospecting: A complete guide, Clay, www.clay.com/blog/ai-sales-prospecting (archived at https://perma.cc/GC66-4BWG)

07

Lead capture and AI

What you will gain from this chapter

Understanding of the following:

- understanding lead capture
- lead capture stages
- how to create lead magnets with AI tools
- how to use AI chatbots for lead capture
- AI and call to actions

Introduction

In the previous chapter we looked at AI for prospecting, which was about researching accounts, finding and identifying relevant accounts; in this chapter we look at the next stage, which relates to the step of capturing and generating the lead; literally how we capture their first details such as email address and role.

Lead capture is when we capture a detail (or details) about the prospect which we can use later to engage them further.

The stage of lead capture occurs usually where the prospect provides some details in exchange for something, e.g. information, some compelling content or where a customer is interested in understanding more information about an organization, and its products and services.

Lead capture can occur through multiple different marketing vehicles or a combination of them; the main vehicles employed are door openers, webinars, email with call-to-actions, events, outbound calls, content syndication, content downloads in the form of infographics, access to information, white papers or other, SEO, paid search, public relations, social, direct email, advertising, mobile and print advertising.

Lead capture mechanics

This stage of lead capture is important in terms of getting timings right and getting the method right. In terms of lead capture methods, there are various options available to B2B marketers such as capturing through live chat, using gamified content such as quizzes to entice prospects to leave their details, inviting prospects to leave their details or using native capture options on third party sites such as LinkedIn lead forms.

Auto-capturing of leads is also another way where technologies can be used for sign-up forms, phone calls, referrals sites, social media, landing pages to capture information about the prospect. Companies like LeadSquared or MyMedLeads offer this option to provide a tailored approach to capturing leads. Sources of lead capture can vary. Leads can be captured through PPC ads, social media, phone inquiries, chat inquiries, lead gen sites, API and webinars.

The evolution of lead capture techniques

Lead capture can occur in many different ways through basic level capturing of emails, through forms, through native capture of forms on third party sites and through prompting website visitors. Lead capture is also about the 'how' in terms of designing forms, designing landing pages, etc.; but there are also elements of lead capture content which appeal to specific target audiences as well as identifying and attracting relevant target audience on first-party and third-party websites.

Key benefits of using AI technology for lead capture

There are many ways AI can benefit lead generation; AI can improve efficiency and reduce costs and workloads.

AI technologies can be used to trawl through large amounts of data and data types, and identify customer behaviours and related preferences. AI can also help predict likelihood of a lead to convert, i.e. convertibility of leads, and thus help businesses and marketing focus their efforts more. AI-powered chatbots also act as virtual assistants and improve engagement with potential leads (see Figure 7.1 for areas where AI can support lead capture).

AI role in lead generation

AI tools can leverage more sophisticated web-scraping techniques to analyse online platforms and identify individuals and businesses which match your ideal target audience; these algorithms navigate through vast amounts of data, such as social media profiles, industry forums and business directories, to curate a prospect list. This automated outreach process enables sales and marketing teams to find potential customers in a highly efficient and personalized manner and maximizes conversion opportunities.

AI's role in the stage of lead capture includes the following sub areas.

- AI for lead magnet creation
- Ai chatbots for capturing leads
- AI in testing landing pages and in testing lead magnets

AI tools can also set up effective lead capture mechanisms, such as more tailored interactive content like forms, quizzes and surveys, which engage users and collect lead information in a more interactive and less intrusive manner. Additionally, AI can enhance lead scoring by analysing vast datasets and identifying patterns indicative of high-quality leads.

FIGURE 7.1 AI for lead capture

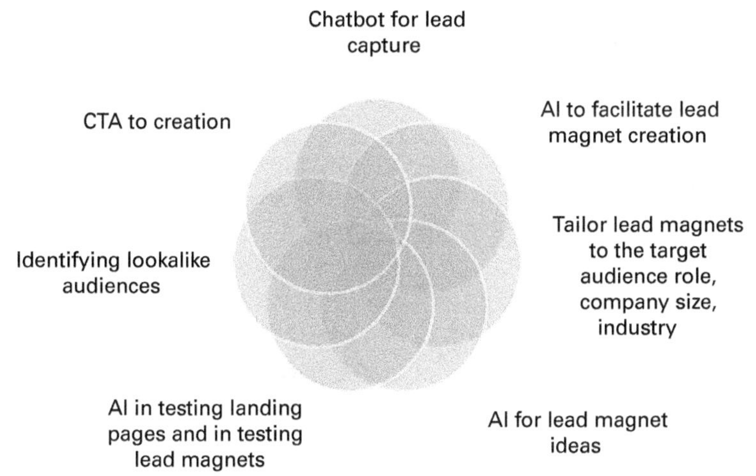

Lookalike audiences

In the last chapter we looked at lookalike accounts; now we turn to lookalike audiences (see Figure 7.2). We can use AI tools to find people or personas which match our ideal customer profile (as opposed to ideal account profile)

Note for some of the tools we discussed in the past chapter we can use the ideal account profile to then find ideal profiles of people, e.g. through using Oppwiser we can then drill down into the account and look for the names of people in roles we're interested in. Other possible AI tools include Lemlist and M1-Project.

Lead magnets

What is a lead magnet?

Lead magnets are a type of incentive you provide to prospects in exchange for some personal details usually an email address. The goal is to 'capture' leads, i.e. capture details of people who might be interested in your product or service.

What makes a good lead magnet?

Good or effective lead magnets tend to be personalized, provide educational or actionable content, provide high value content and are visually appealing. Other points which make effective lead magnets is that they solve a problem, they are easy to understand and can be accessed easily, and also include clear calls to actions.

FIGURE 7.2 Lookalike audiences

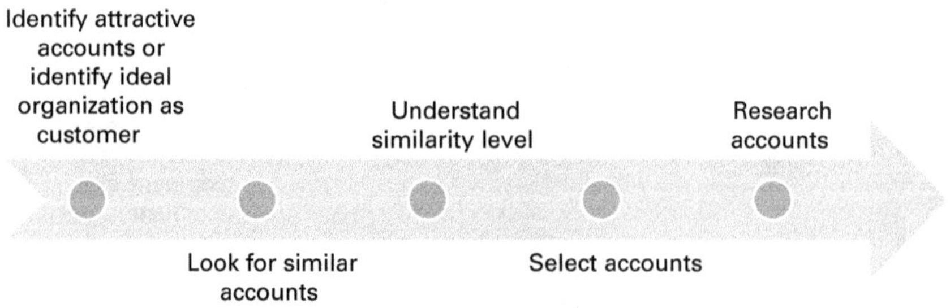

Lead magnet examples

Please find in Table 7.1 popular lead magnet examples including ebooks, white papers, case studies, webinars and templates, etc.

Where AI can help

AI can help with lead magnets in different areas. Here are the main ones.

- Idea generation: AI tools can help in generating ideas for lead magnets based on industry trends, interests of target audiences and their challenges.
- Personalization: AI can be used to analyse user data to tailor the lead magnets to the target audience role, company size, industry or other according to other individual criteria.

TABLE 7.1 Lead magnet

Lead magnet type	Lead magnet description
Case studies	Real-world examples of how your product or service has helped other companies.
Industry reports	In-depth data and insights specific to your target industries.
Webinars with industry experts	Live or recorded sessions providing valuable business insights.
ROI calculators	Tools to help users calculate the financial benefits of your product or service.
White papers	Comprehensive guides or research papers addressing industry challenges.
Templates	Ready-to-use business templates like project management frameworks or sales scripts.
Cheat sheets/checklists	Quick, actionable tools for a specific task (e.g. 'Checklist for Building a Successful SaaS Product').
Product demos	Free trials or personalized demos that let leads experience the value of your offering.
Toolkits	A collection of resources bundled together, such as a guide, worksheet and video tutorial on a specific topic.
Competitor analysis tools	Free tools or reports that allow businesses to compare their performance to competitors.

FIGURE 7.3 AI for lead magnet creation

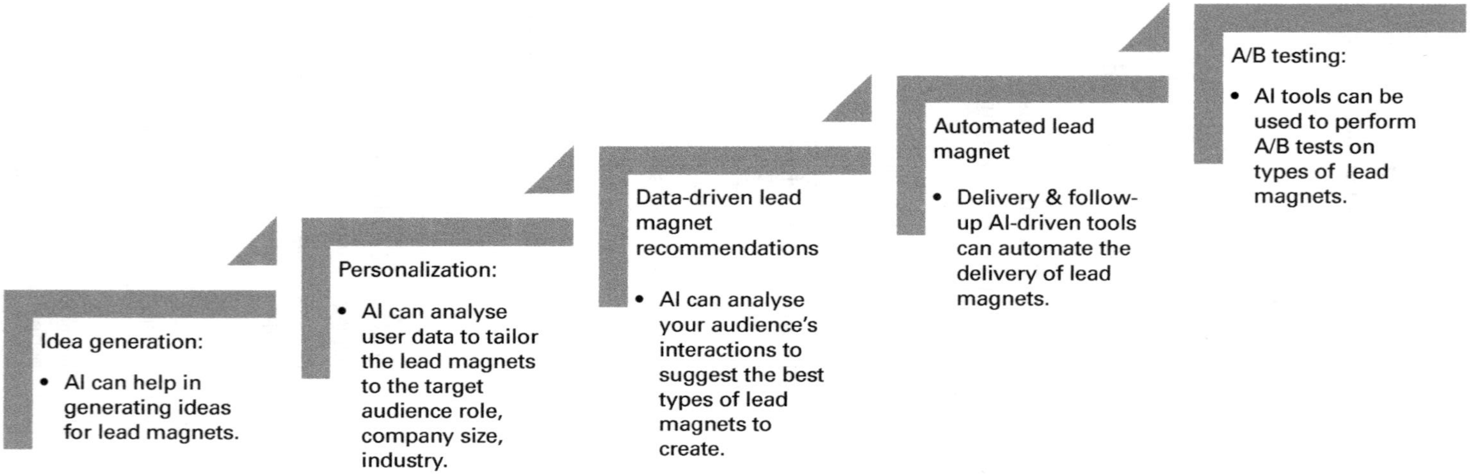

Idea generation:

- AI can help in generating ideas for lead magnets.

Personalization:

- AI can analyse user data to tailor the lead magnets to the target audience role, company size, industry.

Data-driven lead magnet recommendations

- AI can analyse your audience's interactions to suggest the best types of lead magnets to create.

Automated lead magnet

- Delivery & follow-up AI-driven tools can automate the delivery of lead magnets.

A/B testing:

- AI tools can be used to perform A/B tests on types of lead magnets.

- Data-driven lead magnet recommendations: AI can be used to analyse your audience's interactions with your website, emails and other marketing materials to suggest the best types of lead magnets to create.
- Automated lead magnet delivery and follow-up: AI-driven tools like Drift and ActiveCampaign can automate the delivery of lead magnets as well as the follow-up steps.
- A/B testing: AI tools can be used to perform A/B tests on types of lead magnets to understand which ones work better in real time. This helps business optimize content and delivery of lead magnets. An example is Google Optimize which uses AI to help run A/B tests on different versions of lead magnets or landing pages.

PUT INTO PRACTICE: CREATING A WEBINAR LEAD MAGNET

Let's turn to the stages of creating a webinar as a lead magnet.

Step 1: Identifying a webinar topic:

Prompt: *We are a B2B marketing department specializing in cloud-based IT solutions for medium to large businesses. Can you suggest five potential webinar topics that would attract IT decision-makers, focused on industry challenges and new trends?*

Step 2: Crafting webinar content:

Prompt: *Create an outline for a 45-minute B2B webinar on the topic of 'Maximizing Cloud Infrastructure Efficiency'. Include sections for industry challenges, best practices, case studies and a Q&A session.*

Step 3: Writing webinar promotional materials:

Prompt: *Write a compelling email invitation for a B2B webinar titled 'Harnessing the Power of AI for Cloud Cost Optimization.' The email should focus on how this session will help IT managers and CTOs reduce cloud infrastructure costs.*

Step 4: Creating webinar landing page copy:

Prompt: *Write engaging copy for a webinar landing page promoting an event titled 'The Future of Remote Work: How Cloud Solutions Are Shaping the New Workplace'. Emphasize the value to IT leaders and provide a clear call-to-action for signing up.*

We can see the various stages for lead magnet creation in Figure 7.3. We can also use AI NLP and machine learning tools for other types of lead magnet creation, e.g. blog posts, white papers, ebooks or checklists.

AI and call to actions (CTA)

What are CTAs?

Any content we use in lead capture, e.g. for lead magnets or other related content, should include call to actions; these are statements which aim to evoke an action. CTAs guide potential customers toward completing an action that aligns with your business goals, such as downloading a resource, signing up for a webinar or subscribing to a newsletter.

Examples of CTAs

Below are some examples of CTAs; they will vary by type of content, type of audience, type of industry.

- Download now
- Get your free guide
- Sign up for the webinar
- Request a demo
- Join our newsletter
- Watch this webinar
- Make use of this exclusive training
- Complete a survey

Why CTAs are important

CTAs guide recipients to next steps in their buying process; they have been shown to improve conversion and encourage engagement with lead magnets and personalized CTAs have shown even higher conversion rates than standard CTAs. CTAs can also create urgency and influence users to act quickly. Phrases like 'Limited Time Offer' or 'Register Now – Only 50 Seats Left!' can nudge leads to avail of lead magnets or other to download and engage content.

AI for CTAs

AI-driven tools can help CTAs overall and help businesses come up with ideas; they can also support the tailoring of CTAs to specific preferences and behaviours of potential leads, ensuring that the messaging resonates with the target audience. An example of a platform is Involve.me which uses AI to personalize interactive content such as forms and surveys.

Moreover, AI-powered CTA features, e.g. included in Narrato and Frase, can simplify the process of creating stronger and more effective CTAs. These features help marketers save time as well as improve effectiveness of the CTA themselves.

Timing of gating content and AI

Gated content is where prospects or visitors need to enter some details in order to download a piece of content; the following are different ways AI can be used to gate content at lead capture stage.

Dynamic lead form optimization

AI can analyse user behaviour and optimize lead forms in real time. Based on the user's actions, it can adjust the number of fields, the type of questions or even offer suggestions to increase form completion rates.

One example might be for returning visitors or existing contacts in the CRM, the form dynamically shortens to only ask for updated or additional fields (e.g. job title, company size).

Other examples might be adaptive field removal, e.g. if the AI detects that certain fields, like 'Phone Number', tend to decrease form completion rates in this user segment, it dynamically removes or makes those fields optional, which in turn keeps the form as short and relevant as possible.

Personalized gated content recommendations

AI-driven personalization can recommend specific gated content (like a white paper or ebook) to each visitor based on their behaviour, preferences or industry. This increases the likelihood of users finding content valuable enough to exchange their contact information.

One example is where a visitor from the healthcare industry browses the company's site, AI identifies their industry through domain recognition (e.g. from their IP address, cookies or LinkedIn profile integration) and then recommends a white paper titled 'Ensuring HIPAA Compliance in Cloud Solutions for Healthcare' rather than a generic cloud security white paper.

Adaptive gating based on user profiles

AI-driven adaptive gating uses sophisticated algorithms to dynamically adjust how much information users must provide to access gated content. By analysing user profiles, behaviours and historical interactions, AI can tailor the user experience to maximize engagement while capturing valuable lead information.

Some examples of how adaptive gating works:

- Profile analysis: AI tools such as HubSpot CRM or Marketo Engage use machine learning to analyse user demographics, firmographics (e.g. company size, industry) and digital behaviour (e.g. pages visited, time spent on site). This helps classify users as high-quality leads or less-engaged visitors.
- Dynamic form customization: Tools like ZoomInfo Form Complete enrich lead forms automatically by populating data from external databases. For high-quality leads, forms are shortened to one or two fields. For unqualified leads, the system might require additional inputs, such as job title or company revenue.

AI-powered chatbots for content gating

AI chatbots can engage users on the site, qualify them with a few questions and then provide access to gated content based on their responses. By asking tailored questions, these chatbots can assess the potential value of a site visitor and provide personalized access to gated content based on their responses. This approach not only enhances user experience but also ensures that high-value leads receive appropriate content quickly, while less-qualified leads are encouraged to share more information for better targeting.

HOW AI CHATBOTS QUALIFY SITE VISITORS IN B2B MARKETING IN STAGES

Step 1 – Engagement through contextual questions: AI chatbots like Drift, Intercom or HubSpot Chatbot initiate conversations with visitors by asking relevant, non-intrusive questions. For instance:

- *Are you looking for solutions to streamline your project management processes?*
- *What's your primary goal today exploring our services, learning more about [specific topic], or booking a demo?*

- *Which industry does your business operate in?*
- *Can you share your role? For example, are you in operations, IT or procurement?*

Step 2: Dynamic qualification based on responses: Based on the visitor's answers, the chatbot dynamically categorizes their qualification level. For example:

- Qualified lead: A visitor who identifies as a C-suite executive from a mid-sized tech firm looking for enterprise solutions.
- Potential lead: A site visitor exploring general solutions with limited details about their company or goals.

Step 3: Personalized content delivery: Once qualified, the chatbot provides immediate access to relevant gated content tailored to the visitor's needs. Examples include:

- For a highly qualified lead (e.g. IT director from a software company): Access to a white paper on 'Optimizing Cloud Infrastructure for Mid-Sized Tech Firms' or an invite to an exclusive webinar.
- For a potential lead (e.g. small business owner inquiring about general features): Access to an introductory case study or a 'Beginner's Guide to SaaS Solutions.'

See Figure 7.4 for more information on how AI chatbots can be used across different stages of the B2B buyer journey.

Sentiment analysis for optimizing gated content

AI tools can analyse user feedback, comments or interactions to gauge sentiment and determine which types of gated content resonate most positively with your audience, refining what content should be gated.

An example might be where the company analyses user feedback from different sources and finds that prospects are often frustrated with their current tools' lack of integrations. The optimized content offer based on this sentiment insight is via creating a gated ebook titled *Integrating Project Management Tools with Your Workflow: A Guide for Faster Adoption and Productivity*, addressing a specific frustration. This content is positioned to resonate with leads who previously expressed dissatisfaction with integrations, capturing their attention effectively.

FIGURE 7.4 How AI chatbots qualify site visitors in B2B marketing in stages

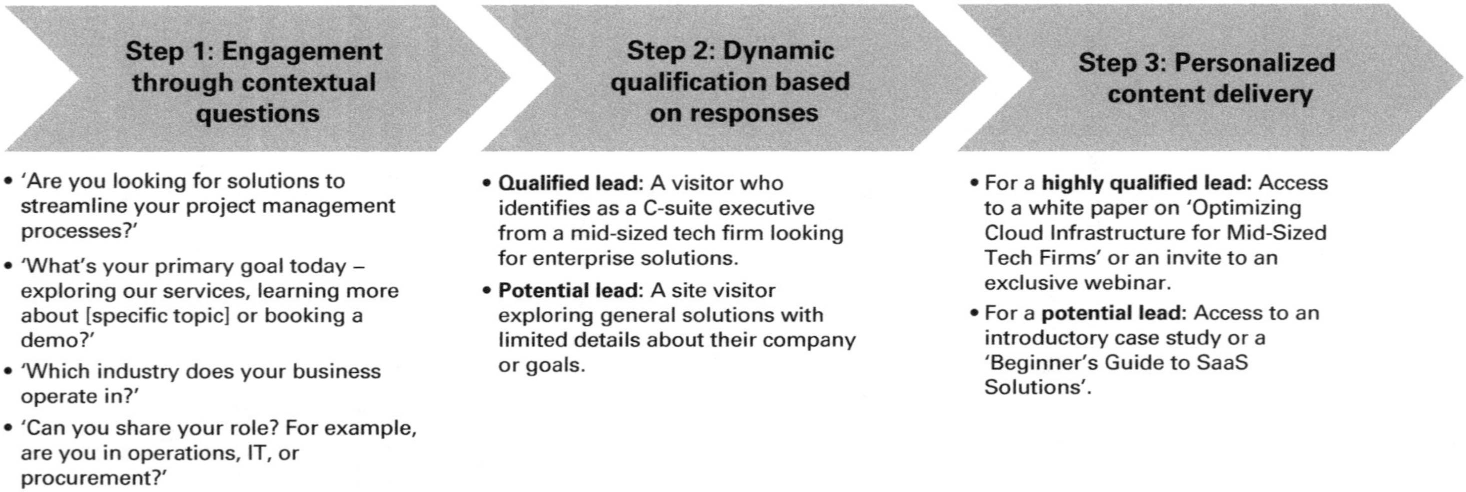

Step 1: Engagement through contextual questions

- 'Are you looking for solutions to streamline your project management processes?'
- 'What's your primary goal today – exploring our services, learning more about [specific topic] or booking a demo?'
- 'Which industry does your business operate in?'
- 'Can you share your role? For example, are you in operations, IT, or procurement?'

Step 2: Dynamic qualification based on responses

- **Qualified lead**: A visitor who identifies as a C-suite executive from a mid-sized tech firm looking for enterprise solutions.
- **Potential lead**: A site visitor exploring general solutions with limited details about their company or goals.

Step 3: Personalized content delivery

- For a **highly qualified lead**: Access to a white paper on 'Optimizing Cloud Infrastructure for Mid-Sized Tech Firms' or an invite to an exclusive webinar.
- For a **potential lead**: Access to an introductory case study or a 'Beginner's Guide to SaaS Solutions'.

Behavioural analysis for triggering gated content offers

AI can analyse user behaviour on your site (e.g. time on page, scroll depth) to trigger the presentation of gated content when the user is most likely to convert. For example, if a user spends a lot of time on a product page, AI can recommend relevant white papers or case studies as gated content.

Lead enhancement and data cleansing

AI also plays a part in being able to enhance data as well as cleanse data.

Data cleansing

Data cleansing is about locating and fixing inaccuracies in the data relating to leads; examples of inaccuracies include duplicate data, old data and incorrect contact information. AI tools can streamline and automate the process of checking data using different sources, so data is kept up to date real-time. This activity of data cleansing means companies can improve audience targeting and engagement.

One example in B2B marketing might be a software company targeting enterprise clients that finds that its CRM contains duplicate records for several leads due to manual data entry errors. Additionally, many email addresses in the database are no longer valid. Without addressing these issues, marketing campaigns are wasted on inactive or incorrect contacts. B2B marketers can make use of the following approaches to resolve this issue.

- Deduplication and validation: Tools like Openprise or Talend Data Fabric use AI to identify and merge duplicate records by comparing fields such as name, email and phone number.
- Real-time updates: Platforms like ZoomInfo check CRM data against their databases to ensure contact information (e.g. phone numbers, job titles) is current.
- Error detection: AI algorithms in tools like IBM Watson Studio can flag and correct anomalies, such as phone numbers with incorrect country codes or incomplete addresses.

Lead enhancement

Lead enhancement is about complementing existing data about leads through additional data, which ultimate leads to more complete profiles of prospects. AI tools can enrich lead data through online source such as social media sites, company websites.

An example could be a cybersecurity firm targeting CTOs at mid-sized companies that has basic contact details for its leads but lacks critical insights like the size of the prospect's IT team or the company's annual revenue. Without these details, the firm struggles to craft personalized outreach campaigns.

To resolve this issue a B2B marketing department can make use of the following AI tools and features.

- Social media enrichment: AI-driven tools like LinkedIn Sales Navigator can pull job roles, skills and activity insights from LinkedIn profiles.
- Firmographic data: Tools such as InsideView or D&B Hoovers enrich records with firmographic data like company size, industry and revenue.
- Real-time enrichment APIs: Platforms like Breeze provide APIs that pull additional details (e.g. company structure, technology stack) into existing CRM records.

Integration and automation

Tools used to enhance data and cleanse data can also be integrated easily with CRM systems, e.g. Salesforce Einstein uses AI to automatically enhance lead data within the Salesforce platform, allowing account managers to have the most up to date information.

There are different ways to improve integration; one way might be to use Zapier AI Integrations. This tool enables businesses to create workflows that connect data cleansing tools with CRMs like Zoho or Dynamics 365.

PUT INTO PRACTICE

Data cleaning can be inbuilt into existing tools such as Prospecting and web identification tools like Happierleads; or AI tools such as Salesforce Einstein; or AI features in CRM tools such as Zia the AI assistant from Zoho which is integrated into Zoho CRM.

There are also dedicated data cleaning applications such as Scrub AI which automates the process of data scrubbing, particularly for the insurance industry. Alternative dedicated applications include the following.

- WinPure: A popular and cost-effective data cleaning tool that handles large volumes of data, eliminates duplicates and standardizes information across various formats including databases, spreadsheets and CRMs.

- OpenRefine: An open-source tool (formerly Google Refine) that can clean, manage and manipulate data. It's free and can handle several hundred thousand rows of data.
- Data Ladder: Known for its speed and accuracy, Data Ladder offers an easy-to-use visual interface for matching, cleaning and deduplicating data.

Using AI chatbots for lead capture

AI chatbots can be very effective tools for capturing B2B leads, offering personalized interactions and efficient data collection.

Lead qualification on landing pages

On lead capture landing pages, AI chatbots can serve to qualify and check the suitability of the visitor; this can be done via asking qualifying questions. Examples might be that the chatbots ask for the following:

- ask about company size
- ask about industry
- ask about specific pain points
- ask about stakeholders needs, timing of needs

Lead qualification can also involve collecting further contact details or integrate with applications to schedule demos or calls for those prospects who have a more urgent enquiry.

Product page Q&A

AI chatbots can capture leads based on product page Q&A and information requests.

On product pages, AI chatbots can serve as interactive product specialists. They can include the following:

- Answer frequently asked questions about product features and specifications.
- Provide pricing information or custom quotes based on user requirements.
- Offer comparisons with competitor products.

- Collect email addresses for sending detailed product information or case studies.
- Schedule product demonstrations for interested leads.

Personalized content recommendations

AI chatbots can analyse visitor behaviour and engage them with personalized content offers in the following ways.

- Suggest relevant white papers, case studies, or webinars based on browsing history.
- Offer exclusive content in exchange for contact information.
- Provide personalized product recommendations based on stated needs.
- Collect lead data while delivering value through tailored content suggestions.

Webinar registration

For B2B companies hosting events or webinars, AI chatbots can streamline the registration process by providing webinar details and answering questions about the agenda or speakers, guiding users via the registration process, collecting necessary information, and sending reminders and follow-up information post-registration.

Automated lead qualification and segmentation

We mentioned above how AI chatbots can be used to qualify leads at lead capture stage; lead qualification can be further improved through AI tools in the following ways.

- AI can use data in real time to score leads which then serves to prioritize leads on an ongoing basis.
- AI tools can automatically route qualified leads to the appropriate sales representatives, ensuring that leads are handled efficiently and by the most suitable team members.
- Advanced AI models, e.g. Lift AI can segment website visitors based on their buyer intent, even for anonymous visitors. This allows for tailored engagement strategies for different segments.

Landing pages

Landing pages in B2B are specialized web pages designed to convert visitors into leads or customers. They typically focus on a specific product, service or offer and are optimized to encourage a particular action, such as filling out a form, requesting a demo or making a purchase.

Landing page creation can be a timely process which may also involve a lot of trial and error, typically involving testing out features to improve effectiveness of landing pages.

AI-based landing page tools can play an effective role through analysing user behaviour and suggesting layout improvements for better conversion rates. AI can also dynamically adjust content based on visitor characteristics or behaviour. For example, Landingi's built-in text generator and regenerator, based on ChatGPT, can produce customized copy directly within the landing page builder. Another example is Lift AI, which can segment website visitors based on buyer intent, even for anonymous visitors.

Some of the main AI features which are supported by AI-enabled landing page tools are described below.

Smart Traffic routing by Unbounce

One of the standout AI features for landing page optimization is Smart Traffic from Unbounce. This AI-driven tool automatically routes visitors to the most relevant landing page variant based on their individual characteristics, such as location, device type, behaviour or referral source.

Personalized landing pages at scale by Instapage

Another key AI feature for landing page creation is the Thor Render Engine from Instapage. This machine learning-driven tool enables businesses to create and serve personalized landing pages at scale. Thor analyses user data, including demographics and browsing behaviour, and generates personalized content on-the-fly.

Real-time suggestions with Leadpages Leadmeter

Leadmeter from Leadpages is an AI-powered tool that provides real-time suggestions to improve landing page performance. By analysing various metrics such as visitor behaviour, time spent on the page and interaction rates, Leadmeter offers actionable insights to optimize landing page design, copy and CTAs.

AI-powered A/B testing by Landingi

A key AI feature in landing page creation is AI-powered A/B testing, as seen in tools like Landingi. This AI feature automatically identifies the best-performing landing page variants and allocates more traffic to them without manual intervention. The AI constantly tests different page elements, such as headlines, images or CTAs, and uses machine learning to determine which combinations are most likely to drive conversions.

Examples of AI-enabled landing pages

Several industry leaders have already implemented AI-driven features to optimize their landing pages, and their examples highlight how AI can be used to create a more personalized and effective user experience; one example is Semrush's Free Trial Page: SEMrush uses AI to personalize content and CTAs based on a visitor's industry and search history. This personalized approach ensures that visitors see the most relevant offers and information, which in turn increases the likelihood of conversion. By understanding each visitor's unique background, the AI customizes the landing page content to boost relevance and engagement.[1]

AI and social media lead capture

Social media platforms have become essential tools for B2B lead generation, with many of them leveraging advanced AI features to optimize lead capture activities. These AI tools enhance the effectiveness of capturing potential leads by personalizing interactions, analysing behaviour and improving engagement. Here, we will explore how AI is used for lead capture on various social media platforms, including LinkedIn, YouTube, Instagram and others.

LinkedIn: AI for B2B lead capture

LinkedIn's InMail feature uses AI to optimize outreach efforts. The AI analyses historical data to suggest improvements in message content, tone and structure, as well as determining the optimal times to send InMails for higher engagement. This improves response rates and increases the likelihood of engaging with decision-makers.

Furthermore, LinkedIn has implemented the Smart Replies feature, which utilizes AI to generate suggested responses to incoming messages. These AI-generated replies help users maintain consistent and timely engagement with potential leads, reducing the manual effort required and ensuring that interactions remain fluid and responsive.

YouTube: AI-driven insights for lead generation

YouTube, another vital platform for lead generation, uses AI to help businesses optimize their content for better lead capture. Through AI-enabled insights into viewer behaviour, YouTube provides creators with valuable data that can be used to tailor content more effectively. By analysing watch patterns, engagement rates and demographics, AI helps identify the type of content that resonates with viewers, allowing businesses to create targeted videos that are more likely to convert viewers into leads.

One of the most notable AI features for lead generation on YouTube is TrueView for Action. This tool uses machine learning to optimize CTAs during video playback. Based on the viewer's interests, TrueView for Action displays personalized CTAs that encourage viewers to take the next step in the lead generation process, whether it's signing up for a newsletter, requesting a demo or downloading a resource. By tailoring CTAs to individual viewer preferences, YouTube increases the likelihood of converting video viewers into qualified leads.

Instagram: AI for enhanced lead engagement

Instagram, widely used for its visual appeal, also offers AI tools that support lead capture for businesses, particularly in the B2B sector. The platform's AI-driven ad targeting leverages data about users' behaviours, interests and interactions to deliver highly personalized advertisements. AI helps businesses target the right audiences by identifying users who are most likely to engage with the brand's content, thus optimizing lead generation efforts.

Additionally, Instagram's AI-powered chatbots are increasingly used for automated direct messaging, providing an efficient means of engaging with potential leads. These bots can answer common queries, direct users to resources or even schedule consultations, all while learning from each interaction to refine their responses over time. This not only speeds up the lead qualification process but also ensures that potential leads receive timely and personalized communication, increasing the chances of conversion.

Facebook: AI for dynamic lead generation campaigns

Facebook, which still remains a significant player in B2B marketing, has integrated several AI features for effective lead capture. Facebook Lead Ads utilize AI to automatically fill in lead form fields based on user data from their profiles, streamlining the process for potential leads and improving conversion rates. By reducing the friction in the lead capture process, Facebook's AI makes it easier for businesses to gather contact details from interested parties with minimal effort.

AI also plays a crucial role in advertising targeting (ad targeting) on Facebook. The platform's machine learning algorithms analyse vast amounts of data, including browsing history, past interactions and demographic information, to ensure that ads are shown to users who are most likely to engage. This precise targeting not only boosts the effectiveness of ad campaigns but also ensures that businesses are reaching the right prospects, ultimately improving lead quality.

Other B2B social platforms: leveraging AI for lead capture

Several other B2B-focused social platforms, such as XING and Slack, also utilize AI features for lead capture. For example, XING, which is popular in Europe for professional networking, offers AI-based job matching tools that connect businesses with relevant talent and potential leads. By using AI to analyse professional profiles and activity, XING recommends job opportunities and potential partners, helping businesses identify leads for recruitment or partnership purposes.

Slack, while typically a communication tool, uses AI to enhance team collaboration but also has opportunities for lead generation through integration with bots and apps. By utilizing AI tools in Slack, businesses can engage with potential leads through personalized recommendations, alerts and real-time updates, which can help nurture relationships and generate leads.

Real-world example: Visum's successful outbound strategy – how they achieved a high response rate

Visum is a SaaS company specializing in software that identifies a company's technology stack based on an email address. Initially, Visum relied on content marketing, particularly through LinkedIn, to acquire clients. However, seeking to expand their customer base, they decided to explore cold email outreach as a new strategy.

Transitioning from content marketing to cold email outreach presented several challenges for Visum. One challenge was to identify target audiences and determine which market segments would benefit from their solution; another challenge was to develop effective messaging that would resonate with diverse prospects.

To resolve these and other challenges Visum partnered with Lemlist, a platform known for personalized cold email campaigns. With Lemlist they began by defining their value propositions, focusing on two primary targets: companies selling tools integrated with specific CRMs and CRM companies themselves.

To enhance their approach, Visum also developed ideal customer profiles (ICPs), focusing on personas like Heads of Sales and Sales Development Representatives. Following this Visum implemented a phased outreach strategy, initially conducting manual outreach to test and refine their approach to ensure they were targeting the right prospects with tailored messaging at optimal times before scaling their process.

By leveraging Lemlist's platform and expertise, Visum achieved significant results. Their personalized and targeted cold email campaigns yielded a 19 per cent response rate, demonstrating strong engagement from prospects. This strategic approach also enhanced their lead-generation efforts, resulting in a higher volume of qualified leads and an expanded customer base. Additionally, the insights gained from their initial manual efforts enabled Visum to develop a scalable and efficient cold email outreach system.[2]

References

1 SEMrush (2024) 8 Things You Can Do with a Free SEMrush Account, 21 June, www.semrush.com/blog/what-can-i-do-with-a-free-account-from-semrush/ (archived at https://perma.cc/87DP-CU2H)

2 Lemlist.com (2021) Visum case study, www.lemlist.com/visum-case-study?r=0 (archived at https://perma.cc/Y7D8-TPLD)

Further reading

Barron, J (2024) AI for B2B lead generation: The ultimate guide, Cognism, www.cognism.com/blog/ai-lead-generation (archived at https://perma.cc/4NAY-K565)

Dang, Patrick (2024) How to use AI for lead generation in 2025, YouTube, www.youtube.com/watch?v=sxuf4WudHZc (archived at https://perma.cc/9HTY-G7TK)

improvado.io (n.d.) 10 ways to acquire high-quality leads using AI lead generation tools, improvado.io/blog/ai-lead-generation-tools-best-practices (archived at https://perma.cc/SXP6-3VD2)

Lemlist Blog (2024) AI lead generation: Definition, tips and 7 tools for 2025, www.lemlist.com/blog/ai-lead-generation (archived at https://perma.cc/R6U9-7XFK)

Ravi Abuvala (2023) How to use AI for lead generation, YouTube, www.youtube.com/watch?v=fHvYGKcZZ_0 (archived at https://perma.cc/ALA2-A4Y6)

08

AI-powered lead nurturing

What you will gain from this chapter

Understanding of the following:

- AI role in nurturing leads
- how to use AI to create email nurture campaigns
- using AI to analyse digital behaviours and segment leads
- learn how to optimize workflows with AI
- lead scoring and AI
- how to use LinkedIn for lead nurturing

Introduction

Lead nurturing is defined as anything which is done to progress prospective customers in their buyer journey. Lead nurturing takes place after a lead has been captured and typically spans from that point through to the purchase stage. Typically, we talk about lead nurturing within the pre-purchase stages of the buyer journey, but aspects of lead nurturing could also apply to existing customers post purchase when they buy additional products and services.

Importance of lead nurturing

Lead nurturing is particularly important in the B2B relationship as the time between lead capture and purchase can last a long time. On average this period for B2B companies is around 12–18 months. The challenge for the organization therefore is to keep customers interested in the organization's products. For B2B marketers it is important to understand roughly the length of this lead nurture period as it will help with the lead nurturing planning. We can also think of lead nurturing as being about improving the possibility of conversion through keeping leads 'warmer' (more interested).

How to do lead nurturing

As we saw from earlier in the book, different customer segments have different buyer personas and different paths in their journeys; with the current digital environment offering a matrix of possibilities in terms of channels and content for customers to progress in their buyer journeys, lead nurturing in turn also needs to be more sophisticated. Figure 8.1 shows different visuals in terms of how lead nurturing can be facilitated or optimized based on a better understanding of the customer and the customer journey; illustrated are three options such as adding another touchpoint, removing touchpoints or even providing an alternative path. Aside of these options we can improve lead nurturing through better integration of content and channels through integrating links or integrating social media widgets where social media is involved.

AI role in lead nurturing

Now we understand lead nurturing and what it can mean we can look at where AI can help; the following are some main areas where AI can play a role (see Figure 8.2 for an overview).

- Lead scoring: AI can more accurately identify the position of the lead in the buying process and more accurately score it.
- Digital conversations: AI tools can be used to facilitate and support conversations and the relationship building process.
- Intent signals tracking: AI can help by understanding intent signals across the lead nurture period, through understanding where the prospect is in the customer journey, i.e. through scoring of leads as well as better automating response and signals.
- Account tracking: AI tools can be used to monitor stakeholders within an account.

FIGURE 8.1 Lead nurturing options

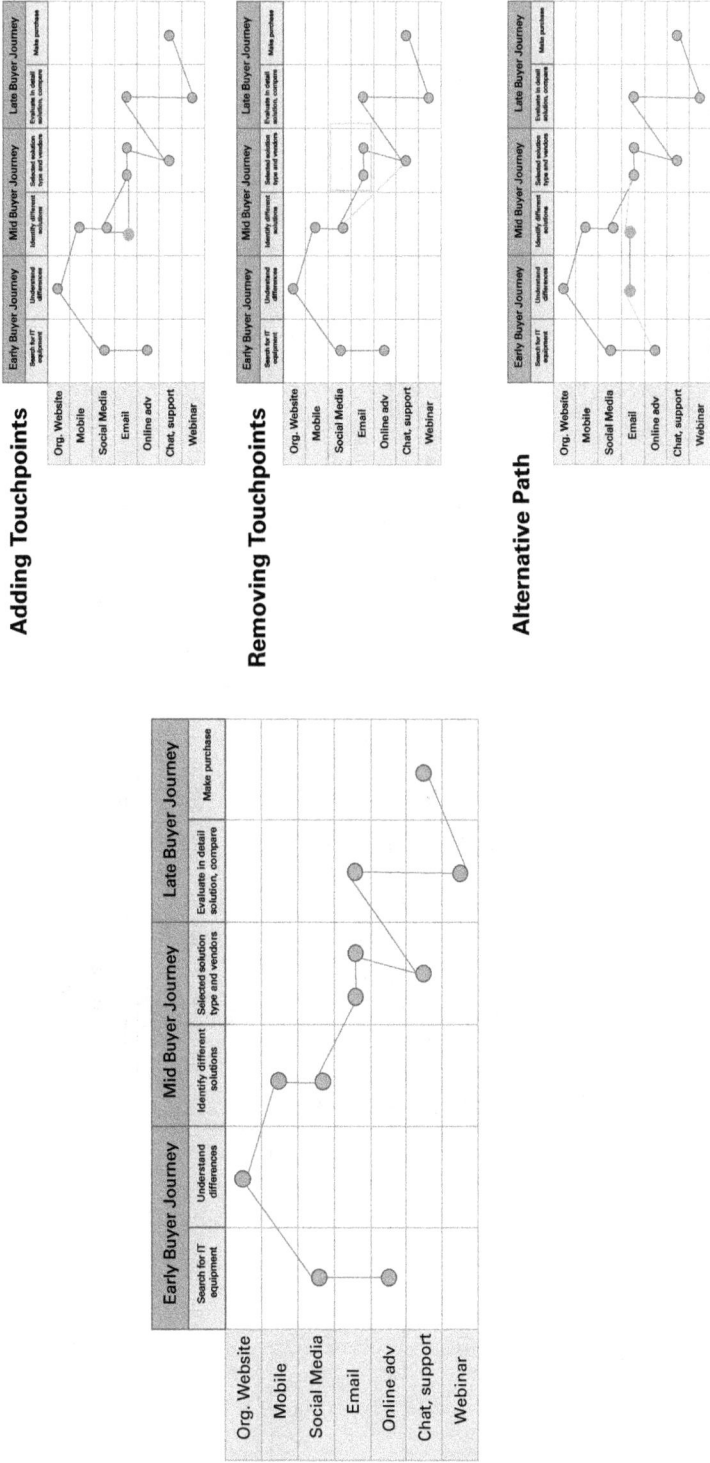

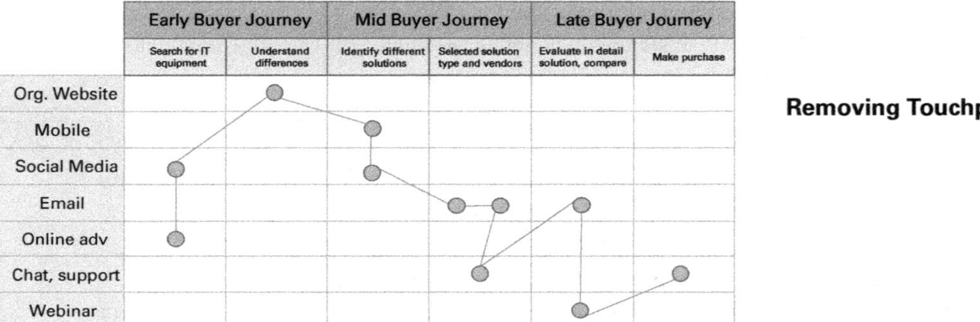

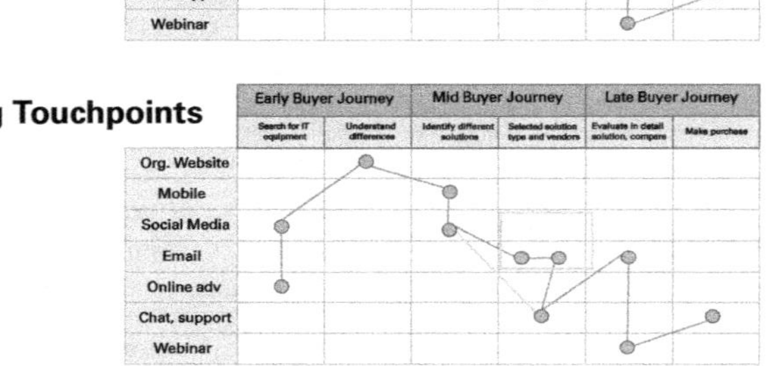

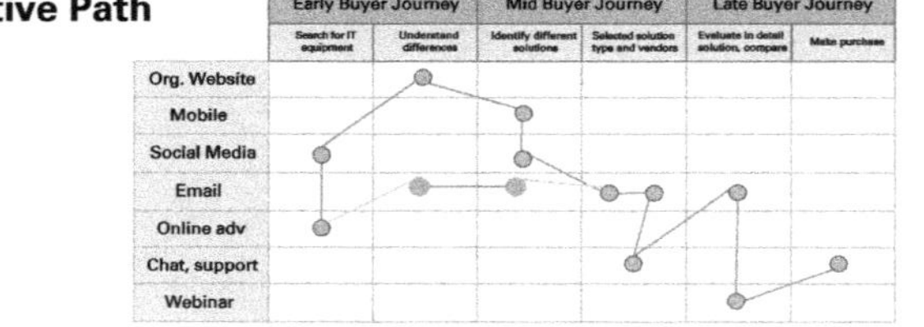

FIGURE 8.2 Areas of AI for lead nurturing

Lead nurture area	Description	AI tool or feature
Content tailoring	AI tools use NLP and machine learning to analyse user behaviour, past interactions, and preferences, enabling the creation of personalized content that resonates with individual recipients	e.g. Phrasee, Copy.ai
Automation	AI-driven automation helps streamline content creation, audience segmentation, and performance optimization, reducing manual efforts and improving scalability.	e.g. ActiveCampaign, Marketo
Segmentation	AI enhances segmentation by analysing customer data to identify patterns, enabling marketers to create targeted segments based on behaviours, demographics, or preferences.	e.g. Klaviyo,Customer.io
Optimizing send times	AI tools analyse recipient engagement patterns to automatically determine the best times to send emails, maximizing open rates and engagement.	e.g. Mailchimp, Sendinblue
Automated A/B testing	AI-driven A/B testing tools automate the process of testing different email variations, helping marketers quickly identify the most effective content.	e.g. Optimizely

Lead nurture campaigns

As we've seen in Chapter 5, AI can play a role in creating various forms of content; in the area of lead nurturing, we can use generative AI for lead nurture campaigns. Consider that you want to create an email or messenger app which covers four to five emails to support a nurture campaign; first, you could use some of the prompts in an NLP/ML tool to come up with ideas and themes for an email campaign; then look at ideas for different topics to support the email nurture campaign; then come up with ideas for templates and use the AI tool itself to write the main part of each of the emails.

PRACTICAL TIP FOR EMAIL NURTURE CAMPAIGN CREATION: PROMPTS

Prompt 1: *Please provide ideas for an email nurture campaign; the campaign is due to last nine months and should span five emails or more; the nurture campaign is targeting HR managers looking to buy pension services for their business employees.*

Prompt 2: *Please suggest five different email topics for an email nurture campaign.*

Prompt 3 : *Please provide five different topics for a messenger nurture campaign.*

Prompt 4: *Suggest five email topics and related paragraphs for an email nurture campaign across five emails.*

Prompt 5: *Please suggest five topics and related paragraphs for a messenger nurture campaign across five messages sent via WhatsApp for a B2B prospect*

Next steps might be to personalize the content to an individual, industry and relate to a product solution the vendor is trying to market; this may relate to a new product launch or a new solution.

See the example below for a response to Prompt 1 – the first two are in full; the remaining emails are summarized in Table 8.1.

Campaign theme: empower HR managers to make confident pension decisions

Email 1: Introduction & Overview of Pension Solutions

Timing: Month 1

Subject: 'The Future of Your Employees Starts Here – Explore Pension Solutions'

Content:

Welcome email introducing your pension services and highlighting why selecting the right pension plan is crucial for both the business and employees.

Outline key benefits of offering a great pension plan (e.g. retention, employee satisfaction).

Include a downloadable guide or infographic on the 'Top 5 Benefits of a Strong Pension Plan for Your Workforce'.

CTA: 'Download the Guide' or 'Schedule a Consultation'.

Email 2: Addressing HR Pain Points in Pension Management

Timing: Month 2

Subject: 'Solving Your Pension Plan Challenges – A Simple Approach for HR Managers'

Content:

Acknowledge common HR challenges (compliance, cost, complexity) when managing pensions and explain how your service simplifies this process.

Provide insights or a short case study of a company that streamlined their pension services with your solution.

Offer a checklist on 'What to Look for When Choosing a Pension Provider'.

CTA: 'Download the Checklist' or 'See How We Help Companies Like Yours'.

Other emails are summarized in Table 8.1.

TABLE 8.1 Email nurture campaign Part 2

Emails 3– 5	Email 3: Personalizing Pension Solutions for Your Business	Email 4: Financial Wellness and Employee Retention	Email 5: Simplifying Compliance and Regulatory Requirements
Focus topic of emails	Timing: Month 4 Subject: 'Tailoring Pension Plans to Meet Your Employees' Needs'	Timing: Month 6 Subject: 'Boost Employee Retention with Financial Wellness Programs'	Timing: Month 7 Subject: 'Stay Compliant with Ease: Navigating Pension Regulations'

Behavioural analysis and segmentation

Behavioural segmentation break-up leads into groups based on behaviours; these can be interests, digital or other engagement patterns. In the area of lead nurture engagement patterns relate to how prospects interact with email, website, social media or other channels; this can also be related to campaign response, e.g. reacting to messages and projected value. AI can digest large amounts of data to for segmenting leads; the segmentation step itself can be according to more specific preferences, needs or according to likelihood to convert. AI can also be used real time in updating information related to the lead, e.g. by providing most relevant content and information.

Content preference analysis

AI tools can be used to identify content formats which are most engaged or preferred by individuals; through identification of personal content preferences the response rates and effectiveness of content can be improved. Examples of AI tools or tools with AI enabled features include Pathfactory and 6sense.

Automated workflow creation

Let's first define workflows: workflows are automated sequences of steps designed to guide prospective customers through stages of the buying process. We typically would use workflows in marketing or mail automation platforms which allow us to structure, organize, automate and sequence the sending of emails.

AI-enabled workflow creation

AI can significantly enhance and optimize automated workflows in marketing automation by improving execution and enabling more precise, efficient activities across the entire lead generation and nurturing process. AI enabled workflow automation can improve various routine tasks in the areas of workflows including data entry and data analytics; each of these tasks can be done faster and typically more accurately than through non-AI-based tools thus improving overall efficiency of this activity as well as reducing errors in the process. See Figure 8.3.

FIGURE 8.3 Workflows and AI

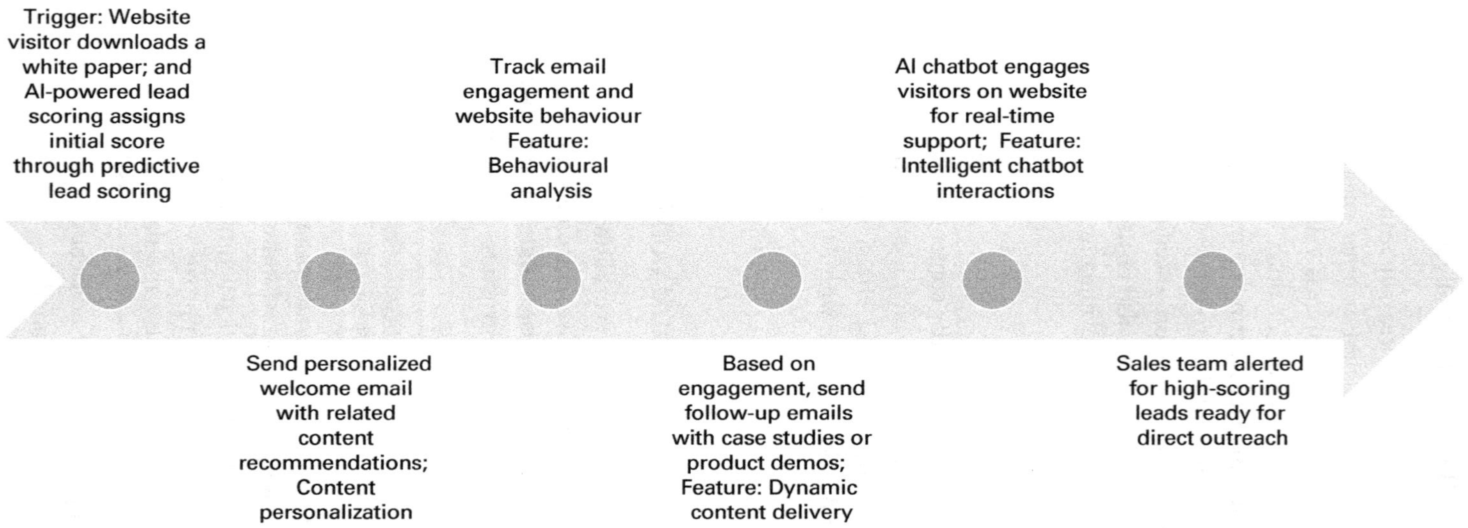

Trigger: Website visitor downloads a white paper; and AI-powered lead scoring assigns initial score through predictive lead scoring

Send personalized welcome email with related content recommendations; Content personalization

Track email engagement and website behaviour Feature: Behavioural analysis

Based on engagement, send follow-up emails with case studies or product demos; Feature: Dynamic content delivery

AI chatbot engages visitors on website for real-time support; Feature: Intelligent chatbot interactions

Sales team alerted for high-scoring leads ready for direct outreach

So, what are we talking about exactly?

Tools like FlowUp and ClickUP can support B2B marketers in creating much tailored workflows; the workflow means follow-up is more consistent and leads remain warm or become increasingly warmer as they proceed through the buyer journey. It should be noted that not all workflows should be automated or AI automated; consider tasks which are repetitive in nature, are low in productivity and time-consuming See Table 8.2 for examples of workflows.

TABLE 8.2 Workflows

Step	Automated lead qualification	Personalized email nurturing	Event follow-up workflow
1	Lead enters system via form submission or website visit.	Import leads into the CRM from form submissions or past interactions.	Capture attendee information during webinar or event registration.
2	Marketing automation assigns an initial lead score based on predefined rules.	Segment leads into categories based on static rules like industry, job role or form answers.	Segment attendees by predefined criteria such as job title or event session attended.
3	Enrich lead data using manual research or integrations with third-party tools.	Personalize welcome emails by selecting prewritten templates tailored to each segment.	Send a 'Thank You for Attending' email with static links to resources related to the event.
4	Monitor behaviour like email opens or link clicks through marketing software.	Schedule follow-up emails at fixed intervals using automation workflows.	Identify interested attendees through email engagement (opens, clicks).
5	Set a fixed lead scoring threshold, e.g. 50 points for opening three emails.	Offer downloadable resources such as ebooks or white papers through email links.	Provide static access to event recordings or materials as a follow-up.
6	Notify sales teams via automation when leads reach the score threshold.	Route leads who respond positively to emails to a sales team for further nurturing.	Invite attendees to a demo or consultation session through automated email campaigns.

Multi-channel nurturing

According to Lead Forensics, 72 per cent of consumers prefer connecting with brands through multiple channels such as websites, mobile apps and social media.[1] AI technologies play a pivotal role in optimizing multi-channel nurturing by tracking behaviours, identifying the most effective channels and allocating resources efficiently. Here's how AI enhances multi-channel nurturing in practice and examples of specific tools and features that enable this transformation.

Tracking customer journeys across channels

AI technologies provide a holistic view of the customer journey by aggregating and analysing data from multiple communication channels. In practice AI tools are collecting and integrating behavioural data from sources such as social media interactions, email engagement, website visits and app usage. By piecing together this data, businesses gain insights into how prospects interact with their brand. Examples of AI tools and features include.

Optimizing the channel mix

AI identifies which communication channels are most effective for specific customer segments, enabling marketers to tailor their strategies to maximize impact. This works in practice via AI algorithms that analyse historical engagement data to predict which channels yield the highest response rates for different audience groups. For example, younger prospects might respond better to social media ads, while executives prefer personalized email campaigns.

Personalization across channels

AI enables personalized content delivery across multiple channels, ensuring that prospects receive relevant messaging based on their preferences and behaviour. AI analyses data such as past interactions, purchase history and preferences to craft tailored messages. For example, a lead who downloads a white paper on a website might later receive a personalized email or a retargeted social media ad promoting a relevant webinar.

Lead scoring

Lead scoring is the process of rating leads usually relating to the readiness of the prospective customer to engage with sales or to purchase something. Lead scoring is usually according to a pre-determined criteria whereby the criteria are assigned a point or number; the aggregate of which gives you a score (see Figure 8.4).

Ways to lead score

There is no 'one' way to score; each company does this differently and depends on what makes sense. One can score leads based on implicit criteria or explicit criteria; implicit lead scoring is lead scoring based on observed behaviours and inferred information. Observed behaviours can be anything from attending a trade show or webinar, downloading an asset or visiting certain web pages.

The idea behind implicit lead scoring is that people who buy your product will exhibit certain behaviours indicating their intent to purchase. To set up an implicit lead scoring model, a company will typically review all actions that a person can take and assign positive and negative values to those actions. For example, a person downloading a white paper may be worth 10 points. If they request a demo, that may be worth 20 points. But, if they don't interact with the website for a month, they may lose 15 points.

Explicit scoring is based on account demographics, firmographics rather than based on behaviours such as digital behaviours; examples of explicit scoring might be their industry, role and size of company.

FIGURE 8.4 Lead scoring

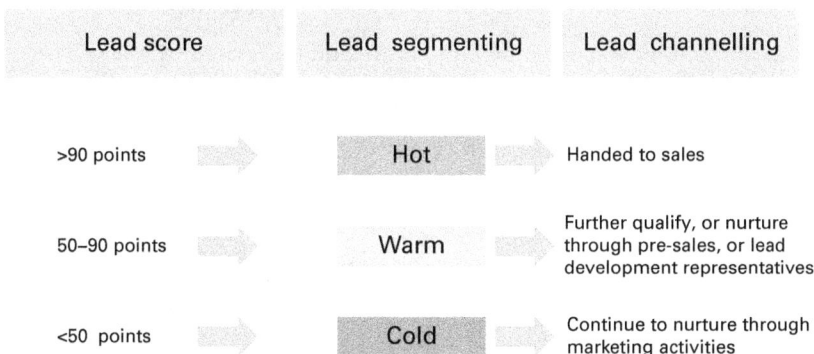

Lead score	Lead segmenting	Lead channelling
>90 points	Hot	Handed to sales
50–90 points	Warm	Further qualify, or nurture through pre-sales, or lead development representatives
<50 points	Cold	Continue to nurture through marketing activities

AI for lead scoring vs traditional non-AI based lead scoring

AI lead scoring can improve on traditional methods or non-AI methods by using inbuilt learning where they can learn and evolve from new data thus fine tuning and updating lead scoring; this means lead scores remain as relevant as possible.

DYNAMIC LEARNING AND ADAPTABILITY - HOW AI IMPROVES TRADITIONAL SCORING METHODS

Traditional lead scoring often involves assigning fixed points to specific actions (e.g. +10 for downloading an ebook or +5 for opening an email). While effective to some degree, this method becomes outdated as customer behaviours evolve. AI-led scoring, in contrast, uses machine learning to adapt to new data in real time. It learns from patterns in historical data and continuously refines its scoring model. For example:

- AI algorithms can adjust the importance of specific actions based on trends (e.g. webinar attendance becoming a stronger predictor of conversion over time).
- AI ensures that lead scores remain relevant and reflective of the most recent customer behaviours and market conditions.

ANALYSIS OF MULTIPLE DATA TYPES

Traditional scoring methods often rely on a limited set of data points, such as demographic details or basic engagement metrics. AI can process and analyse complex, multi-dimensional data, including:

- **Behavioural data:** Website visits, time spent on pages, email interactions and social media activity.
- **Firmographic data:** Industry, company size and revenue potential.
- **Technographic data:** Technology stacks and tools used by a lead's organization.
- **Sentiment analysis:** AI tools can even assess the tone of a prospect's communication (e.g. positive sentiment in emails).

By identifying relationships and patterns between these data points, AI reveals factors most strongly correlated with lead conversion.

Some platforms which support AI-based lead scoring include Hubspot, Infer, Marketo and 6sense.

Social media automation and AI

AI-based social media can automate social media posts, response and can boost site traffic by up to five times; in the form of applications like Sproutsocial, Buffer AI and SocialBee. SocialBee is an example of an AI-enabled social media automation tool which enables B2B businesses to manage social media presence and social media content.

A feature of SocialBee is its AI post generator which can generate captions, content ideas, video scripts and more. Through SocialBee one can schedule and automatically promote content at optimal times.

Here are other examples of areas of social media automation in addition to content scheduling.

- Audience targeting and personalization: This feature is about analysing audience behaviour, segment followers and personalizing content in real time. More specifically, AI can monitor comments, likes and shares to determine best performing posts or types of posts which drive higher engagement. AI can help businesses target specific demographics, interests or even predict future engagement patterns.
- AI chatbots for social engagement: AI-driven chatbots can automate real-time interactions with users, responding to common inquiries, handling customer service questions and engaging with prospects.
- Social listening and sentiment analysis – we covered this in previous chapters; please refer to Chapter 3.

Integration

To ensure a more holistic view of the buyer journey and of lead nurturing; these applications can be integrated with marketing automation platforms and CRM systems. In synchronizing the data with other platforms, this allows sales and marketing to have a more comprehensive view.

PUT INTO PRACTICE: HASHTAG IDEAS

One can use AI-based text tools to come up with hashtag ideas.

Hashtag suggestions: *Recommend the top five hashtags related to [topic] to increase engagement.*

Promote: *Please recommend 10 related hashtags for a B2B marketing training company targeting marketing departments working in industrial gas companies.*

AI and email nurturing

When we consider what lead nurturing is and apply this to email marketing, we can see that nurturing via email involves building relationships, listening to emails in terms of content and digital behaviours, more personalized and segmentation of emails as well as more accurate automation of email-based tasks.

So how can AI help? What are we talking about and how do we go about implementing practically?

In terms of email, AI tools can help better interpret email marketing metrics to identify what needs to be optimized in terms of elements of emails.

Different areas of AI for email nurturing

Content tailoring: Tailored email content using NLP/machine learning tools like ChatGPT. AI tools can help to create more personalized email content based on customer data. Past email campaigns can be reviewed to understand how to optimize aspects of the email, e.g. subject lines, structure, etc. See Table 8.3 for an example of email template types of email nurturing.

TABLE 8.3 Email template types for email nurture campaign

Email	Key focus of email	Key contents in email
Email 1: Introduction & Awareness	Introduce your company and build brand awareness	– Brief company introduction and focus on solar farm solutions. – Highlight commitment to quality, sustainability, and technical expertise. – Link to an informative blog or guide: 'The Basics of Solar Farms for Engineers.'
Email 2: Industry Trends & Insights	Educate on current trends and solar farm technology advancements	– Overview of recent solar energy trends and innovations relevant to engineers. – Key insights on efficiency, cost-effectiveness, and sustainability advancements. – Link to an industry report or whitepaper: 'How Solar Technology Is Evolving in 2024.'

(continued)

TABLE 8.3 (Continued)

Email	Key focus of email	Key contents in email
Email 3: Technical Product Overview	Introduce key solar farm products and solutions with a technical focus	– Detailed overview of solar products (e.g. panels, inverters, storage solutions) and their technical specifications. – Comparison with industry standards or competing technologies. – Link to product data sheets and case studies.
Email 4: Case Study & Real-World Application	Showcase successful implementations and real-world results	– Case study of a successful solar farm installation using your products. – Highlight engineering challenges overcome and quantifiable benefits achieved (e.g. energy output, ROI). – Link to full case study download and customer testimonial video.
Email 5: Engineering-Specific Benefits	Dive deeper into product benefits for engineering teams	– Benefits focused on engineering needs, such as ease of installation, maintenance, durability and scalability. – Technical advantages (e.g. efficiency ratings, adaptability to different climates, integration ease with other technologies). – Link to an in-depth technical FAQ or product webinar registration.
Email 6: ROI and Cost Savings	Address ROI and financial benefits for solar farm projects	– Breakdown of potential cost savings, ROI and TCO (total cost of ownership) for solar farm projects. – Examples of how choosing your products can maximize ROI and reduce operational costs. – Link to ROI calculator or downloadable financial planning guide.

Automation: AI can revolutionize email marketing campaigns by automating processes such as content creation, audience segmentation and performance optimization. Here are specific examples of how AI tools can automate and enhance email marketing.

Let's look at Table 8.3 where we ask for a generic email introduction and first paragraph and the personalized email introduction.

Segmentation: AI tools like Klaviyo can help to improve segmentation of emails; for example, the smart audience segmentation feature in Klaviyo automates audience segments through data such as past purchases, browsing behaviour and email engagements

Optimizing sends times: Brevo is an AI tool that automates the process of determining the best times to send emails for each recipient. This is done by looking at engagement data and behavioural data to identify the most likely times for recipients to open emails, ensuring optimal email send times.

Automated A/B Testing: Mailchimp has integrated AI-powered A/B testing features that automate the testing process for email marketing campaigns. The tool can automatically test different versions of subject lines, images and email content, and determine the winning variations based on performance metrics. By automating A/B testing, Mailchimp reduces the time marketers spend on manual testing and ensures that only the best-performing versions of emails are sent to larger audiences.

LinkedIn and lead nurturing

So, what features can we use within LinkedIn to do better lead nurturing, considering that lead nurturing is mainly about building relationships with prospects as well as better understanding and responding to needs of prospects? Here are the main AI features.

AI-powered profile building

LinkedIn has implemented an AI tool that provides personalized writing suggestions. This feature identifies key skills and experiences and recommends ways to present them in users' 'About' and 'Headline' sections, while respecting each user's unique writing style. This reduces the effort required in profile building, offering a more user-friendly experience.

Simply open any text field on LinkedIn, such as the 'About' section of your profile or a comment on a post. At the bottom of the text field, you will see a new button that says, 'Get AI-Powered Suggestions'. Click on this button to get started.

Smart audience targeting

One of the key AI-powered features in LinkedIn's Campaign Manager is Smart Audience Targeting, which analyses a vast array of data to segment LinkedIn users into relevant groups. The platform considers factors such as job title, industry, company size, skills, location and interests to create audience segments that are highly aligned with a business's objectives.

A feature within LinkedIn's smart targeting capabilities is the Lookalike Audience tool. This AI-driven feature allows marketers to identify and target users who share similar traits and behaviours to their existing customers. By analysing data from current customer profiles and engagement history, LinkedIn's AI identifies key attributes such as skills, job titles, company sizes and professional interests that are common among the brand's top clients.

To illustrate how LinkedIn's AI-driven targeting works in practice, consider a scenario where a B2B technology company is promoting its latest enterprise software solution. The company can use LinkedIn's Smart Audience Targeting to segment users based on their job titles, such as IT managers, CTOs or technical directors, as well as company size, location and industry. Additionally, with the Lookalike Audience feature, the company can upload a list of existing customers or website visitors to find users who share similar characteristics. This allows the company to reach a wider but highly relevant audience, increasing the chances of conversion.

Automated messaging through InMail

LinkedIn Sales Navigator uses AI to significantly enhance the effectiveness of outreach efforts by automating and personalizing InMail messages. The platform leverages AI to analyse lead data, including job titles, industry, company size and engagement history, to craft highly tailored messages. By understanding the context of previous interactions, such as whether a lead attended a webinar, downloaded a white paper or engaged with certain content, Sales Navigator's AI personalizes the communication to increase relevance and impact. (See Figure 8.5.)

FIGURE 8.5 Messenger campaign – LinkedIn

Message 1: Introduction & Awareness
• Subject: Exploring Advanced Solar Farm Solutions
Message 2: Industry Trends & Insights
• Subject: Stay Ahead with the Latest Solar Farm Trends
Message 3: Technical Product Overview
• Subject: Technical Solutions to Optimize Your Solar Projects
Message 4: Real-World Application – Case Study
• Subject: See How Our Solar Solutions Deliver Real Results
Message 5: Engineering-Specific Benefits
• Subject: Solar Solutions Built for Engineering Excellence
Message 6: ROI and Cost Savings
• Subject: Maximize ROI with Solar Solutions Designed for Efficiency
Message 7: Strong CTA & Conversion
• Subject: Ready to Enhance Your Next Solar Project?

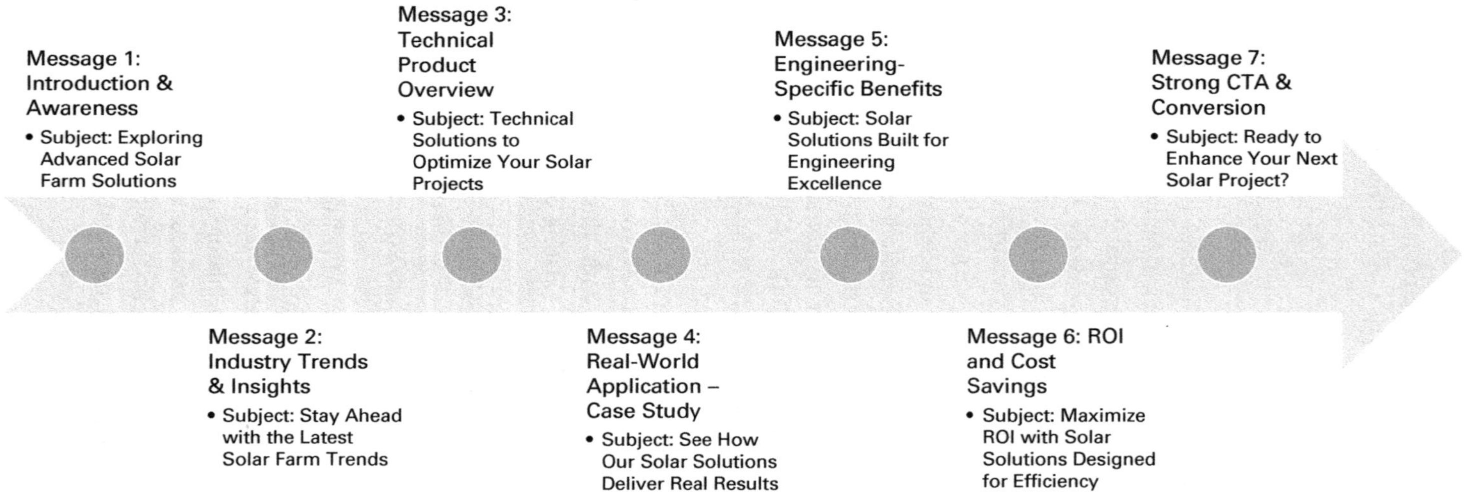

A B2B example of this in action might be a software company offering a cloud-based project management solution. Using LinkedIn Sales Navigator, the company's sales team can use AI to identify key decision-makers in the marketing department of large enterprises, such as chief marketing officers or directors of marketing operations. The AI analyses their LinkedIn profiles, engagement history and any prior interactions with the brand, helping the sales team craft a personalized InMail message. This could include mentioning a relevant case study, addressing the lead's pain points or referencing a recent webinar they attended, making the outreach feel more tailored and valuable.

LinkedIn-based AI tools

LinkedIn is one of the major social media platforms used in B2B. As a result, B2B marketers should consider not only embedded features in LinkedIn for lead nurture but also consider LinkedIn-based AI tools, i.e. AI tools which work with LinkedIn.

Types of LinkedIn AI tools include:

- LinkedIn-based InMail/messenger tools
- LinkedIn and profile optimization tools
- LinkedIn posting tools
- LinkedIn data scraping tools

LinkedIn-based InMail/messenger tools

An example of such a tool is Dux Soup. Dux Soup is an AI-enabled tool that automates LinkedIn prospecting and lead generation. Dux Soup can be thought of in the terms of a marketing automation tool on LinkedIn; if we can consider how marketing automation platforms automate email campaigns, we can think of Dux Soup as an automation tool which automates LinkedIn-based messaging campaigns although there is a lot more to Dux soup than that.

In 2024, it rolled out new features like managing multiple clients from one dashboard, enhanced campaign customization with triggers and branching, and seamless integration with third-party tools.[2]

Alternatives to Dux Soup include LinkedIn Helper and Kanbox.

LinkedIn and profile optimization tools

Profile optimization tools help users enhance their profiles for visibility, engagement and impact. These tools provide personalized recommendations, keyword insights, personality analysis and content suggestions to make LinkedIn profiles more attractive to recruiters, clients or potential leads.

Popular examples are as follows:

- Crystal Knows: Crystal Knows uses AI to analyse LinkedIn profiles and predict personality traits using the DISC framework, which categorizes personality types as Dominance, Influence, Steadiness and Conscientiousness. This feature helps users understand how to best communicate with their audience on LinkedIn. In addition to personality insights, Crystal Knows offers message-tailoring suggestions, enabling users to personalize their outreach based on the inferred traits of their prospects or connections.
- Taplio: Taplio is designed to help users optimize their LinkedIn profiles through consistent, engaging content. Its AI-powered content suggestion feature analyses industry trends and recommends LinkedIn posts that align with the user's expertise, supporting engagement with their target audience. Taplio also tracks post-performance, providing insights into what types of content are resonating with the user's network.

LinkedIn posting tools

Several AI-powered tools can help users optimize their LinkedIn posts, utilizing various techniques such as content generation, engagement analytics and engagement pods to maximize performance. Examples include the following.

- Taplio: AI-powered content suggestions for LinkedIn posts. Tools like Taplio use AI to analyse industry trends and generate content ideas tailored to the user's expertise and audience.
- Shield Analytics: AI-driven performance insights. Shield Analytics is an AI-powered tool designed to provide in-depth insights into how LinkedIn posts are performing. Shield uses AI to track engagement metrics such as likes, comments, shares and audience demographics, helping users identify trends and patterns in their content's success.
- Lempod: AI-powered engagement pods to boost visibility. Another AI tool that can enhance LinkedIn post-performance is Lempod, which

focuses on engagement pods. Lempod connects users with like-minded professionals who agree to engage with each other's posts by liking, commenting and sharing.

LinkedIn data scraping tools

LinkedIn data scraping tools automate processes such as profile data extraction, connection automation and engagement tracking, enabling users to efficiently gather actionable insights and build targeted databases. One of the most popular LinkedIn data scraping tools is Phantombuster, which provides a range of automation and data extraction features to streamline lead generation and engagement efforts. Phantombuster's AI allows users to automate tasks such as visiting profiles, collecting LinkedIn profile data and extracting contact details, including names, job titles and email addresses, to build highly targeted lead lists. For example, a sales team looking to generate leads from a specific industry can use Phantombuster to scrape data from LinkedIn profiles within that sector, making it easier to find potential prospects for follow-up.

Another tool is Octopus CRM which combines LinkedIn automation with data scraping capabilities, making it a comprehensive tool for marketers and sales professionals. Octopus CRM allows users to automate LinkedIn tasks, such as profile visits, connection requests and personalized messaging, while also extracting valuable LinkedIn profile data like job titles, company names and industry information.

Automated follow-ups

Automated follow-ups play a crucial role in lead nurturing by ensuring consistent and timely communication with potential customers. AI plays a key role in automating follow-ups; follow-ups can be by email, on messenger apps and on social media platforms where messages are sent, e.g. LinkedIn InMail, SMS and website-based follow-up (see Table 8.4).

The benefits of automated follow-ups are that one can see improved lead conversion as a result. Studies have shown that automated follow-ups can significantly increase lead conversion rates. Timely follow-ups demonstrate that automated follow-ups free up time to focus on more strategic tasks, such as developing new leads and closing deals. AI-powered tools can personalize follow-up messages based on individual lead behaviour and preferences, improving engagement and relevance.

Different areas of automated follow-ups

LinkedIn follow-up: Alfred is an AI tool which can automate repetitive tasks like sending connection requests and following up; LinkedIn helper is another AI tool which is used on LinkedIn to automate tasks like sending connection requests, messages and endorsements.

Email follow-up: AI-driven tools like HubSpot and Drip enable businesses to automate follow-up email sequences tailored to the recipient's behaviour. For example, if a lead downloads a white paper, AI can trigger a series of follow-up emails offering related resources, gradually nurturing the lead with relevant content.

Web-based/chatbot-based follow-up: Tools like Drift or Intercom use AI chatbots to automatically follow up with website visitors. These chatbots can initiate conversations, answer questions and even schedule meetings based on user interactions, providing instant follow-ups and keeping the lead engaged in real-time.

Automated SMS follow-ups: AI can automate SMS follow-ups based on customer actions. For instance, platforms like Twilio use AI to send personalized text messages as follow-ups after key events, such as a webinar registration or abandoned cart. This automation ensures timely communication without requiring human effort.

Automated task reminders for sales teams: AI-driven CRMs like Pipedrive automate task reminders for sales teams, ensuring that they follow up with leads at the right time. These reminders are often based on AI's analysis of the lead's activity, making sure that no follow-up opportunities slip through the cracks.

TABLE 8.4 Types of automated follow-up

Follow-up type	Description	Example AI tools or tools with AI embedded features
LinkedIn Follow-Up	Automates LinkedIn actions like sending connection requests, follow-up messages, helping maintain contact with prospects on LinkedIn.	Dux Soup, LinkedIn Helper

(continued)

TABLE 8.4 (Continued)

Follow-up type	Description	Example AI tools or tools with AI embedded features
Email follow-up	Sends automated, behaviour-based follow-up emails. Triggered by actions like downloads or page visits, it nurtures leads with tailored content over time.	HubSpot
Web-based/chatbot follow-up	Uses AI chatbots to engage website visitors, answer questions or schedule meetings in real-time, ensuring instant follow-up based on visitor behaviour.	Drift, Intercom
Automated task reminders for sales teams	AI-driven CRMs provide automatic reminders for sales teams to follow up with leads based on activity, ensuring timely engagement without missing any leads.	Pipedrive, Salesforce Einstein

REAL-WORLD EXAMPLE: GEOVENT'S JOURNEY WITH AI-BASED LEAD SCORING

A case study

Geovent, a company specializing in ventilation and extraction solutions, sought to optimize its lead generation and sales processes by leveraging AI-driven lead scoring. In 2021, the company intensified its focus on online advertising and SEO optimization but encountered challenges in correlating these digital efforts with lead generation. Traditionally, Geovent relied on manual methods such as searching databases, initiating contact through meetings, fostering relationships, following up and eventually providing quotations. While effective, these methods were resource-intensive and slow, and they did not scale efficiently with the company's growth.

One of the main challenges Geovent faced was the inefficiency of its lead qualification process. Leads generated through online activities were forwarded to sales representatives without categorization or prioritization, forcing them to manually assess each lead. This lack of segmentation meant that all leads were treated equally, resulting in wasted time and effort. To address these inefficiencies, Geovent implemented ActiveCampaign's AI-based lead scoring system, which provided deeper insights into which digital and other activities contributed to high-quality leads. This technology enabled the company to allocate resources more effectively, reducing the time and effort needed to secure potential customers while improving overall efficiency.

The implementation of AI lead scoring began with a pilot test in the UK market, where a sales representative was actively involved in discussions to ensure alignment with existing processes. Initially, without automated lead scoring, the workload remained similar to the manual approach. However, once automation was integrated, the marketing team took charge of generating leads, while the sales representative followed up when leads met a predetermined score threshold. During this process, Geovent identified the need to improve its website structure, as inconsistencies caused by various updates hindered lead tracking. A significant update was necessary to ensure accurate lead tracing and a seamless user experience.

Before implementing AI-based lead scoring, lead evaluation was entirely dependent on the subjective judgement of individual sales representatives. ActiveCampaign introduced a structured framework that allowed significant customization to align with Geovent's needs. The AI model evaluated leads based on email engagement, such as sending inquiries or submitting forms and website activity, including the number of pages visited, visit frequency and time spent on specific pages. High engagement indicators, such as repeat visits within a short period, further contributed to the overall score, with time spent on the website carrying the most weight as a sign of strong interest. This AI-driven approach transformed Geovent's lead management by reducing time wasted on unqualified leads, increasing the percentage of hot and relevant leads by approximately 80 per cent, and enabling a more targeted sales process.

Following the success in the UK, Geovent plans to expand AI-led scoring to markets in Denmark and Germany, with structured training sessions ensuring smooth adoption. The sales team's response has been overwhelmingly positive, recognizing the long-term benefits of reduced workload and improved lead quality. The impact of AI-based lead scoring is evident in strategic insights, such as identifying a UK business that visited Geovent's website eight times in two weeks, leading to an expected long-term customer relationship. By leveraging data-driven insights, Geovent now prioritizes high-value prospects, streamlining sales efforts and improving customer retention. Through ActiveCampaign's AI-powered lead scoring, Geovent has achieved greater efficiency, allowing sales teams to focus on converting high-potential leads and driving business growth.

References

1 Flairlane (2024) 9 Statistics about cross-channel marketing you should know, 19 September, blog.flarelane.com/nine-statistics-about-cross-channel-marketing-you-should-know (archived at https://perma.cc/ZL7T-6KXD)

2 Tegze, J (2024) LinkedIn features you can't miss in 2024, 2 July, www.linkedin.com/pulse/linkedin-features-you-cant-miss-2024-jan-tegze-y6lve/ (archived at https://perma.cc/YRD5-FGVE)

Further reading

Colburn, L (2023) How multichannel marketing and AI elevate the customer experience, Persado, www.persado.com/articles/multichannel-marketing-and-ai/ (archived at https://perma.cc/6Q3M-UAWB),

kissflow.com (n.d.) How to automate workflows with AI: A complete guide for modern businesses. kissflow.com/workflow/how-to-automate-workflows-with-ai/ (archived at https://perma.cc/JV6W-E6ML)

Sivek, SC (2023) What is predictive lead scoring with AI?, Pecan AI, www.pecan.ai/blog/predictive-lead-scoring-with-ai/ (archived at https://perma.cc/DMH9-T4AT)

PART FOUR

AI for optimizing customer relationships

09

Personalization and AI

What you will gain from this chapter

Understanding of the following:

- understand how AI can be used in B2B marketing personalization
- learn how to personalize different content formats
- understand different approaches to content personalization

Introduction

Personalization marketing is about using persona-specific information to create or improve bespoke experiences through marketing. It involves individualizing content or parts of content for target customers through collecting and analysing data. In an era where digital marketing is increasing and customers use or consume more marketing channels within shorter times, the demands on personalization have also increased.

Benefits of personalization

Personalization can help build better relationships by adapting content, messages and interactions to better speak to prospective or current customers.

As the benefits of personalization have become evident in improved ROI, reduced acquisition costs and revenue increase, attention should also be paid as to how to adopt and integrate this into B2B marketing efforts.

Personalization can help drive sales and understand customer segments as well as grow the business. Personalization marketing is still evolving in B2B and is specific to the industry, product or service type, and even country.

FIGURE 9.1 Types of B2B personalization

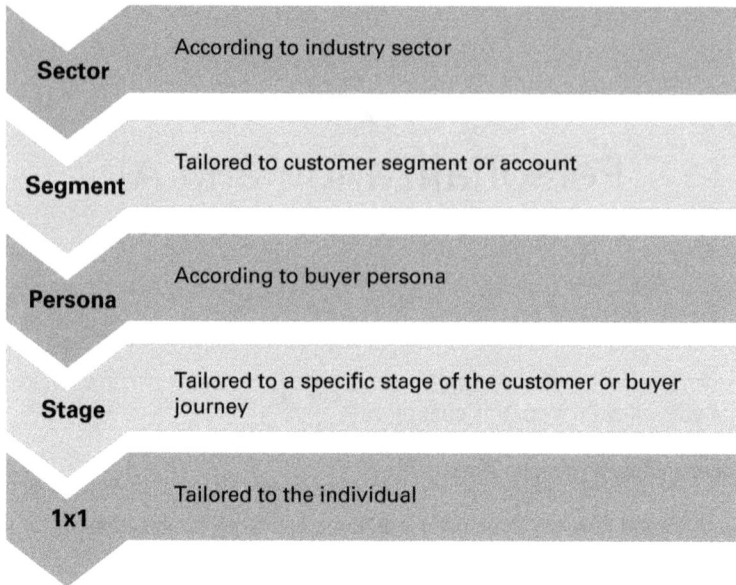

Sector	According to industry sector
Segment	Tailored to customer segment or account
Persona	According to buyer persona
Stage	Tailored to a specific stage of the customer or buyer journey
1x1	Tailored to the individual

Levels of B2B personalization

There are also different levels of personalization in B2B marketing; not all personalized marketing is fully tailored or comprehensively detailed to a person. See Figure 9.1 which illustrates the different forms of B2B marketing personalization from segment and sector personalization through one-to-one personalization.

Role of AI in personalization

The following are some of the main roles of AI in personalization B2B marketing.

AI and dynamic marketing

Digital technologies can make personalization easier by automating some tasks required in the background, for example dynamic or adaptive websites. Such technology supports recognition of customer interest and provides tailored messages and content accordingly, a process that would not be scalable or feasible without digital means. Hence digital technologies and digital marketing go hand in hand with many forms of personalization.

Enhanced customer engagement

AI-based personalization improves customer engagement as it can provide more detailed insights into customer behaviours and needs. Through this higher degree of customization one can capture the attention of prospects and also nurture stronger customer relationships,

Real-time adaptation and predictive analytics

Adapting in real time is one of the main advantages of AI tools for personalization. AI can instantly analyse customer interactions and preferences, supporting businesses to adapt their communication to prospects.

Content personalization with AI

We'll be looking at the aspect of personalizing content using AI. For this following section we could consider a particular industry sector and a type of buyer persona, for example:

- A purchase manager in the pharmaceutical industry looking to buy lab equipment.
- A finance manager in the healthcare sector looking to buy IT equipment.
- An HR manager looking to buy marketing training from a marketing training provider.
- A CFO in the manufacturing sector evaluating a solution.

Some of the content we can personalize and use for our lead generation and lead nurturing initiatives include the following.

- blogs
- posts
- webinar scripts
- podcast scripts
- emails
- slide decks
- polls
- surveys

Blogs and personalization

Blogs are cost-effective content which can also build more traffic for your website; some blogs are used to turn prospects into leads through embedded calls to actions. Blogs are great ways to demonstrate thought leaderships for B2B marketing, while at the same covering long-tail search terms, attracting prospects in the awareness and consideration stages of the buyer journey.

Often the issue with blog writing comes down to two main areas: what to write about and two how to write this for a specific audience. Here's where AI can help, as well as optimizing and improving the blog content. We can break the blog creation process into the following steps (see Figure 9.2).

FIGURE 9.2 Blog creation process

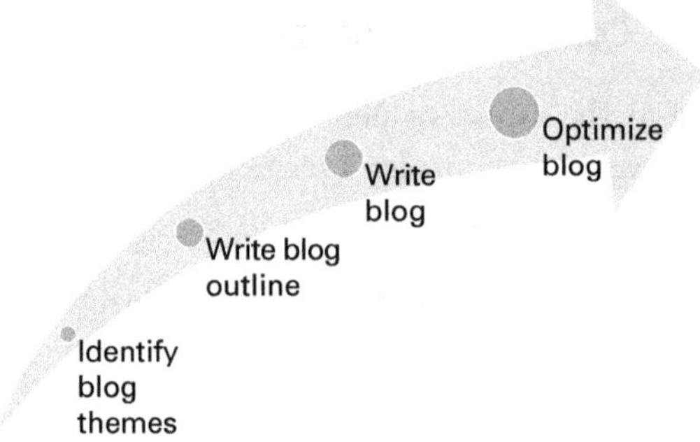

Step 1: Identify blog themes

The first step in the blog creation process is to identify blog themes; to come up with ideas for blog titles we can use NLP/ML AI tools like ChatGPT and Gemini; please consider the following prompts.

- *Please provide 10 possible ideas for blogs on the topic of challenges a purchase manager faces in buying laboratory; please try to rank the different blog titles in terms of market trends.*
- *Please provide five engaging themes regarding the use of IT equipment in the healthcare sector.*

See below the response to step 1 above which highlights two of the top 10 themes.

- Navigating supply chain disruptions: How purchase managers in pharma can secure critical lab equipment.

  - Trend focus: Supply chain challenges and geopolitical tensions.
  - With global supply chain disruptions becoming more frequent, this blog can address how purchase managers can overcome delays and shortages in sourcing lab equipment.
- Sustainable procurement in the pharmaceutical industry: Challenges in sourcing eco-friendly lab equipment.
  - Trend focus: Sustainability and green procurement.
  - As companies aim to reduce their environmental footprint, purchase managers need to find sustainable equipment without compromising quality.

Step 2: Writing and tailoring the blog

Now we have themes which relate to the sector and persona we can select a theme and ask for the blog to be written out; assuming we select theme two let's input the following query.

Prompt: *Please write an 800-word blog on the topic of 'Overcoming Budget Constraints in the Pharma Industry: Smart Solutions for Purchasing Essential Lab Equipment in an Era of Tight R&D Budgets'. Explore ways to optimize equipment purchases without sacrificing quality or functionality.*

Of course, we can adjust the prompt to our needs, e.g. ask for a bullet-point outline, or ask for 500 words or more than 800 words; we can include more specifics in the prompt by asking for a particular focus in the blog.

Step 3: optimizing the blog

We can now fine tune the blog further by asking the AI tool things like the following.

Prompt: *For the response to the previous prompt please include data and statistics for each main area of the blog; also, please include anecdotes, analogies and any specific practical tips as well as references and citations.*

Videos

In terms of personalizing and tailoring videos using AI we can do this by looking at three main areas: video scripts, video generation and avatar-based video generation.

Video scripts

AI-powered video tools can be used to tailor videos in different ways; we can tailor videos to industries and buyer personas by personalizing video scripts making the content more engaging for specific audiences.

Taking the blog example from before let's say we now want to create a video on the same theme; we'll keep the theme generic.

Here are some prompts we could use to create video script outline.

Prompt: *Please provide a video script for a 10-minute video regarding challenges a purchase manager from the pharmaceutical industry encounters in buying laboratory equipment; please show a breakdown of the script by minute.*

Once we are happy with the video script outline we can then ask the AI tool to write out the video script in full. See below the outline for the first minute; notice how without asking for specifics in this case the NLP/ML tool already highlights elements of a video script, i.e. scene, voice over, host, etc. We can also ask for advice on other possible elements which a video script should incorporate.

INTRODUCTION (0:00 – 1:00)

- Scene: Bright, modern office background with a purchase manager seated at a desk reviewing equipment catalogues on a laptop. The video host stands beside the desk.
- Voiceover: 'Welcome to today's video, where we explore the challenges a purchase manager faces when buying laboratory equipment in the pharmaceutical industry. These professionals play a vital role in ensuring that R&D labs are well-equipped while dealing with budget constraints, compliance and market fluctuations. In this video, we'll dive deep into the main challenges they encounter and smart solutions to overcome them.'
- On-screen text: 'Challenges in Procuring Lab Equipment for Pharma Companies.'

Video generation

Beyond just video script generation which we can use NLP/ML tools for, like ChatGPT, Gemini and Copilot, we can also look to AI video-generating tools. One of the most ground-breaking applications of AI is the ability to generate videos directly from textual input. Tools like Invideo, Runway and Pictory allow users to input text scripts, which the AI converts into engaging video content. These platforms use pre-trained models to generate visuals, animations that align with the provided narrative. An example is Runway which enables the creation of custom video clips from text descriptions using generative models.

Other AI features of generative AI tools include customizable background music from tools such as Epidemic Sound and Artlist; scene customization and style transfer from tools like Runway ML; and AI-powered video editing from AI tools like Adobe Sensei integrated into Adobe Creative Cloud.

PUT INTO PRACTICE: AVATAR-BASED VIDEOS

Avatar-based AI tools can be used to tailor video content. Synthesia offers an AI script generator that creates video scripts based on user-defined topics, objectives and tone of voice. With Synthesia one can choose from over 60 video templates.

For this practice example we'll look at a purchase manager in healthcare looking to buy IT equipment.

Personalization features

- Tailored video scripts with Synthesia: One can tailor video scripts to unique challenges of purchase managers in healthcare IT procurement. For instance, the script could focus on compliance with healthcare regulations, cybersecurity concerns or the need for scalable IT infrastructure in hospitals.
- Dynamic video content: Synthesia allows you to insert variables into your video script, such as the company name, the name of the purchase manager or specific IT challenges related to healthcare. Example: 'Hi [Name], as the purchase manager at [Hospital Name], you're responsible for selecting the most reliable IT solutions while maintaining compliance with healthcare regulations like HIPAA. In this video, we'll explore how our IT solutions ensure data security and scalability for healthcare organizations like yours.'
- Custom avatars for buyer personas: Synthesia allows you to choose avatars that resonate with specific personas. For example, you could select an avatar dressed in a healthcare-appropriate environment to make the content feel more relevant to a purchase manager working in the sector.

- Localization and language options: If you're targeting global clients, Synthesia's avatars can speak multiple languages, which adds another layer of personalization. You could create videos for a healthcare purchase manager in different regions, adapting the content to their native language.

Personalizing email

Through AI technology and tools, one can register ideal send times for email, create optimal content and write the email content as well as come up with ideas for the email campaign. In the last chapter we already discussed the email nurture campaign and AI, so we'll turn our attention to other areas.

Data driven introductions

AI NLP and LLM tools use advanced natural language processing and machine learning algorithms to analyse publicly available data about prospects, enabling businesses to craft highly personalized email introductions. This personalization increases the likelihood of engagement.

AI tools like ChatGPT tailor email content by gathering and analysing data from sources such as follows:

- Social media profiles (e.g. LinkedIn, Twitter): Details about professional background, recent posts or updates shared by the prospect.
- Company websites and blogs: Information about the company's recent milestones, products or press releases.
- News articles: Insights about the individual or their organization, such as awards, partnerships or funding rounds.
- Online forums or industry events: Participation in discussions or speaking engagements.

PUT INTO PRACTICE: EXAMPLE OF A TAILORED EMAIL INTRODUCTION USING PUBLIC DATA

A SaaS company wants to reach out to a prospect, 'John Sanches', who is the VP of Marketing at 'Techx', a mid-sized software company.

Publicly available data found:

- LinkedIn: John recently posted about his excitement regarding the Techx launch of a new AI-driven product for predictive analytics.

- Company website: Techx announced a partnership with a Fortune 500 company in a press release.
- Twitter: John shared an article about innovative AI use cases in marketing.
- Industry news: Techx secured $10M in Series B funding last month.

From the above the AI tool can generate an email introduction with the subject 'Excited about Techx's Innovations in AI' and the following email.

Hello John

I came across your recent LinkedIn post about Techx new AI-driven predictive analytics product – congratulations on such a forward-thinking launch! It's clear that Techx is setting a benchmark in leveraging AI for actionable insights.

I also noticed your recent partnership with [Fortune 500 company name], which is an incredible milestone. As someone deeply interested in how AI is transforming marketing, I believe there's a unique opportunity for [SaaS company name] to support Techx's growth trajectory.

If you're open to exploring ways we can collaborate, I'd love to schedule a quick chat next week. Let me know what works best for you!

Best regards,

[Your Name]

Hyper personalizing with AI

Imagine the scenario that you are looking to target HR managers who are deciding on buying office space from a flexible office space provider.

AI tools can support hyper personalizing; AI tools like Drift or Intercom can be integrated into email marketing to dynamically personalize office space recommendations based on company size, number of employees or location preferences. For example, an email might highlight flexible workspace options in specific cities where the HR manager is focused on recruiting new talent.

Example personalized email segment: 'Dear [Name], as [Company Name] expands, your HR strategy is likely focused on creating adaptable workspaces that inspire your team. Our flexible office spaces in [City/Area] are perfect for a hybrid workforce, offering the room to grow while maintaining a modern, adaptable environment.'

Better subject lines and email body content personalization

Subject lines are critical for engagement. AI tools like Phrasee can analyse preferences of the target audience and then recommend subject lines that appeal to HR managers, focusing on employee well-being, office culture and flexibility.

- Example personalized subject line: 'Boost Employee Satisfaction with Flexible Office Spaces at [Company Name]'
- Email body: 'Hi [Name], we know that retaining top talent means offering more than just competitive salaries – it's about creating a workspace where your employees can thrive. Our flexible office solutions provide the balance of professionalism and comfort, giving your team the ideal environment to work productively. Let's explore how we can help your company create a workplace people love coming to.'

White papers

A white paper is a comprehensive and authoritative document designed to inform, persuade or educate its audience about a specific topic, often within a professional or technical field. These documents are typically aimed at decision-makers, stakeholders or a specialized audience, and they are crafted to establish the authoring organization or individual as a credible expert in the subject matter. White papers are commonly used in industries such as technology, healthcare, finance and engineering, where complex concepts or emerging trends require explanation and context. Unlike marketing brochures or blog posts, white papers are in-depth and research-driven, often including data analysis, case studies and evidence-based arguments. They provide a deep dive into the topic, offering a blend of technical detail and practical advice. The goal is to persuade the reader of the validity of the proposed solution or framework, often encouraging them to adopt a product, service or methodology.

Personalizing white papers

White paper personalization can be approached a few ways via AI tools.

- **Approach 1**: Building a personalized white paper from scratch; ultimately this involves building the structure, themes and defining the flow, outline, structure of the white paper as well as tailoring it to an industry and/or buyer personas needs. Following on from that, this would typically be handed on to someone to write up, adjust and tweak. The final stages would be non-AI-based.

- **Approach 2**: This would be the inverse to approach 1 where the white paper has been written already; to personalize this one could input the white paper into the NLP/ML AI tool and ask it to adapt and personalize for a specific buyer persona and their main needs.
- **Approach 3**: This approach is taking the existing white paper and enhancing the content by drawing out some of the specifics through expanding on points, adding data and statistics; this enhancement of the white paper can be done through AI NLP/ML tools.

Webinars

Webinars are video-based content formats typically lasting up to one hour; they tend to be live with some degree of interaction, though the majority of the webinar tends to be for viewers to watch and listen.

Here are different ways AI can be used to help personalize webinars.

- Suggesting specific topics: Rather than just identifying themes for webinars we can use AI NLP/ML tools to suggest webinar topics which are specific to an industry and/or a buyer persona's needs.
- Writing webinar scripts: In the planning and outline of the webinar we can use AI NLP/ML tools to develop the webinar script in the same way we create scripts for videos.
- Webinar analysis by leveraging advanced machine learning algorithms. Tools like BigMarker and Zoom AI Companion analyse various aspects of webinars, including audience interactions, engagement rates and participation trends.
- Additionally, real-time AI-powered polling tools like Vevox, Pollfish and Slido allow presenters to gather instant feedback during the webinar. AI processes this feedback to identify trending topics, frequently asked questions or areas where the audience sought further clarification.

Personalizing content

Tools like ClickUp AI, Pathmatics and Optimizely help organizers analyse attendee data such as professional backgrounds, industry interests or prior engagement with the brand. This data enables the generation of personalized content that speaks directly to the needs and preferences of distinct audience segments. AI can also help design interactive elements such as quizzes or polls tailored to audience profiles, making webinars more engaging and interactive. For example, if the AI detects that a segment of the audience frequently engages with content on digital marketing trends, it can recommend incorporating a live demo or case study on that topic during the webinar.

Creating slide decks for webinars

AI can automate the creation of presentation slides by organizing content into a coherent and visually appealing format. Tools like Pitch and AEvent use AI to analyse existing content and generate slides that highlight key points and insights, ensuring that presentations are both informative and engaging. Alternative tools could be slides.ai or others.

Post-webinar engagement

After the webinar, AI can support automated follow-up processes by sending personalized content and recommendations to attendees based on their participation and interests. AI-powered tools can analyse feedback and engagement data to create customized follow-up emails, surveys and content suggestions, ensuring that the relationship with participants continues to develop beyond the live event.

PUT INTO PRACTICE

An event uses AI to analyse audience behaviour and preferences across various platforms. It examines past webinar attendance and engagement rates as well as user behaviour on hosting platforms. Using this analysis, it provides post-webinar suggestions in the following ways.

- Recommends optimal days and times for future webinars.
- Suggests preferred topics and content types for follow-up communications.
- Provides insights on audience preferences to tailor post-webinar messaging.

> PUT INTO PRACTICE
>
> We can ask AI to create an outline for a webinar; we can do this by writing this out as one long prompt or typing in successive commands which build on each other.
>
> Prompt: *Please write a webinar brief in a guiding, coaching tone of voice focused on the latest challenges which purchase managers face in the B2B transportation sector.*

Tools

There are different ways to approach AI for webinar personalization; one way is to use generic NLP/machine learning tools like ChatGPT, Gemini or others and use these to create webinar briefs, webinar scripts and then use other AI tools to create webinar slide decks.

The other root is to look for webinar platforms which include AI functionality and AI guidance such as WebinarGeek.

Ebooks/guides

In the context of B2B marketing, ebooks are powerful digital assets that serve multiple strategic purposes such as lead generation, lead nurture and establishing thought leadership. Their format is typically 10–30 pages long, downloadable as a pdf, with some interactive features.

AI can be used to personalize ebooks in a similar way as white papers, although there are some differences:

- Create a tailored ebook from scratch: AI tools like ChatGPT, Jasper, can generate content for an ebook based on specific prompts or target audience needs.
- Tailor an existing ebook: AI tools like Grammarly Business can assist in editing and rephrasing content to better align with the preferences of different audience segments. For example, an existing ebook on cybersecurity could be tailored for small businesses by including specific threats and solutions relevant to smaller IT budgets.
- Enhance existing ebook through personalized aspects such as expanding sections, including data/statistics relating to the industry.

- Create the ebook from a long-form blog: AI tools like Surfer SEO and Frase can identify key points and structure a blog into an ebook format, ensuring logical flow and expanded depth.
- Expand the blog to become a long form blog and then convert to an ebook.

Creating an ebook from scratch

One can using AI writing assistants like Jasper.ai and Narrato.io to generate content based on specific inputs, allowing for the creation of highly personalized ebooks.

Some inputs or steps in creating the ebook from scratch might be as follows.

- Input industry-specific keywords, target audience details and desired tone.
- AI generates chapters, sections and content tailored to the specified parameters.
- Refine and edit the AI-generated content to ensure accuracy and brand voice.

Tailoring existing ebooks

For tailoring existing ebooks, tools such as Designrr.io and Piktochart AI ebook generator can modify content to fit new target audiences or industries, adjusting language, examples and case studies as needed.

Enhance existing ebooks

To enhance existing ebooks with personalized aspects, Wordgenie (integrated with Designrr.io) and EbookMaker AI can expand specific sections and incorporate relevant data, automatically sourcing industry-specific statistics and seamlessly integrating new content with existing material. AI can expand specific sections to include updated or industry-relevant data. For example, tools like Tableau or Power BI can integrate fresh statistics or visualizations into an ebook's content. AI can also add tailored callouts or examples that resonate with the reader's industry. Tools like Grammarly Go or Narrato.io can suggest new sections or elaborate on existing content. Once expanded, the content can be reorganized and formatted into an ebook using tools like Canva or Scrivener, with AI handling design suggestions, layout improvements and even cover design.

Leveraging a blog to create a personalized ebook

For those looking to create an ebook from a long-form blog, tools like Typeset and Canva (with AI features) can transform blog content into a structured ebook format. These tools analyse the content, suggest an ebook structure and automatically format it into chapters and sections, complete with a table of contents and design elements. Alternatively, to expand a blog into a long-form piece before converting it to an ebook, AI writing assistants like Rytr and ShortlyAI can suggest additional topics and subtopics, generating new sections and paragraphs to create a comprehensive long-form blog. Once expanded, tools like Designrr.io can be used to convert the long-form content into an ebook.

Presentations

AI tools can significantly enhance the personalization of B2B presentations, making them more relevant and engaging for specific audiences and industries. Here's how AI can be used to personalize presentations, along with examples of supporting tools.

Creating from scratch

Tools such as Pitch can create a slide deck based on an inputted paragraph providing suggestions in terms of flow, sequence, imagery and other aspects. One can then use the suggested slide deck to further optimize content.

Content customization

AI-powered tools like Beautiful.AI and Canva's Magic Studio can tailor B2B marketing content to specific industries and audience profiles. Beautiful.AI, for example, analyses audience data, such as job roles, pain points and sector trends, to recommend industry-specific content. A B2B marketing firm targeting the healthcare sector might use Beautiful.AI to generate slides featuring examples like case studies on medical device implementation or tailored terminology such as 'patient care pathways' instead of generic business terms.

Data visualization

AI tools like Visme's AI Presentation Maker enable businesses to transform raw data into visually compelling charts and graphs. For example, a SaaS company presenting to a retail client could use Visme to create heatmaps showcasing regional sales performance or bar graphs illustrating e-commerce growth.

These tools also offer customization options, such as adjusting the style of visuals to match industry expectations. In the financial sector, Visme might generate clear and precise line graphs with clean fonts and muted colour palettes to convey professionalism. In contrast, a marketing firm might use more vibrant and creative infographics to capture the dynamic nature of their industry. By converting complex datasets into easily digestible visuals, AI helps B2B marketers convey their message effectively and make data-driven insights actionable for their audience.

Modify existing presentations

AI tools like Tome simplify the process of adapting existing presentations for different B2B audiences or industries. Users can upload a slide deck and input specific audience details, such as 'manufacturing executives' or 'HR leaders'. Tome then adjusts the content, replacing general examples with industry-specific case studies or refining terminology to match the new audience.

For example, a generic presentation on digital transformation can be adapted for the manufacturing sector by adding slides on predictive maintenance and IoT-enabled production lines. Similarly, targeting HR professionals might involve integrating content on AI-driven talent acquisition and workforce analytics. Tome's ability to generate supplementary slides ensures that the presentation is not only tailored but also enriched with relevant insights, enhancing its impact for B2B stakeholders.

Survey and poll personalization

The following section is considering how we personalize surveys as content to use in B2B marketing (as opposed to conduct market research in a pure sense). In survey and poll personalization this is about how we create questions which are specifically designed for the industry and buyer persona; the personalization should serve to create questions which resonate better and thus facilitate a response; even if these are non-text responses through personalized survey questions the response rate would increase.

Generating surveys

AI-powered survey creation tools, such as Zonka Feedback, Beautiful.AI and SurveyMonkey Genius, can generate tailored surveys based on specific inputs. These tools use AI to analyse the survey's purpose, target audience and industry to create relevant questions and structure. For example, SurveyMonkey Genius can create surveys in as little as 30 seconds by using AI to recommend question types and autofill balanced answer choices.

AI can also optimize surveys in real time. AI tools like Fillout can analyse existing surveys and suggest improvements for better clarity, flow and effectiveness. This dynamic optimization can lead to higher completion rates and more valuable data collection.

Personalizing

For deeper personalization, AI tools can create unique customer profiles based on survey responses and behaviour. Qualtrics, for instance, uses AI to analyse not just the content of responses but also to analyse factors like answer times to create comprehensive customer experience profiles. These profiles are built not only from survey responses but also by analysing factors like response times, sentiment and patterns in behaviour. Qualtrics, for instance, uses AI to evaluate survey data comprehensively. For example, if a survey identifies a B2B customer as a mid-sized tech company interested in scaling operations, Qualtrics can create a profile highlighting this need. It can also factor in slower response times to specific questions, signalling uncertainty or a need for additional resources, which can guide follow-up interactions. AI can also personalize the survey-taking experience itself.

EXAMPLES OF CUSTOMER PROFILES IN B2B MARKETING

A B2B survey aimed at manufacturing clients might reveal respondents focused on automation and efficiency. AI tools like Medallia or SurveyMonkey could generate a profile for 'manufacturing operations managers' who prioritize cost-saving solutions. This profile would guide personalized marketing campaigns showcasing case studies on automation ROI and webinars on lean manufacturing practices.

In the financial services sector, survey results might highlight concerns about regulatory compliance. Tools like Survicate could create profiles for 'risk-averse CFOs', emphasizing their preference for robust, secure solutions. Marketing materials for this profile could include compliance-focused white papers, consultations with experts and product demonstrations that highlight risk mitigation features.

Data analysis and insights

AI can also assist in data analysis and insight generation. Many tools offer AI-powered analysis features that can identify trends, patterns and sentiments in survey responses. This can help in quickly understanding the overall sentiment of respondents and provide actionable insights for decision-making.

Removing bias

Some AI survey tools, like BlockSurvey, focus on removing bias from surveys. By using AI to generate questions, these tools can help create more objective surveys, especially for sensitive topics where human bias might influence question formulation.

Podcasts and scripts

AI technologies can also be used to tailor B2B podcasts for specific industries and buyer personas. By leveraging AI, podcasters can create more targeted, engaging content that drives better results. For example, in the healthcare technology industry, a podcast targeting hospital IT directors might use AI tools to analyse industry trends and generate relevant topic ideas. Riverside.fm's Magic Tools suite could be employed to transcribe episodes with 99 per cent accuracy and create short-form clips highlighting key points about cybersecurity in healthcare or the implementation of new electronic health record systems. These clips could then be shared on LinkedIn or in email newsletters to attract the target audience.

Another example might be a podcast aimed at chief financial officers in the manufacturing sector, AI tools like Podcastle could be used to generate industry-specific content. The AI could analyse financial reports and economic indicators to suggest topics around supply chain optimization or cost-reduction strategies.

Enhancing audio quality with Podcastle

Podcastle's AI-driven audio editor offers powerful tools to enhance audio quality as it automatically removes background noise, balances audio levels and improves clarity, creating polished podcast episodes that resonate with discerning audiences such as C-suite executives. For example, in a healthcare IT-focused podcast, Podcastle can ensure that discussions around complex technical topics are delivered with crisp and professional audio, enhancing the listening experience for hospital IT directors or decision-makers.

Repurposing podcast content with Castmagic

Castmagic is a versatile AI tool that transforms podcast content into multiple formats, making it an invaluable resource for extending the reach of B2B podcasts. It allows businesses to repurpose key insights and conversations into formats tailored to specific audiences and platforms.

By following these steps and utilizing AI tools, B2B podcasters can create highly tailored content (see Table 9.1).

For instance, a healthcare IT podcast could use Inflection AI to research emerging trends in hospital data management, then use ChatGPT to draft

TABLE 9.1 Podcast and AI personalization

Step	AI Tool	Function
Topic research	Inflection AI	Generate industry-specific topic ideas
Content creation	ChatGPT	Draft outlines and scripts
Recording	Riverside.fm	High-quality remote recording with AI enhancements
Editing	Descript	Text-based editing with AI transcription
Audio enhancement	Podcastle	AI-powered noise reduction and voice enhancement
Repurposing	Castmagic	Generate multiple content assets from each episode
Distribution	Podpage	Create AI-optimized podcast websites

an outline for an episode on implementing AI in diagnostic imaging. The episode could be recorded using Riverside.fm's high-quality audio capabilities, then edited in Descript using its AI transcription and text-based editing features. Adobe Podcast could be used to enhance the audio quality, ensuring it meets the professional standards expected by hospital IT directors. Castmagic could then repurpose the episode into a series of LinkedIn posts, each focusing on a specific aspect of AI in healthcare imaging, tailored to resonate with the target audience. Finally, Podpage could be used to create an SEO-optimized website for the podcast, making it easily discoverable by healthcare IT professionals searching for information on e topics.

Further reading

Hayes, M and Downie, A (2024) AI personalization, IBM, www.ibm.com/think/topics/ai-personalization (archived at https://perma.cc/6D4T-PHD5)

IOVOX (2024) 6 Applications of AI personalization in marketing you need to know, www.iovox.co.uk/blog/ai-personalization-marketing (archived at https://perma.cc/6GP4-TT67)

Lee, M (2024) AI Personalization: 5 examples + business challenges, Bloomreach, www.bloomreach.com/en/blog/ai-personalization-5-examples-business-challenges (archived at https://perma.cc/73CZ-W9ZE)

10

Conversational technology

> What you will gain from this chapter
>
> Understanding of the following:
>
> - understanding conversational technology
> - learn about chatbots and AI chatbots
> - how to go about implementing an AI chatbots
> - virtual assistants and their use in lead generation

Introduction

Conversational technology refers to technologies which allow machines to interact with humans over communication channels; these include the following:

- chatbots
- revenue assistants
- virtual assistants

Benefits of conversational AI

Conversational AI is used increasingly in customer service, allowing businesses to provide 24/7 support. Through conversational AI-based technology, businesses can automate routine activities such as enquiries and as such they lower operational expenses and reduce the number of physical employee hours needed by a business.

The main benefit of conversational AI is its ability to scale and meet growing business needs and increasing numbers of customers expecting a more personalized support. Without investing in additional resources, this personalized support can be achieved through conversational technology. Conversational technology uses vast amounts of data together with machine learning to imitate human interactions; for example, they can help users book appointments, answer FAQs, qualify leads, nurture leads, help capture leads and much more.

Main use cases for conversational technology

Below are some of the main use cases of conversational technology in marketing split out by areas of the buyer journey (see Figure 10.1).

Pre-purchase or both: supporting lead capture and nurturing

AI chatbots can play an important role in the pre-purchase phase of B2B marketing by enhancing lead capture and nurturing efforts. Often, prospects don't have the time to thoroughly explore a company's website or may struggle to find the information they need. In such cases, chatbots can provide immediate assistance without the need to engage directly with a sales representative.

1. OPTIMIZING WEBSITE EXPERIENCES

For businesses with complex products or services, chatbots can improve the website experience by offering real-time assistance. When a prospect encounters a product or service that requires more explanation, a chatbot can provide a brief summary, direct the visitor to relevant content (such as videos, case studies or webinars) or even answer common questions directly.

2. LEAD DEVELOPMENT AND COMMUNICATION

AI chatbots can be employed across various channels such as email, SMS or messenger apps to initiate and maintain communication with prospects. Instead of waiting for a potential lead to reach out to a salesperson to intervene, chatbots can proactively send relevant information or answer queries before the customer needs to interact directly with a human.

3. LEAD QUALIFICATION AND NURTURING

One of the most powerful features of AI chatbots is their ability to qualify and nurture leads automatically. By asking targeted, predefined questions, chatbots can collect critical data such as company size, industry, budget and pain points. This information can then be used to segment leads and personalize further interactions. For example, leads from the finance industry may be offered different content or communication compared to leads from the healthcare sector. By automating this qualification process, businesses save time and ensure that sales teams focus on high-potential leads.

4. CONTENT RECOMMENDATION

AI chatbots can also personalize the content experience for each visitor based on their industry, role and previous interactions with the brand. If a visitor has previously looked at a case study or webinar on a particular topic, the chatbot can recommend related content such as blog posts or white papers.

Post-purchase: enhancing customer onboarding and beyond

After a purchase is made, chatbots can continue to provide value by guiding customers through the onboarding process and supporting them throughout their journey with the product or service.

1. CUSTOMER ONBOARDING

AI chatbots can be incredibly useful in the post-purchase phase by helping new customers get up to speed with the product or service. During the onboarding process, chatbots can assist customers with setting up their accounts, completing initial configurations and walking them through tutorials or training resources.

2. CONTINUOUS CUSTOMER SUPPORT AND ENGAGEMENT

Beyond onboarding, AI chatbots can play a vital role in ongoing customer support. As customers continue using a product or service, they may encounter issues or have questions about advanced features.

3. UPSELLING AND CROSS-SELLING OPPORTUNITIES

Chatbots can also be used post-purchase to identify opportunities for upselling or cross-selling. By analysing the customer's past interactions, preferences and purchase history, chatbots can recommend additional products, features or services.

4. GATHERING FEEDBACK FOR CONTINUOUS IMPROVEMENT

Post-purchase chatbots can be used to gather customer feedback on the product, service or overall experience.

FIGURE 10.1 Use case of chatbots

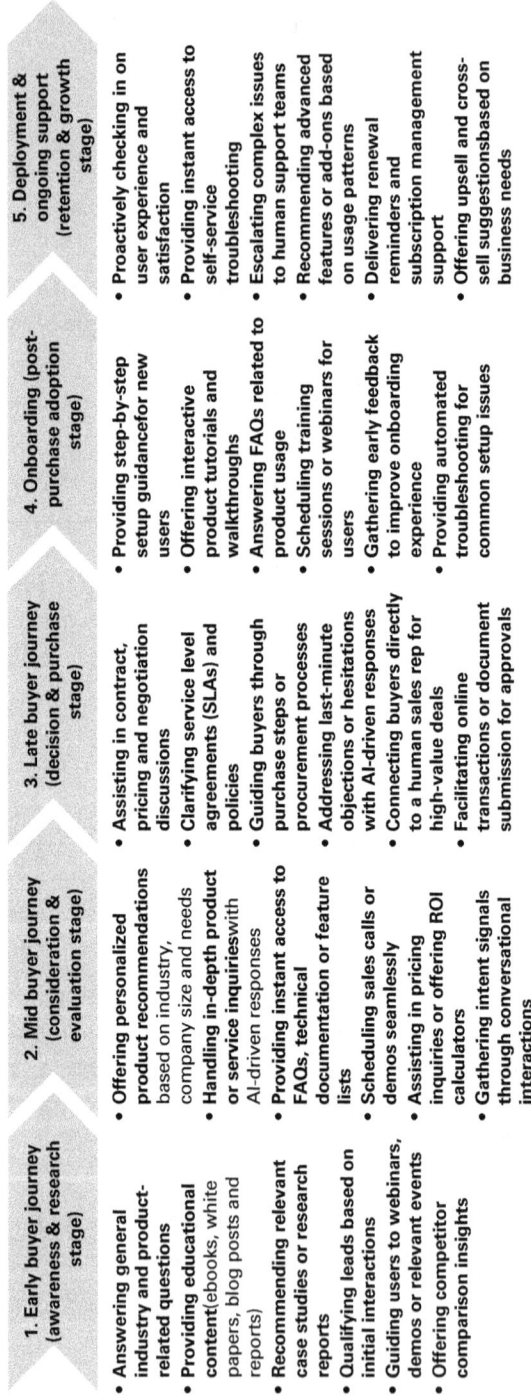

1. Early buyer journey (awareness & research stage)

- **Answering general industry and product-related questions**
- **Providing educational content**(ebooks, white papers, blog posts and reports)
- **Recommending relevant case studies or research reports**
- **Qualifying leads based on initial interactions**
- **Guiding users to webinars, demos or relevant events**
- **Offering competitor comparison insights**

2. Mid buyer journey (consideration & evaluation stage)

- **Offering personalized product recommendations** based on industry, company size and needs
- **Handling in-depth product or service inquiries**with AI-driven responses
- **Providing instant access to FAQs, technical documentation or feature lists**
- **Scheduling sales calls or demos seamlessly**
- **Assisting in pricing inquiries or offering ROI calculators**
- **Gathering intent signals through conversational interactions**

3. Late buyer journey (decision & purchase stage)

- **Assisting in contract, pricing and negotiation discussions**
- **Clarifying service level agreements (SLAs) and policies**
- **Guiding buyers through purchase steps or procurement processes**
- **Addressing last-minute objections or hesitations with AI-driven responses**
- **Connecting buyers directly to a human sales rep for high-value deals**
- **Facilitating online transactions or document submission for approvals**

4. Onboarding (post-purchase adoption stage)

- **Providing step-by-step setup guidancefor new users**
- **Offering interactive product tutorials and walkthroughs**
- **Answering FAQs related to product usage**
- **Scheduling training sessions or webinars for users**
- **Gathering early feedback to improve onboarding experience**
- **Providing automated troubleshooting for common setup issues**

5. Deployment & ongoing support (retention & growth stage)

- **Proactively checking in on user experience and satisfaction**
- **Providing instant access to self-service troubleshooting**
- **Escalating complex issues to human support teams**
- **Recommending advanced features or add-ons based on usage patterns**
- **Delivering renewal reminders and subscription management support**
- **Offering upsell and cross-sell suggestionsbased on business needs**

Now we're going to look into the two main areas of conversational technology: chatbots and virtual assistants.

Chatbots

Chatbots are software tools which are created to simulate human conversations; they tend to be mainly text-based, although some now include voice. Initially, chatbots were basic rule-based programs only capable of dealing with basic customer inquiries. In the past decade we've seen a rapid shift to more sophisticated AI-powered tools that play a crucial role in B2B marketing strategies. They can be used in various functions including sales, marketing and customer service. Chatbots can be placed anywhere online including business websites, on social media platforms, messaging apps or even via the phone.

Traditional chatbots

Traditional chatbots are software which operate on a predefined set of rules, scripts. Through these rules the chatbot can respond to 'specific' queries or inputs from users. Traditional chatbots use keyword matching techniques to match a response to the user query. They can be useful for dealing with simple and repeated queries, although their limitation is that they can only respond to predefined situations and queries, i.e. if a user asks something not programmed into the tool, then the chatbot is unable to respond appropriately.

AI chatbots

AI chatbots leverage artificial intelligence, i.e. NLP and machine learning algorithms. AI chatbots are able to understand more complex inputs as well as wide range of questions. They are very flexible, and they can also adapt, i.e. through repeated interactions they improve their capabilities and understanding of context. AI chatbots can identify patterns in queries in order to provide more precise and suitable responses.

AI chatbots go beyond predefined rules; they can also understand the intent behind a user query; they can also adapt their response based on the context of the conversation. AI chatbots as a result support personalization.

Types of chatbots

Typically, non-AI:

- rule-based chatbots
- keyword recognition-based chatbots
- menu-based chatbots

AI-based:

- contextual chatbots (intelligent chatbots)
- hybrid chatbots
- voice-enabled chatbots

Rule-based chatbots (decision tree chatbots)

Rule-based chatbots, aka decision tree chatbots, are rule-based chatbots that work on the basis of predefined rules and decision trees.

Keyword recognition chatbots

These bots employ keyword recognition techniques to make sense of queries and offer predefined responses. They offer more flexibility than rule-based bots but still rely on matching user input with specific keywords to generate a response.

FIGURE 10.2 Types of chatbot

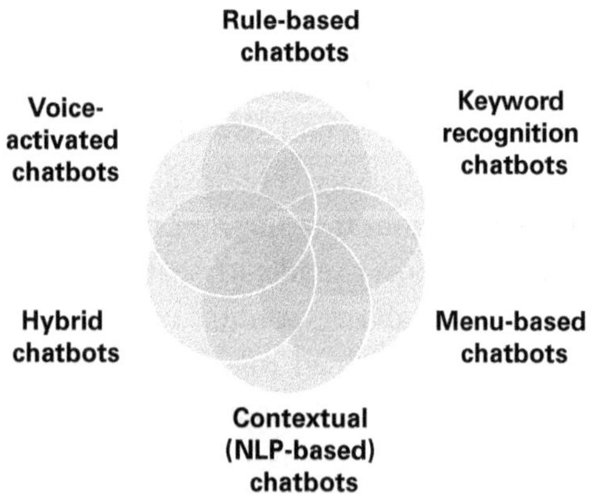

Menu-based chatbots

These bots guide users through a series of menus or buttons, allowing users to make selections to navigate through information or options. They are often combined with rule-based flows. They can be found supporting content delivery, e.g. a menu-based chatbot can offer different options like case studies, white papers or product demos, allowing users to select the content most relevant to them. They are also used in customer onboarding guiding new users through setup processes. Examples of menu-based chatbots include FlowXO and Intercom.

Contextual chatbots (NLP-based chatbots)

These chatbots leverage AI or more specifically NLP to grasp context as well as intent, NLP based chatbots can deal with more complicated conversations. They also employ machine learning to learn from previous prompts and conversations, which in turn improves their capabilities as well as allow them to offer more personalized answers. Examples where NLP chatbots can be found include IBM Watson assistant, Microsoft Azure Bot Service and Drift.

Hybrid chatbots (AI + human interaction)

Hybrid chatbots are a mix of AI-based chatbots and in-person engagement; the idea is that if the AI chatbot is unable to handle the question or identifies elements in the question and discussion which require human interaction, it is able to switch or escalate so humans can take over. They provide automated responses but can seamlessly hand off the conversation to a human representative when queries become too complex for the bot. They can be used as follows.

- Customer support escalation: Start with AI to handle routine queries and seamlessly escalate to human agents when complex or high-value leads need personal attention.
- Sales conversations: Hybrid chatbots can initiate a conversation and qualify leads, then pass them to sales reps for more in-depth discussions if a lead shows high interest.

Examples of technology which support this hybrid features include LivePeson, Ada and Zendesk.

Voice-activated chatbots

Voice-activated chatbots can enhance B2B interactions by leveraging voice recognition and speech-to-text technologies. They can enable users to engage through voice commands, making them particularly valuable in hands-free environments and for enhancing accessibility. Notable examples in this space include Amazon's Alexa for Business, which can handle voice-activated tasks like booking meetings or retrieving business information. Google Dialogflow, integrated with Google Assistant, offers a platform for building voice-activated chatbots tailored to B2B needs.

Selecting the most suitable chatbot

Using Table 10.1, we can see different side-by-side comparisons of the main types of chatbots; one consideration is that typically the more sophisticated the chatbot the higher in price it'll be, but of course more sophisticated chatbots tend to provide better customer experience.

TABLE 10.1 Chatbot comparison

Chatbot type	Pros	Cons
Rule-based chatbots	– Simple to build and deploy – Predictable responses – Good for FAQs and lead qualification	– Limited flexibility – Can't handle complex queries – No learning or context understanding
Keyword recognition chatbots	– More flexible than rule-based bots – Can handle variations in questions – Easy to implement	– Struggles with complex or ambiguous queries – May miss intent if keywords aren't recognized
Menu-based chatbots	– Clear, structured flow for users – Easy to set up – Effective for content recommendation	– Limited interactivity – Frustrating for users with specific or complex questions
Contextual (NLP-based) chatbots	– Understands context and user intent – Personalized interactions – Handles complex queries	– Requires more advanced setup – May need training for optimal performance – Can be more expensive

(continued)

TABLE 10.1 (Continued)

Chatbot type	Pros	Cons
Hybrid	– Best of both worlds: AI efficiency with human fallback – Can handle complex queries with escalation – Ensures a seamless user experience	– Requires human support availability – More complex setup and integration – Higher cost due to human involvement
Voice-activated chatbots	– Hands-free, convenient – Great for accessibility and mobile users – Can engage users in real time	– Struggles with accents, noise or unclear speech – Limited use cases in some B2B environments – More complex to build

The first step in the process of implementation is to consider the focus of usage, e.g. whether this is about dealing with a simple query or queries that are repetitive or is this about dealing with more complex queries.

The following are the main use cases in B2B marketing of chatbots specifically; we've already mentioned some of the use cases at the start of this chapter, i.e. lead generation/lead capture, lead qualification, personalized recommendations, etc. Here are additional use cases.

- Customer support: AI chatbots provide instant, 24/7 support by answering frequently asked questions, resolving common issues and guiding users through troubleshooting processes.
- Appointment scheduling: AI chatbots help schedule meetings and demos by accessing calendars and setting up times that work for both the prospect and the sales team.
- Product demos and information: Chatbots offer personalized product demos or explain product features in detail, helping prospects make informed decisions without requiring human intervention.
- Post-purchase support: After a customer makes a purchase, chatbots assist with onboarding, answer product-related questions and provide training resources to ensure a smooth transition.
- Survey and feedback collection: Chatbots conduct surveys and collect customer feedback, enabling B2B companies to gather insights for improving products, services and customer experiences.

- Event registration: AI chatbots simplify the event registration process by answering questions about the event, capturing attendee information and sending confirmation details.

PUT INTO PRACTICE: SETTING UP AN AI CHATBOT

After the selection of the type of chatbot based on its role, one can decide on 'how' to implement. The following are the main steps for implementing an AI chatbot on a website page of the company (see Figure 10.3).

Step 1 – Define business objectives and use case: Establish the specific goals of the chatbot. Is it lead generation, product recommendations or event registration? For the goal, what is the specific role? In our case here we are looking at a product/solution understanding in lead generation.

Step 2 – Analyse and select the suitable web pages: In this step we review website analytics to understand visitor behaviour, bounce rates and time spent on various pages. Criteria we may use to select the web page might include:

a. Pages with high exit rates, indicating confusion or unanswered questions.
b. Pages with key conversion opportunities (like sign-ups, purchases or demos) where a chatbot could nudge users to take action.

Example: A pricing page may benefit from a chatbot that answers questions about different pricing plans and offers to schedule a demo.

Step 3 – Select the type of chatbot: Choose the appropriate chatbot type based on complexity and desired functionality.

- NLP-based: For understanding complex queries and delivering personalized responses.
- Hybrid: For more comprehensive support with human escalation.

One should consider if the chatbot is for lead qualification; a rule-based or keyword recognition bot may suffice, although customer experience may be impacted. Alternatively, if we were looking at both customer support and or an area of marketing an NLP-based or hybrid chatbot might be needed to handle a range of questions.

Step 4: Design the conversation flow and script: Create user-friendly, natural conversation scripts tailored to your business objectives.

Step 5: Customize, integrate and test the chatbot: Embed the chatbot on your site and connect it with CRM and analytics tools. Ensure the chatbot works smoothly and effectively across devices.

FIGURE 10.3 Steps for implementing a chatbot on ones's website

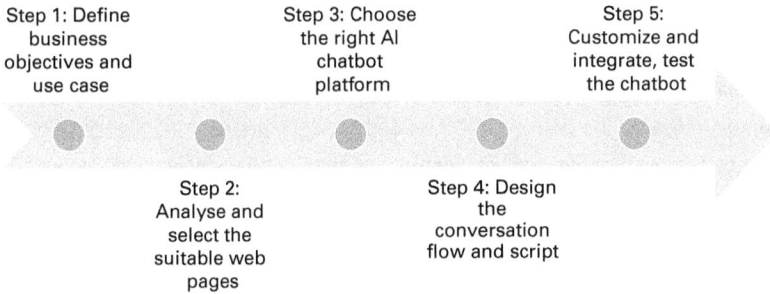
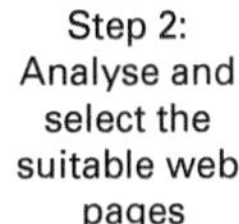
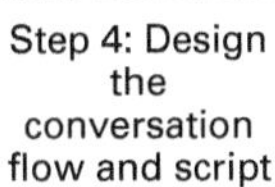

Step 3: Choose the right AI chatbot platform

OTHER AREAS OF LEAD GENERATION AND AI CONVERSATIONAL TECHNOLOGY

Let's explore the expanded applications of AI chatbots in lead generation, along with B2B marketing examples and relevant statistics.

Lead nurturing

AI chatbots are very suitable at automating lead nurturing by sending personalized follow-ups via emails or messages after initial conversations. This ensures consistent engagement throughout the customer journey.

Let's take the example of a software company implementing an AI chatbot that engages website visitors interested in their enterprise solution. After the initial interaction, the chatbot sends tailored follow-up emails based on the prospect's specific interests and pain points discussed during the chat. These emails might include relevant case studies, white papers or product demos.

Data collection and lead qualification

One can collect lead contact information, preferences and other data to qualify leads more effectively through AI chatbots. An example could be a manufacturing equipment supplier uses an AI chatbot to gather crucial information from potential clients. The chatbot asks about the prospect's industry, current equipment, production volume and budget. This data is then used to qualify leads and route them to the appropriate sales team.

Personalized content recommendations

AI chatbots can analyse user behaviour and preferences to recommend relevant content, nurturing leads through the sales funnel. For example, an IT services company uses an AI chatbot to guide visitors through its extensive resource library. Based on the visitor's interests and previous interactions, the chatbot suggests relevant white papers, webinars or case studies, increasing engagement and lead quality.

Automated appointment scheduling

The process of scheduling meetings or demos with sales representatives can be streamlined through AI chatbots, reducing friction in the lead generation process. A marketing automation platform employs an AI chatbot that can access the calendars of sales representatives. When a qualified lead expresses interest in a demo, the chatbot can instantly schedule a meeting based on mutual available calendar availability.

Qualifying leads

Lead generation chatbots can be used to collect particular information from leads. This can be done by setting up qualifying questions; before we continue let's define an MQL and SQL (sales qualified lead). An MQL is a marketing qualifying lead. In B2B we would typically go further than just defining a qualified as someone who has expressed an interest; we would also want to understand whether the lead is suitable or even a potential customer. We may also want to understand whether the prospect fits the criteria of an ideal target audience, e.g. an ideal customer profile.

So, in qualification we should set up questions for the following different areas.

- Qualifying stage of lead MQL vs SQL.
- Qualifying whether the MQL lead has intent to buy.
- Qualifying whether the MQL lead fits the ideal customer profile.
- If SQL qualifying whether there is a need or interest to talk to a salesperson.

PUT INTO PRACTICE: QUALIFYING THE STAGE OF MQL OR SQL

The following are possible questions we can use for this situation.

- 'Are you currently researching options or are you ready to take the next steps in purchasing?' Helps identify whether they are in the early discovery phase (MQL) or closer to purchasing (SQL).
- 'Have you already evaluated similar solutions or vendors in the market?' This reveals how far along they are in the buyer's journey.
- 'Do you need more information about our product or are you ready to discuss pricing or a demo?' Distinguishes between those still gathering information (MQL) and those ready to talk specifics (SQL).
- 'How soon are you looking to implement a solution?' A lead looking for a solution within a short timeframe might be closer to the SQL stage.

Qualifying whether there is an intent to buy

We might use the following questions to understand buyer intent. Here, the aim is to assess if the MQL has a genuine interest in purchasing or if they're just gathering information.

- 'What challenges are you looking to solve with this solution?' Helps to understand if they have a pressing need and whether your solution can solve it, indicating intent.
- 'Are you currently using any similar products or services, and are you looking to replace or upgrade them?' A lead that's actively looking to switch or upgrade may have stronger intent to buy.
- 'Do you have a timeline for when you'd like to make a decision?' A lead with a defined timeline is likely further down the buying journey and has serious intent.
- 'Who else will be involved in the decision-making process?' If they mention other stakeholders, it can indicate they are serious and moving forward with internal discussions.

Other more specific qualifying questions might relate to the quality /temperature of the lead in terms of right stakeholder, budget level, timing of need, e.g. an AI chatbot can start a conversation with a B2B prospect by asking to give a budget range or to provide a timing in terms of when something is needed and then according to the response can direct them to a sales person or continue to ask more qualifying questions.

Other considerations in setup

Defining your chatbot's tone of voice is crucial, and this process is closely tied to understanding your audience. The tone should align with your brand guidelines to ensure consistency in messaging and build trust among users. Another key aspect to consider is how to target your chatbot effectively. This involves deciding on which pages your lead generation chatbot should appear and determining the optimal moment for it to be triggered. You can fine-tune your targeting based on various factors, such as the specific page a visitor is viewing, their origin (previous page, campaign URL or traffic source), geographical location, device type (desktop, mobile or tablet) and the number of times they've visited your website. By carefully considering these elements, you can create a more personalized and relevant chatbot interaction, increasing its effectiveness in engaging visitors and achieving your business objectives.

Conversational/revenue assistants

AI revenue assistants and virtual assistants provide AI-driven services that help businesses perform specific tasks; they differ from chatbots as chatbots are generally more limited and specific in their capabilities. AI-based virtual assistants and AI-based revenue assistants are AI-powered tools designed to automate various tasks that traditionally require human involvement.

AI-based revenue assistants: capabilities

Main capabilities of AI-based revenue assistants are as follows.

- Automated outreach: AI-based virtual assistants can initiate contact with prospects through emails, chat or social media messages, following predefined scripts.
- AI-based conversations: Automates lead engagement through natural language conversations, primarily over email and SMS. It interacts with leads, responds to inquiries, asks questions and follows up, mimicking human interaction.

- Lead qualification: Qualifies leads by gathering information through conversation and determining whether the lead is ready to engage with the sales team.

Let's take a look at some of the specific features of AI revenue assistants.

AI-based meeting scheduling

These intelligent assistants can analyse the user's calendar, identify optimal meeting times and send invitations based on the availability of all parties involved. By understanding individual preferences, such as preferred meeting times or communication channels, the AI assistant can adapt and optimize the scheduling process without requiring manual input. This can significantly reduce administrative overhead and improve efficiency.

AI-based customer service

AI-powered virtual assistants are also used to automate customer service tasks by understanding user intent and context, which helps provide more accurate and relevant responses. These virtual assistants can interact with customers in real time, resolving inquiries or directing them to the appropriate resources. By continuously learning from previous interactions, AI chatbots improve their ability to handle complex queries and offer human-like conversational experiences, all while reducing response times. Examples include inbenta and Kore.ai.

AI-based sales automation

AI virtual assistants are increasingly used to automate sales processes by guiding potential customers through the sales journey and collecting key information that can later be used by sales teams for follow-up. These AI tools can engage prospects in personalized conversations, answer product-related questions and help qualify leads by analysing responses to tailored queries. With their learning capabilities, these AI assistants can continuously improve their understanding of customer behaviour and adapt their approach for greater sales success.

PUT INTO PRACTICE

Practical example 1

Lead qualification and enrichment: AI tools like Conversica engage with prospects and ask specific questions to qualify them as potential buyers. These questions might focus on their company size, budget, needs or decision-making timeline. Example of data relating to purchase readiness or pain points might be as follows.

- Purchase readiness: Time frame for purchase, budget and authority in decision-making.
- Pain points and needs: What challenges they are trying to solve.

Taking the example of the SaaS industry and a mid-level IT manager looking for a new cloud-based data security solution: After showing interest in a product through a website form, the AI chatbot reaches out to the IT manager. It asks questions like:

- 'What size is your IT team?'
- 'Are you looking for a solution immediately or within the next six months?'
- 'What's your estimated budget range?'
- 'What specific data security challenges are you facing?'

This interaction helps the company qualify the lead by collecting key information about the prospect's readiness to purchase and specific needs.

Practical example 2

Customer feedback and surveys

Take the situation of a product demo or purchase; after a product demo or purchase, an AI revenue assistant can send a follow-up message asking for feedback on the experience. This data can be used for improving the product or customer service.

The type of data collected might be as follows.

- Customer satisfaction ratings: Rating on a scale (e.g. 1–10).
- Qualitative feedback: Open-ended responses on what went well and what can be improved.
- Net Promoter Score (NPS): How likely the customer is to recommend the product.

- Customer pain points: Specific areas where the customer experienced problems.

Potential questions might be.

- 'On a scale of 1–10, how would you rate your overall experience?'
- 'What could we have done better to make your buying experience smoother?'
- 'How likely are you to recommend our product to a colleague?'
- 'Did the product meet your expectations in terms of quality?'

Challenges in implementing chatbots

Implementing AI chatbots presents several key challenges for B2B marketing including understanding NLPs, integration and the ongoing training of the chatbot itself.

One of the most significant hurdles is for chatbots to accurately interpret human language. This includes addressing ambiguities, handling various dialects and phrasing variations, understanding context, sarcasm and implied meanings, as well as processing slang, typos and abbreviations. Integration is another challenge; this can include integrating with existing business systems like CRMs and ERPs to ensure a consistent user experience.

Ongoing training and maintenance are also critical for the success of chatbots. Organizations must collect and curate training data continuously while updating the bot's knowledge base to reflect changes in user behaviour and expectations. Monitoring performance to fix errors and adapting conversational flows to feel natural are essential components of user experience optimization. Ensuring that chatbots maintain user attention without providing repetitive or irrelevant responses is crucial for engagement.

Finally, cost considerations can complicate the implementation process. Organizations must account for initial development or purchase costs, ongoing maintenance expenses and the potential need for human oversight to handle complex queries. By systematically addressing these challenges, organizations can successfully implement AI chatbots that enhance customer service and improve operational efficiency.

Limitations of AI conversational technology

In addition to the challenges mentioned above there are some other limitations of AI conversational technology.

One area is the functionality; AI assistants are often constrained in their functionality, they do well with routine tasks but struggle with complex or creative activities. Most cannot detect or respond appropriately to emotional cues, and their knowledge is limited to their training data, which may become outdated.

Another limitation is text-based limitations; AI revenue assistants tend to be mainly text-based and even those few that offer voice don't offer voice functionality at a reasonable quality.

AI assistants may record and store sensitive user information without explicit consent. The potential for data breaches or misuse of personal information remains a concern. Additionally, AI assistants lack the human touch, unable to fully replicate genuine emotional intelligence, empathy or the ability to build authentic rapport with users. They may also struggle with context-dependent decision-making.

Chatbots and GDPR

The use of AI chatbots and revenue assistants in B2B marketing raises several concerns regarding GDPR compliance. While many chatbot platforms claim GDPR compliance, the onus remains on organizations to ensure their implementation aligns with GDPR requirements.

There are various things which B2B marketers can do to ensure GDPR compliance while using such AI tools as follows:

- selecting GDPR-compliant platforms
- implementing clear consent mechanisms
- providing transparent information about data usage
- limiting data collection to what's essential
- regular reviews of data protection practices, staff training on GDPR requirements

Marketers should also stay informed about evolving AI regulations and adjust their practices accordingly. While achieving 100 per cent certainty of compliance may be challenging due to the complexity of GDPR and the rapidly evolving AI landscape, following these guidelines and working closely with legal and compliance teams can help B2B marketers strive for GDPR compliance in their use of AI chatbots.

Real-world example

IRON MOUNTAIN OVERCOMES LEAD ENGAGEMENT CHALLENGES

Iron Mountain is a global leader in information management services, specializing in secure storage, data protection and workflow automation. With a presence in over 60 countries, the company serves a diverse range of industries, helping businesses manage their critical information efficiently.

Iron Mountain faced significant obstacles in managing its marketing and sales processes. The company struggled with a growing backlog of unworked leads, particularly at the enterprise level. Many leads were left unattended due to shifts in account ownership, staff turnover or premature handoffs to Sales. Given that Iron Mountain's sales cycle often stretched six to eight months, the Sales team prioritized leads closer to conversion, leaving earlier-stage opportunities untouched.

The challenge intensified during the pandemic, which increased the number of touchpoints required to convert leads. The Sales team lacked the bandwidth to sift through dormant leads and identify high-potential prospects. To address this issue, Iron Mountain implemented Conversica's Revenue Digital Assistant™ in late 2021. This AI-driven tool helped reactivate dormant leads, engage post-event attendees and nurture early-stage inquiries through automated outreach. Through the integration of Conversica with salesforce CRM and the Eloqua Marketing Automation Platform, Iron Mountain established an always-on lead engagement process. Active leads were guided through Conversica-driven conversations for immediate nurturing, while less-engaged prospects entered passive nurture campaigns within Eloqua. When these leads re-engaged, they were funnelled back into Conversica for personalized follow-up, ensuring no prospect was left behind.

The results were significant. A notable example occurred in late 2023 when a dormant lead reactivated over Labor Day weekend while the Sales team was out of the office. Conversica's digital assistant maintained communication, answered questions and flagged the lead as 'hot'. When the sales rep returned on Tuesday, they quickly engaged the prospect, securing a $500,000 deal by the end of the week.[1, 2]

References

1 Conversica (2024) Iron Mountain revives dormant leads and closes $500K deal with Conversica, www.conversica.com/customers/iron-mountain (archived at https://perma.cc/VXW5-NTQL)

2 Wood, C (2024) How Iron Mountain implements conversational AI to drive engagement and revenue, MarTech, martech.org/how-iron-mountain-implements-conversational-ai-to-drive-engagement-and-revenue/ (archived at https://perma.cc/Q6QH-LUX9)

Further reading

Bloomreach (2025) Conversational AI: Everything you need to know, www.bloomreach.com/en/blog/conversational-ai-everything-you-need-to-know (archived at https://perma.cc/2L89-CXGD)

Google Cloud (n.d.) What is conversational AI: examples and benefits, cloud.google.com/conversational-ai (archived at https://perma.cc/8UTE-EZV7)

IBM (2021) Conversational AI, www.ibm.com/think/topics/conversational-ai (archived at https://perma.cc/DJY5-RW68)

11

B2B events and AI

What you will gain from this chapter

Understanding of the following:

- main AI use cases for B2B events
- how to use AI for event outline
- AI and event promotion
- AI for optimizing events on the day
- post-event marketing and AI

Introduction

A marketing event in B2B is an activity revolving around a themed display or presentation leveraging people engagement, either virtually (via webinars) or physically. Events can occur on- or offline and can be participated in, hosted or sponsored.

For the purposes of this chapter, we'll be focusing on mainly in-person and virtual events, with some reference to webinars.

Events trends

The main trends include the following shifts between in-person to virtual to hybrid events. In 2020/2021 we saw a large shift to virtual events due to Covid-19, and this virtual event usage is here to stay, i.e. 59 per cent of event professionals agree that virtual events are a permanent fixture of their event strategy.[1] Aside of this mega shift a majority of companies (61 per cent of companies) were also webinars as part of their events marketing.[2]

Since 2022 we've seen other trends such as the rise of hybrid events. Hybrid events combine in-person and virtual events as they cater for those that can physically attend as well as those that attend remotely.

Types of events

B2B events can be categorized under online and virtual events, and in-person events.

The main types of in-person events are physical trade shows, networking dinners and in-person first party events.

Events data capture

Capturing data prior to the event relates to capturing data about customers who are more likely to attend; where the event is intended to be split by region, the data can be used to understand customer location and invite according to a maximum distance surrounding the event.

Data can be captured during the event by collecting attendance contact details as well as forms for attendees to fill out to understand audience view of presentations. Today this is captured through online event-based forums where audience share comments and inputs about the event.

After the event, data can be captured around the audience rating the event overall, rating speakers, event content and generally capturing feedback as to what can be changed or adapted should the event be repeated.

Data capture at virtual and online events

One major advantage of virtual events and webinars is that you can get a wealth of data from analytics. If you're using a virtual events platform, you can measure each of the aspects of the virtual event such as speakers, networking event, sponsors and chat. The main aspects you can measure are:

- Dwell Time - This metric tells you how long an individual spent in a session.
- Average Content and Presenter Ratings: These tell you how attendees rate the speaker and the content.
- Attendance per session: This metric tells you how many attended each session.

- Chat message: This measures average chat messages per attendee.
- Demographic/Firmographic Data: This provides an overview of level, role, industry, of attendees across the event.

Areas of events marketing

The main areas of events marketing can be broken into the following sub-activities.

- Planning and preparing: Goal setting, target audience identification, identifying themes for the events, promoting events, developing content, determining the event format (conference, seminar, exhibition, etc.), creating a detailed event timeline.
- During event activities include the following activities: Conducting polls, engaging in conversations and lead capture.
- Post-event activities include the following main activities: Research, gathering feedback, lead capture, measuring events ROI, data analysis.

According to the main areas of events we can also see how AI tools and technologies are used, e.g. across pre-event, ongoing and post-event as can be seen in Figure 11.1.

Pre-event planning

If we look at the main areas of events marketing, we can also map the AI role, activity and tool; you'll find a summary in Table 11.1.

TABLE 11.1 AI for events marketing

Event enhancement aspect	AI tools type	Examples of AI tools
Personalized recommendations	Machine learning algorithms	Grip, Brella
Attendee assistance (chatbots)	Natural language processing (NLP)	Drift, Zendesk, HubSpot Chatbot
Real-time polls and Q&A	Sentiment analysis, NLP	Slido, Pigeonhole Live
Networking and matchmaking	Machine learning, predictive analytics	Brella, Grip
Content engagement insights	Data analytics	Pathable, Hopin

FIGURE 11.1 Areas of event marketing – pre, ongoing, post or other and AI

Phases	Pre-event	Ongoing	Post event
Activities	Audience analysis Event theme ideation Event agenda creation Personalized marketing and outreach	AI chatbots to help attendees with queries Live translations & transcriptions Audience engagement & sentiment analysis Smart matchmaking & networking	Event data analysis & reporting Content curation & on-demand access Automated follow-ups & lead nurturing Predictive analytics for future events

In pre-event planning AI can play a role of supporting target audience analysis; tools which can be used include salesforce Einstein. AI tools can be used to analyse customer data such as firmographics, preferences and other characteristics to identify optimum customers. AI can also play a role in identifying optimum location for the in-person event; tools like ArcGIS and Google maps can be used. Such tools can analyse location data of potential attendees and customers to determine the most optimal event location based on accessibility, proximity and target market concentration.

AI tools can also be used to tailor marketing campaigns as well as for predictive lead scoring. Through tools such as Infer and Demand base lead data can be analysed to predict likelihood of conversion and therefore outbound prospect efforts can be prioritized.

Let's take a look at the main areas of pre-event planning in more detail.

Identifying event themes

Just as with blog creation mentioned in previous chapters, we can use NLP/ML tools like ChatGPT to come up with themes for events.

Generating event agendas

One can also use AI tools like ChatGPT to generate event outlines; this can be done in different ways; one way is to input a previous event agenda and ask for it to product an update to the agenda based on more recent trends.

Another way might be just simply to ask it to prepare an event agenda but highlight various parameters such as overall length of event, length and timing of each session and whether any of the event topics are running in parallel.

PUT INTO PRACTICE

Let's start to create an event outline by using the following prompt: *Please provide an event outline for a three-hour in-person event focused on the challenges of identifying flexible workplace solutions; please consider the first hour is for the keynote speech and the subsequent two hours will have two parallel content streams.*

Event outline: navigating the flexible workplace landscape

Event goals:

- Provide insights into the challenges of implementing flexible workplace solutions.

- Explore best practices for creating effective flexible work environments.
- Foster discussion and networking among industry professionals.

Target audience:

- HR professionals
- facilities managers
- business leaders
- workplace strategists

Event structure

Morning session (9:00 am - 12:00 pm)

9:00–10:00 am: Keynote address: The Future of Work: A Flexible Perspective

- A thought-provoking presentation on the evolving nature of work and the importance of flexible workplace solutions.

10:00–12:00 pm: Parallel content streams

Stream A: Technology and tools for flexible work

- **10:00–10:30 am: The role of technology in enabling flexible work**
  - Explore the latest technological advancements that support flexible work arrangements.
- **10:30–11:00 am: Case study – leveraging technology for successful flexible work**
  - A detailed case study showcasing a company that has effectively used technology to facilitate flexible work.
- **11:00–12:00 pm: Q&A session**

We can also look at other aspects for the event outline and extend the prompt to ask for more details based on more input into the event is about.

Prompt: *Assume there is a three-hour event taking place titled 'Identifying flexible workplace solutions*. The conference will include sessions on the latest trends working in flexible workplace solutions, the industry's future, the challenges and limitations, new research and how AI can be used. Create a table for the agenda of this event with the following columns: time bracket, session title and session description.

Creating promotional emails for the event

One can use AI to help create very specific promotional emails for an event, e.g. by describing the event, event details and other specifics such as intended audiences. Through AI machine learning tools one can also come up with a promotional roadmap for the event in terms of email types and email themes in the lead up to the event.

> PUT INTO PRACTICE
>
> Prompt: *Create an introduction email for a trade show happening in three months' time taking place in London; the target of the event is purchase managers looking to purchase healthcare equipment for hospitals.*
>
> Response: 'Dear [Recipient's Name], I hope this message finds you well. I am excited to announce that [Your Company Name] will be exhibiting at the upcoming Healthcare Equipment Trade Show in London, taking place in three months on [specific dates]. This event is a fantastic opportunity for purchase managers like yourself to explore the latest innovations in healthcare equipment tailored for hospitals.
>
> Follow-up prompt: *Please provide suggestions of five types of email one could send in the three months leading up to the event describe described above.*

Matching attendees to sessions

AI tools can be used at large events to enhance the attendee experience by providing tailored recommendations for sessions, meetings and networking opportunities. By analysing attendee data, such as professional backgrounds, interests and other relevant information, AI-powered systems can suggest specific sessions that align with each individual's preferences. The AI tools can also take into account behaviour patterns, such as which sessions or topics attendees engage with the most, to refine and improve their suggestions over time. Additionally, the technology can help attendees discover networking zones or potential meetings with others who share similar interests or professional goals, further enhancing the value of their participation.

For example, platforms like Grip, Swapcard and Glue Up have integrated AI matchmaking features that can automatically recommend optimal matches based on the data collected about each attendee. These platforms analyse attendee profiles, preferences and behaviours to suggest the most relevant sessions, speakers and other event activities. By offering personalized session recommendations, they ensure that attendees can maximize the value of their time at the event, ensuring they don't miss out on opportunities that align with their goals and interests. Whether it's recommending a networking opportunity or highlighting a session on a trending topic, AI matchmaking systems enhance the overall event experience, fostering greater engagement and satisfaction.

AI-powered chatbots for real-time attendee support and FAQs

Consider an event where one can have access to all critical information event timetables, speaker info, FAQs etc.; this is where AI chatbots can add real value to events. AI-based chatbots can deal with all types of questions.

Creating presentations

AI tools can significantly improve the ability and optimize time in webinars and event presentations by helping across all stages of the presentation content creation process, i.e. ideation, outline, scripts, slide decks themselves. Typically, one would need to use a combination of AI tools for the different stages, let's take a look at two main stages.

- Automated script writing: AI-powered writing tools like ChatGPT can help craft engaging scripts for webinars and events. By analysing the topic, audience and objectives, AI can generate personalized and relevant content that aligns with the event's goals. These tools can assist in drafting introductions, key points and conclusions, ensuring that the script flows smoothly and is tailored to the audience's needs.
- Presentation design and visuals: AI software can automate the presentation slides creation itself. Such tools include features such as suggested templates, design elements and suggested visuals. AI can also assist in selecting relevant images, icons and infographics that enhance the overall impact of the presentation. Examples of AI tools include Canva and Beautiful.ai.

We can also see in Figure 11.2 where and how AI-based presentation can be used in events.

FIGURE 11.2 AI-based presentations and events

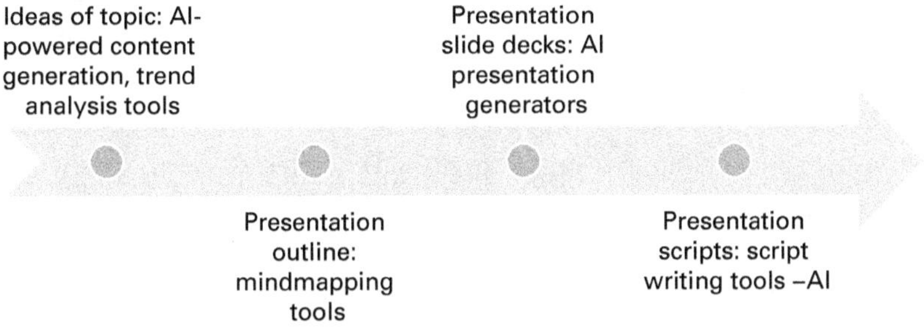

Predictive analytics for attendee engagement and participation

When discussing virtual, hybrid or in-person events, event data can include data such as attendees, engagement, social media coverage and interaction, the impact of event marketing material and many other aspects. Through using predictive analytics from past events and in using past attendees' data, one can make predictions which inform the improvement of future events.

Below are key areas where predictive analytics could be used for events.

1. ATTENDANCE AND ENGAGEMENT PREDICTION

By analysing attendance patterns and engagement metrics, such as participation rates, session drop-offs and audience feedback, one can identify which types of sessions, topics or speakers lead to higher attendance and engagement.

2. AUDIENCE PREFERENCES AND PERSONALIZATION

This involves evaluating which sessions or speakers received the most positive feedback and which event formats were most popular (e.g. panel discussions vs interactive workshops). Through this area of predictive analytics, content can be better tailored to delegate interests; and other aspects of the event can be better personalized.

3. PREDICTING NO-SHOW RATES

Using historical data to understand patterns of registration and actual attendance, including cancellations, organizers can identify no-show risks, enabling them to offer incentives for early attendance, or implement overbooking strategies to optimize participation and revenue.

4. SPONSOR AND EXHIBITOR ROI OPTIMIZATION

Analysing metrics related to exhibitor booth visits, sponsor session attendance and lead generation success during previous events. Predictive analytics can provide insights into which sponsors and exhibitors achieved high ROI. This helps event organizers optimize the layout of exhibitor booths and customize sponsorship packages to provide higher value to partners in future events.

5. CONTENT EFFECTIVENESS AND SPEAKER IMPACT

Reviewing the past performance of different speakers, topics and content formats in terms of attendee ratings, Q&A participation and social media mentions. Can determine which speakers or content formats lead to the highest engagement and satisfaction levels. This information can be used to select better speakers and refine the type of content offered.

During events

We're now going to turn our attention to the use of AI technology during events.

Chatbots and virtual assistants

AI chatbots can also be used for the following main situations during the day of the event itself.

- Instant attendee support and FAQs: AI chatbots can provide real-time support to attendees by answering common questions related to the event, such as session schedules, speaker details, room locations and other logistical inquiries. This allows event organizers to focus on other tasks while attendees receive quick, accurate information at their fingertips. These chatbots can be integrated into event apps or websites, ensuring easy access for all attendees.
- Session recommendations and personalization: AI conversational assistants can analyse attendee data and preferences to recommend specific sessions, workshops or panels tailored to their interests and professional goals. For example, an AI assistant can suggest a session on marketing automation to an attendee from a digital marketing agency, ensuring they have a personalized and valuable experience.

- Networking facilitation: AI chatbots can facilitate networking opportunities by suggesting potential connections based on attendees' professional profiles, business needs and interests. The AI assistant can send messages introducing attendees to each other, schedule virtual or in-person meetings, and suggest networking zones or activities where they might find useful business contacts.

Enhanced engagement interactive features

Incorporating real-time polls and Q&A during sessions is another good approach for boosting engagement. Sentiment analysis and NLP tools using AI can assess attendee sentiment allowing speakers to adjust their presentation style or content based on immediate feedback. For example, using tools like Slido and Pigeonhole Live, attendees can ask questions or vote in polls, making sessions more interactive.

With in-person events, polling can be done via mobile devices or dedicated kiosks; while in virtual and hybrid events, polls can be seamlessly integrated into the event platform, allowing for quick and easy responses.

In virtual environments, polls can be displayed prominently in the user interface to capture attendee attention; while in hybrid events, both physical and digital attendees should be given equal opportunities to participate. This helps bridge the gap between in-person and virtual experiences, ensuring inclusivity for all participants.

Automated transcription and translation of event sessions

AI transcription is about converting speech to text. Previously, humans would transcribe speech to text; now AI transcription makes this activity more manageable and easier thanks to more accurate transcription technology. AI-enabled automated transcription and translation can be powerful tools for event organizers and marketers as they allow for quick transcription of verbal content, sometimes even into multiple languages in one go.

Examples of automated transcription tools include Otter.ai, Rev and Sonix that offer real-time transcription services, converting spoken words during event sessions into written text. These tools leverage advanced speech recognition algorithms to transcribe presentations, panel discussions and Q&A sessions with remarkable accuracy. Other benefits of AI transcription tools are they can make events more accessible to people speaking different languages; the ability to offer real-time translation means attendees can have real-time translations; also, attendees can choose their preferred language for the day. Aside from the language barrier issue, transcription tools also mean those with hearing impairments can attend events.

Real-time feedback during the event

AI technologies can gather real-time feedback from attendees, analysing their behaviour, digital interactions and other data; as a result such tools are able to provide immediate insights allowing event organizers to make adjustments to parts of the event during the event. Examples of tools one can use include Poll Everywhere, Gliss and Mentimeter.

Examples of where feedback during the event can be used:

- Live transcription: Use AI to transcribe comments from live Q&A sessions or discussions.
- Sentiment analysis: Analyse the transcribed comments to identify key themes and sentiment.
- Dynamic survey updates: Incorporate the most common themes or concerns from the comments into a live survey, allowing attendees to provide more detailed feedback.
- Real-time insights: Analyse the survey responses and comments in real time to identify emerging trends or issues.

Post event

After the day of the event itself AI tools also can be used in different ways in the post event phase; below are some of the main areas.

One area of AI usage post event is through automated feedback analysis; AI tools can rapidly sort and categorize survey responses, providing actionable insights faster than manual analysis; as a result, organizers are able to identify comment themes and understand where to improve an event.

Another area is that of sentiment analysis where event-related social media posts, comments and other text-based feedback can be analysed to gauge overall attendee sentiment; this provides a nuanced understanding of how attendees felt about different aspects of the event.

Content summarization

AI can analyse video recordings and transcripts to create concise summaries of event sessions; summaries can be used for post-event summary pages on a company's website, for social media posts, for detailed reports or other post event content and communications.

Examples of tools include Rev.com and Otter.ai which can transcribe audio and video recordings and generate summaries; they are suitable for both in-person and virtual events. For video editing and video summaries one can use Descript and AssemblyAI; it also offers AI-powered transcription and summarization features. It's particularly useful for summarizing video content from events.

Video highlight generation

AI-powered tools can analyse video footage to extract key moments and create engaging event highlights or trailers. This repurposed content can be used for marketing future events or providing value to those who couldn't attend.

Examples of AI tools include Amazon Rekognition Video which can analyse videos to detect objects, scenes and faces. It can be used to identify specific people or objects in event videos and extract relevant clips. Another AI tool is Google Cloud Video Intelligence which uses AI to analyse videos and extract insights. It can be used to identify key moments in event videos, such as speeches, Q&A sessions or product demonstrations.

Automated content tagging

Automated content tagging powered by AI is a powerful feature and/or tool for B2B marketers, particularly in the context of both in-person and virtual events. By analysing various types of event content such as video, audio and text AI can automatically assign relevant tags or keywords. This enables B2B marketers to easily access specific topics, speakers or sessions later on, streamlining content management, improving searchability and enhancing post-event engagement.

Several AI features make content tagging both accurate and efficient, providing valuable insights and enhancing the overall event experience.

1. IMAGE AND VIDEO ANALYSIS

AI tools can analyse video and image content to identify key visual elements, which significantly aids in organizing and tagging event footage. For instance, object recognition can identify and tag specific items such as event logos, speakers or even products featured during a presentation. This is particularly useful for B2B marketers who want to track specific brand mentions, products or key participants.

2. TRANSCRIPTION

AI-powered transcription tools can convert speech from videos or live sessions into text in real time. This process is valuable for both in-person and virtual events, as it enables the creation of searchable transcripts for all spoken content. These transcripts allow marketers to quickly locate specific points made by speakers or discussions about relevant topics, which can be used for post-event content repurposing, like blog posts, summaries or white papers.

3. KEYWORD EXTRACTION

Natural language processing (NLP) algorithms are essential for identifying important terms and phrases in event content. By analysing the text from transcriptions, chat logs or written materials shared during the event, AI can pinpoint key topics, themes or speaker names that can then be used to tag content. For B2B marketers, this functionality can help categorize content based on industry-specific trends or topics of interest, allowing them to quickly identify material that resonates most with their target audience.

4. METADATA EXTRACTION

AI can also extract valuable metadata, such as timestamps, file names or location information, from event content. This metadata adds additional context to the content, which can be helpful when organizing large volumes of video, audio or written materials. For example, metadata can be used to tag content based on the exact time or location of a session, allowing B2B marketers to target very specific moments within an event that might be of particular interest to their audience.

AI TOOLS FOR AUTOMATED CONTENT TAGGING

Several AI tools are available to support automated content tagging, offering powerful capabilities for B2B marketers looking to enhance their event content management. Popular tools include Amazon Rekognition, Google Cloud Vision API and Microsoft Azure Computer Vision. These platforms provide image and video analysis tools that can automatically detect objects, recognize faces, extract text from images and categorize content based on pre-set keywords. By leveraging these tools, event organizers and B2B marketers can efficiently manage, analyse and retrieve content for post-event marketing campaigns, sales enablement and audience engagement.

Personalized follow-up emails

By analysing attendee behaviour and engagement data, AI can help craft personalized follow-up emails for each participant, ensuring that the message resonates with their unique experiences and needs. Personalized follow-ups not only increase attendee engagement but also boost the chances of generating valuable post-event interactions, such as lead conversions or content sharing. Below are four examples of different situations and types of audiences for personalized B2B event follow-up emails:

1. POST-EVENT SURVEY REMINDERS FOR UNRESPONSIVE ATTENDEES

For attendees who haven't yet completed a post-event survey, AI can send a gentle yet personalized reminder, increasing the likelihood of receiving feedback. By reviewing attendee participation and engagement levels during the event, the system can craft an email that reflects their session interests, nudging them to share their opinions. For instance, the email could say:

> Hi [First Name], we noticed you attended [Session Name], and we'd love to hear your thoughts! Your feedback will help us improve future events and make sure we're offering the most valuable content to professionals like you. Please take a moment to fill out our short survey. It only takes a few minutes, and your input is invaluable to us.

2. THANK YOU EMAIL FOR ATTENDEES WITH POSITIVE FEEDBACK

If an attendee has provided positive feedback, AI can generate a thoughtful follow-up email those thanks them for their input while highlighting their specific feedback. This personalized communication shows appreciation and strengthens the relationship with the attendee, turning them into an advocate for future events.

3. FOLLOW-UP FOR PROSPECTIVE LEADS POST-EVENT

For prospective leads who attended sessions related to your product or service, AI can send a tailored follow-up email with additional resources, such as case studies, product demos or an invitation for a one-on-one meeting. These emails are based on the specific sessions attended, ensuring the content is highly relevant.

4. FOLLOW-UP FOR ATTENDEES WITH SPECIFIC CONCERNS OR QUESTIONS

For attendees who voiced specific concerns or had questions during the event, AI can generate a personalized follow-up that addresses their concerns in a thoughtful and solution-oriented manner. This type of follow-up shows that their issues were heard and that the company is committed to providing value.

Using AI to gamify events

B2B gamification has become an increasingly popular way to enhance engagement and create memorable experiences at both in-person and virtual events. In the area of gamification one can use tools like TensorFlow which is an open-source machine learning framework that can be used to build custom AI models for various applications, including event gamification.

- **Interactive quizzes and games:** One can use AI tools to create quizzes and games which test attendees' knowledge and understanding of themes and topics discussed at events; AI can also go further to adapt quizzes and difficulty levels based on individuals and their performance.
- **Augmented reality (AR):** AR can enhance events by incorporating interactive elements like product demos or virtual tours. AI can be used to create realistic AR experiences that engage attendees.
- **Attendee data for gamification experiences:** One can use AI to analyse attendee profiles and create tailored gamification experiences based on individual interests and goals; AI can also be used to dynamically adjust challenges and rewards based on attendee behaviour and engagement levels.

AI and virtual events

Specifically, now turning to virtual events and virtual events software, we can look at how AI is used and how this may differ from in-person events; AI typically is more embedded into virtual events software; for example, virtual events software will include most of the following features:

- attendee matchmaking and networking recommendations
- personalized content suggestions

FIGURE 11.3 Event gamification

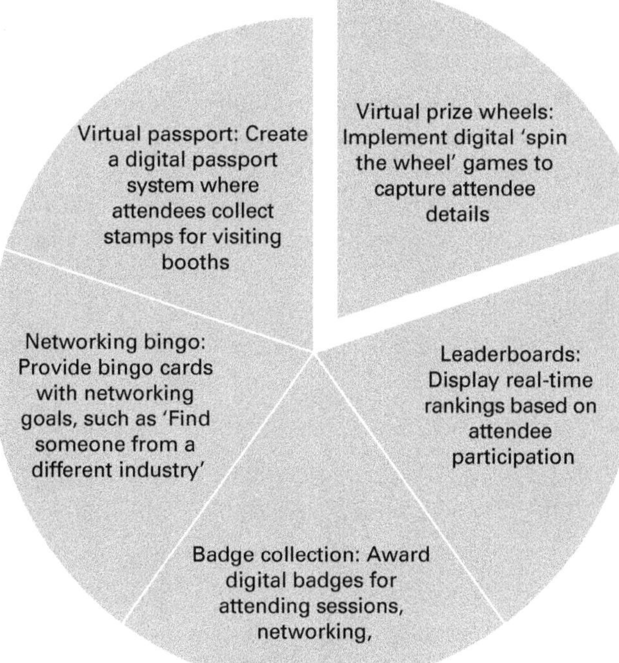

- AI-driven analytics for measuring event performance
- real-time translation and transcription
- personalized agenda recommendations

Examples of virtual events tools which incorporate most of these features include Hopin, Events, Hubilo and StreamAlive.

References

1 Bizzabo (2020) 2021 Event marketing statistics, trends, and data, Bizzabo, www.bizzabo.com/blog/event-marketing-statistics (archived at https://perma.cc/ER7M-PSVU)

2 Salvatori, H. (2025) 42 Webinar Statistics You Need to know in 2025, Cvent Blog, www.cvent.com/en/blog/events/webinar-statistics (archived at https://perma.cc/T5RQ-DMWC)

Further reading

Hire Space (n.d.) Exploring AI's impact on events: A comprehensive guide for event organisers, hirespace.com/blog/the-impact-of-ai-on-events (archived at https://perma.cc/DGN5-E2JL)

prasadGSI (2023) Role of predictive analytics for seamless event management in 2023, www.gevme.com/en/blog/predictive-analysis-in-ai-for-event-management/ (archived at https://perma.cc/9SGW-X7VS)

York, A (2023) 9 AI tools for smoother event management in 2023, ClickUp, clickup.com/blog/ai-tools-for-event-management/ (archived at https://perma.cc/59JD-HP68)

12

AI for customer retention marketing

What you will gain from this chapter

Understanding of the following:

- how to identify customer churn
- using AI to prevent customer churn
- learn about cross selling and upselling
- AI for business development

Introduction

Why the focus on retention marketing?

Customer retention marketing refers to actions, activities and strategies leveraged by marketing to look after existing customers.

Existing customers are easier to target and probably easier to engage. Existing customers are also probably quicker to generate business and profitable business when we think that in most cases the very first purchase is a fraction of their potential purchase possibilities and compared to what they typically spend in the subsequent purchases.

The role of AI in retention marketing

AI tools and technologies can also be invaluable in the retention space. One can use AI tools to predict the next best sale or opportunity, for identifying which customers are more likely to churn or even for predicting overall churn rate from a range of customers.

In the area of loyalty programmes, AI can help business create more targeted and effective B2B loyalty programmes through analysing various online and purchase behaviours of customers as well as identifying better reward structures. AI can also be integrated into CRM tools to enrich existing data and provide more actionable insights.

In the area of personalization marketing, existing customers tend to demand more tailored experiences than prospective customers and so AI can help provide tailored content via NLP/ML tools, more personalized interactions via AI chatbots, tailored interactions and timelier interactions.

Customer churn

It costs much more to acquire customers than to sell to existing customers, yet customers still lapse, often for no good reason. So, what if we can predict the lapsing of customers and use that information to do something about it?

Let's first define lapsing; this is when customers stop doing business with you for whatever reason, essentially they are no longer happy with you. This lapsing of customers is also known as customer churn, customer attrition, customer defection, lapsing, etc.

Why do customers lapse?

Customers can lapse for different reasons, e.g. failing to deliver to an original need; the onboarding process was less than optimal; the product wasn't up to standard; the customers' needs changed; the customer no longer had funding to continue to purchase; competition intercepted and were able to offer better conditions, and or a better product, etc. Understanding a bit of context as to why customers lapse can go a long way to improve chances of re-engaging them as well as re-acquiring them.

What are the signals for identifying churn?

One of the ways to think about decreasing churn is to have a set of signals or indicators which could indicate less engagement or signs which lead to a customer lapsing. These leading indicators of customer churn are basically signals which tell us in advance if a customer is likely to churn. Examples of leading indicators might include decreased time on web pages or on the website overall, reduced purchases, reduced frequency of purchases and reduction in number of emails opened and clicked on. Other leading indicators might be product usage patterns and changes within an account.

Predictive analytics

Identification of churn AI can involve different types of AI implementation; this can be through predictive analytics where customer data is analysed in order to predict likelihood of customers to lapse. As a result of the data analysis, business can then pinpoint those customers more likely to leave and include these in sales and marketing outreach activities.

In the area of predictive analytics, data is collected such as behavioural data, revenue data, purchase frequency data and digital behavioural data. Once collected, AI technologies use machine learning algorithms to analyse the cross section of data and identify signals early on which highlight churn potential. Such insights can also be then integrated into targeted marketing campaigns which accommodate and focus on different messaging and content for different churn signals.

Examples of signals and suitable marketing activities might be as follows.

Churn Signal 1: Decreased engagement – in this case signals might be reduced website visits, email opens or product usage. Corresponding follow-up activities might be personalizing outreach with tailored content, such as product tutorials or case studies relevant to their specific needs.

Churn Signal 2: Increased support tickets – signals might be a rise in support inquiries or complaints. An appropriate marketing activity might be to conduct a thorough investigation of the issues and offer proactive solutions to address customer concerns.

Churn Signal 3: Negative sentiment – signals could be negative feedback in surveys, social media or support interactions. A suitable marketing activity could be to reach out directly to the customer to understand the root cause of their dissatisfaction and offer personalized solutions or compensation.

There are a number of different AI tools one can use to predict churn through predictive analytics; these include mParticle (a CDP platform), Custify (described as a customer success platform) and Pecan AI.

Beyond predictive analytics

Outside of predictive analytics tools, there are other AI tools which can be used to predict customer attrition.

Sentiment analysis tools are an area of AI tools which can be used to analyse customer feedback from surveys and social media. This analysis can bring to light insights relating to customer experience as well as potential indicators of churn.

A second area of AI tools are machine learning tools such as Google Cloud AutoML, which can group customers based on similar characteristics to identify high-risk segments and tailor retention efforts accordingly.

Finally, one can also use tools such as OpenAI Gym and Ray RLlib which use reinforcement learning algorithms to recommend products or services that are tailored to each customer's individual needs and preferences, increasing engagement and reducing churn.[1]

Code-free predictive analytics

As marketers we probably don't have skills for coding or knowledge of using code-based platforms, and this is where code-free predictive analytics becomes really interesting. An example of a code-free predictive analytics tool is PredictEasy. Code-free or no-code AI software means businesses are able to avail of predictive analytics without all the training or technical expertise; tools can be adopted by multiple departments so sharing is more possible.

No-code AI predictive analytics also allows for quicker building of predictive AI models; such tools typically include templates or pre-existing models which one can build from and/or drag and drop features thus reducing development time. Aside of not needing time and people for such activities, costs can be reduced through no-code AI. Development costs are significantly reduced, which makes such technologies ideal for small and medium-sized businesses.

Cross-selling and upselling – development

Marketing for business development is about identifying customers and accounts for growth opportunities. One of the bigger challenges is knowing how to use digital marketing and technologies to support the business or develop customers' businesses. The first step comes down to understanding your customers first and understanding differences using CRM, data analytics and digital technologies.

Cross-sell, upsell

When we think about developing business with customers, we can boil this down to cross-selling and upselling; cross-selling is the action or practice of selling an additional product or service to an existing customer. Upselling is a sales technique where a seller induces the customer to purchase more expensive items, upgrades or other add-ons to make a more profitable sale. Development of customers can follow three different paths: (1) selling to a higher margin products or products, (2) selling a wider range of products in general or (3) a mix of '1' and '2'.

Non-AI methods for identifying opportunities for next sales

There are different non-AI approaches and techniques we can use to understand customers and identify the best opportunities for developing business; these include use of Google Analytics, identifying gaps in a customer's portfolio, understanding buying power potential and understanding share of wallet. These are summarized in Figure 12.1.

AI for identifying business development opportunities

We can use AI in different ways for supporting business development; areas of business development relate to how we can identify areas to grow business through product associations or to gain clues for next best purchase, most likely purchases as well as predicting better timing of next purchases.

Product combinations

AI tools can detect common product combinations frequently purchased together which point to cross-selling patterns. For example, imagine that a B2B customer frequently purchases a number of notebooks together with printers. The AI tool or feature might identify that customers who buy notebooks also often purchase printer ink and paper; using this insight, marketing can then offer printer ink and paper as an upsell when a customer purchases a notebook.

Often-viewed products

AI tools can identify products most frequently viewed by customers, providing valuable insights into upsell opportunities. Machine learning tools including features such as collaborative filtering, and predictive analytics can analyse customer behaviour, including product views, purchases and browsing patterns. For example, a customer who views several high-end

FIGURE 12.1 Methods for identifying business opportunities

notebooks and accessories but ultimately purchases a basic model might indicate interest in premium products. AI tools like TensorFlow, Amazon Personalize or Scikit-Learn can model this data to generate actionable insights. Marketing teams can then use this information to recommend the higher-end models or the accessories that the customer previously viewed, positioning them as potential upsell options.

Timing of purchases

One can also analyse the timing of purchases to identify patterns and trends. Using a time series analysis of a motorsports company buying IT equipment as an example, if the company typically purchases data storage solutions after major races or events, this might indicate a seasonal demand. Other examples of purchase behaviours and purchase patterns that could be identified relating to a motorsports company and the purchase of IT equipment can be found in Figure 12.2.

Intent data for development of accounts

We've discussed intent data earlier on in this book for identifying customer journeys; AI intent data analysis tools such as Bombora can also identify intent for future sales opportunities. By analysing intent data, businesses can pinpoint companies or individuals actively researching products or services they offer. This involves tracking digital footprints such as website visits, keyword searches, content downloads or engagement with online ads. For instance, if a potential customer is repeatedly visiting pages related to a specific product category, it signals interest or need. Tools like Bombora, 6sense or ZoomInfo leverage machine learning to identify these patterns, helping businesses uncover prospects earlier in the buying journey.

Intent data enables businesses to create marketing messages that are highly relevant and resonate with the unique needs of potential customers. By understanding the specific products or services a customer is researching, businesses can craft personalized email campaigns, ads or content that directly address those interests.

Intent data helps sales teams prioritize leads that are most likely to convert, saving time and resources. By analysing behavioural signals, such as frequent visits to pricing pages or repeated webinar attendance, sales teams can identify prospects who are closer to making a purchase decision. Platforms like Outreach or Salesloft, combined with intent analysis, allow sales teams to focus their efforts on these high probability leads.

The following are some examples in practice of how intent data can be used.

- Software purchase: If a company is researching cloud-based CRM software, intent data can reveal their interest in related products like customer support software or marketing automation tools.
- Hardware purchase: If a company is looking for new servers, intent data can indicate their need for additional storage solutions or network upgrades.
- Services purchase: If a company is exploring consulting services, intent data can reveal their specific areas of interest, such as digital marketing or HR consulting.
- Subscription purchase: If a company is considering a subscription-based service, intent data can indicate their budget and preferences for features and pricing.

Customer loyalty

Across this chapter and the last chapter most of what we've been covering should also go to improve customer loyalty in general. Customer loyalty can be understood as the gravitational pull a company has on a customer, or the

FIGURE 12.2 Purchase patterns and behaviours

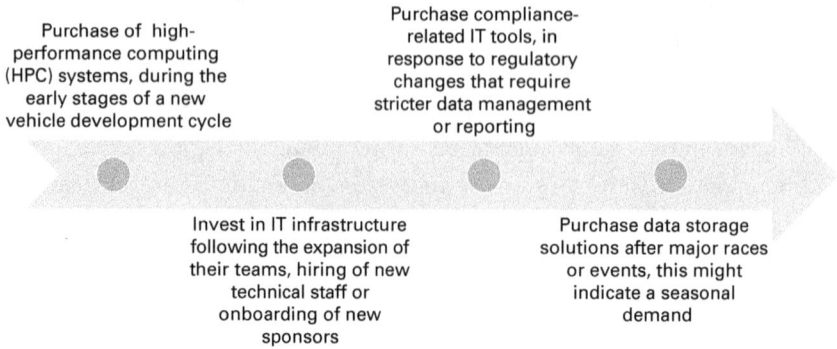

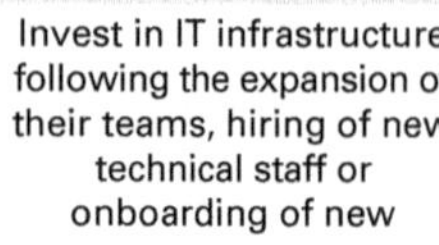

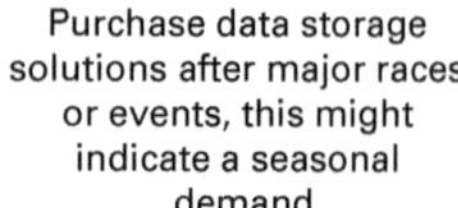

Purchase of high-performance computing (HPC) systems, during the early stages of a new vehicle development cycle
Purchase compliance-related IT tools, in response to regulatory changes that require stricter data management or reporting

Invest in IT infrastructure following the expansion of their teams, hiring of new technical staff or onboarding of new sponsors

bond or attachment a customer has for a company or brand. Customer loyalty can be shaped by many things including sales engagement, salespeople, customer services, operations and both direct and indirect marketing.

When we think of elements that impact our loyalty, a lot of those elements are influenced directly or indirectly by marketing. The following are the main areas where AI tools and technology can help with customer loyalty and improve loyalty are as follows:

1 Personalization at scale: AI tools can significantly enhance customer loyalty by enabling businesses to personalize interactions and offerings at scale.
2 Predictive analytics for customer retention: AI-powered predictive analytics can identify early warning signs of customer churn, allowing businesses to intervene before it's too late. By analysing patterns such as a decline in purchase frequency, reduced engagement with marketing emails or negative sentiment in support interactions, tools like Gainsight can predict which customers are at risk of leaving.
3 Enhancing customer support with AI chatbots: AI chatbots and virtual assistants play a critical role in improving customer loyalty by delivering fast and efficient support.
4 Loyalty programme optimization: AI technology can optimize customer loyalty programmes by making them more engaging and effective. Using tools like Antavo or Punchh, businesses can analyse customer data to design reward systems that incentivize repeat purchases and long-term engagement.

5 Sentiment analysis for improved customer relationships: AI-powered sentiment analysis can help businesses gauge how customers feel about their products, services or overall brand. Tools like Sprinklr and Hootsuite Insights can analyse social media posts, reviews and customer feedback to uncover underlying emotions whether positive or negative. By addressing negative feedback promptly and reinforcing positive experiences, businesses can demonstrate that they care about their customers' opinions.

Customer lifetime value

CLV is about measuring the value of a customer to a company; it measures value across the entire relationship a customer has with a customer, i.e. it doesn't just focus on a purchase at a time. One can measure CLV by looking at how much value a customer means to a company by looking at historical purchases; another way is to categorize a customer and predict the CLV.

CLV is a key measure for the business and for marketing; through identifying and calculating CLV one can distinguish higher value customers from those customers who spend much less; marketing activities can thus be a lot more focused. CLV prediction also helps improve customer retention by identifying at-risk customers and increase profitability through targeted cross-selling and upselling.

AI for CLV prediction

AI employs various machine learning techniques to predict CLV. For example, linear and logistic regression can estimate future customer spend based on historical behaviour. probabilistic Models like Bayesian networks and Markov chains help predict the probability of a customer making repeat purchases or churning.

Aside of these areas one can also use AI frameworks such as TensorFlow, PyTorch and Scikit-learn that make it easy to build and train these models. These algorithms empower businesses to forecast CLV for individual customers or segments, aiding in strategic decision-making.

TOOLS FOR CLV PREDICTION

One can also use CRM tools with embedded AI for CLV prediction. An example of such a tool is Zoho CRM with Zia AI. Zia AI provides predictions about customer behaviour, including CLV predictions based on past transactions, interactions and patterns. Zia can also automate lead scoring and customer segmentation. Zoho offers a straightforward interface with built-in AI capabilities that require minimal setup or coding knowledge. Other examples include Paddle Predict and Optimove.

Customer onboarding

This part of the buyer journey focuses on how customers get to grips with first interacting with the company they've purchased from and how the vendor engages its customers; the onboarding process can involve customers finding and accessing information easily related to using the product. It can also involve providing information in real time.

Onboarding might also involve customer services; sales though marketing plays a role both directly and indirectly via sales and even customer services. Examples of marketing activities might include welcome emails, trigger emails based on website engagement, product educational information, explainer videos and how to relate to the product or services, and a webinar to introduce them to the company or products.

With a more personalized onboarding experience for customers this can make a difference in successive interactions with the customer. Research by Wyzowl found that 86 per cent of customers say their loyalty to a business is increased when they are offered a great onboarding experience.[2]

How can AI be used?

AI can be used to personalize the onboarding path that a customer takes based on their role and goals, including providing recommended relevant features and in-context help and assistance. AI can also be used to automate repetitive onboarding tasks.

Here are examples of some repetitive tasks.

- Customers often need to provide personal details, company information and preferences multiple times during the onboarding process. An example of AI is Formstack, which uses AI-powered form automation to pre-fill forms with data from previous interactions or databases, reducing the time customers spend filling out repetitive fields.
- Customers frequently ask the same onboarding questions about how to use certain features, billing or account settings; one could use AI-driven

chatbots to automatically answer common onboarding questions in real time, providing relevant knowledge base articles or directing users to the appropriate resources.

- Customers often have to go through the same tutorials or product training during onboarding, which can be time-consuming and generic. AI tools such as WalkMe can provide contextual guidance based on the customer's journey, automatically adapting tutorials to their level of experience and previous actions.
- AI solutions like DocuSign Insight can verify signatures, confirm data consistency and flag missing documents, reducing back-and-forth communication and speeding up approvals.
- Tools like Gong.io analyse customer interactions and feedback to recommend personalized onboarding plans based on the customer's industry, size and goals. These platforms automatically suggest training sessions, support resources or key milestones, ensuring a more relevant and streamlined experience for the customer.

See Figure 12.3 for a view of scenarios and types of tools.

Deployment of the product or service can be a journey in itself which overlaps with onboarding; by deployment we mean roll-out and provision of the product or services to users within the organization. For this stage customer service and account management take front-line responsibility though marketing can help again through answering questions or providing standard answers to simple questions through online product FAQs; online chat can be offered for those not wanting to pick up the phone to someone. Marketing can ensure web pages and key documents are ready and made available.

If the product is relatively new, marketing can engage sales and customer service to understand satisfaction level of product and service and use feedback to optimize customer experience. Similarly, marketing can use feedback regarding customers use of online materials and any content and use feedback to optimize content provided.

Content for deployment (and onboarding)

If we consider that the goal is to support customers in understanding products in more detail as they are actively using them, we can divide up content in this phase into educational content, support content and ongoing deployment content.

FIGURE 12.3 AI and repetitive tasks

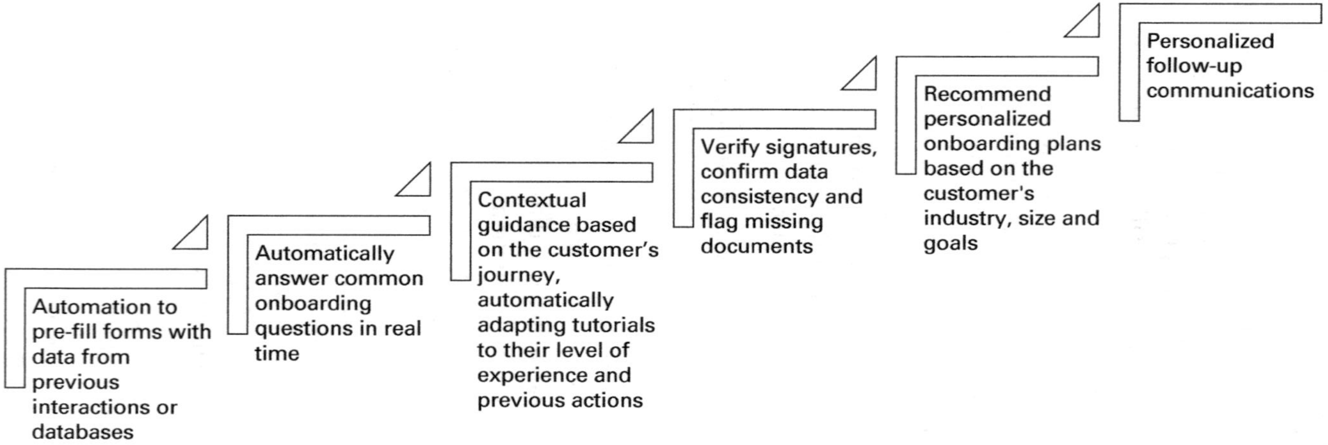

Automation to pre-fill forms with data from previous interactions or databases

Automatically answer common onboarding questions in real time

Contextual guidance based on the customer's journey, automatically adapting tutorials to their level of experience and previous actions

Verify signatures, confirm data consistency and flag missing documents

Recommend personalized onboarding plans based on the customer's industry, size and goals

Personalized follow-up communications

- Education content which can be provided includes (1) how to documents and (2) product demos.
- Follow-up emails can be used to inquire how the customer is getting on with using the product or service; such emails can also be automated and related to customers viewing particular webpages or downloading particular types of content from the website.
- Support content can be provided which involves setup, usage help as well as support with some basic troubleshooting.
- Ongoing product updates and news: Product updates can be provided through an enewsletter, dedicated emails or through posts on social media highlighting new products and services or updates to existing products.

ONBOARDING IN PRACTICE

We can use NLP machine learning tools to help us write onboarding emails; here is a response for the command. *Please provide an example of a B2B customer onboarding email showing two paragraphs.*

Example 1: SaaS onboarding email

Subject Line: Welcome to [Software Name] – Let's Get Started!

Dear [Customer Name],

Welcome to [Software Name]! We're thrilled to have you onboard and can't wait to help your business achieve [specific benefit, e.g. 'streamlined project management' or 'faster data insights']. To get started, we've designed an intuitive setup process to ensure your transition is smooth and hassle-free. Access your [dashboard/account] here.

To help you make the most out of [Software Name], we've created a Quick Start Guide filled with step-by-step instructions and best practices tailored to your needs. If you have any questions, our support team is just an email away at [support email] or through our live chat feature. We look forward to seeing your business thrive with us!

Warm regards,
[Your Name]
[Your Job Title]
[Company Name]

AI for gamification

Gamification is the use of game mechanics and concepts to engage customers and encourage them to take actions.

Gamification is not new and has been used for some time in the consumer marketing space, though this is relatively new to the B2B space. The trend of looking at game mechanics is more about appealing to the human side of target audiences by introducing the fun element into B2B interactions.

Approaches to gamification

Gamification can be rolled out as a bigger initiative or can be implemented on a small scale, i.e. including within activities and tactics. Some gamification techniques include levels, use of badges, digital prizes and leader boards. Here are some thoughts where gamification could be used in B2B marketing.

Types of gamifications

AI tools can come to the aid of B2B marketing by identifying which types of gamified content (quizzes, challenges and competitions) will best engage specific customer segments based on their past behaviour, industry or role. These insights can be used to design highly effective gamification strategies.

Rewards

AI tools can also automate the process of distributing rewards based on predefined rules or customer achievements in the gamification process. This includes badges, points, tiered incentives or exclusive content access. Talon. One is an example of such a tool; it automates loyalty and rewards programmes by distributing points, discounts or prizes based on customer actions and engagement levels.

Real-time feedback and adaptation

AI can track user behaviour in real time during the gamification process and adjust challenges, rewards or content to keep engagement levels high. If the system detects a drop in participation, it can offer incentives or adjust difficulty levels to re-engage users. Pendo uses AI to track real-time user interactions and offers personalized feedback or prompts based on customer activity, ensuring continuous engagement in gamification.

Dynamic leaderboards and competitions

AI tools such as Playlyfe can create dynamic, personalized leaderboards that adapt based on customer performance and engagement, encouraging healthy competition. AI can ensure that each customer sees competitors of similar skill levels, keeping the challenge exciting and fair.

PUT INTO PRACTICE: GETTING IDEAS

One can also come up with ideas for gamification formats via machine learning applications. Let's take the prompt: *Please share 15 ideas for different gamification formats in bullet point format e.g. spin the wheel, etc.*

The response from this was about a 300-word set of ideas including progress bars, leaderboards, treasure hunt, quiz show, etc. The following are five of those ideas suggested by ChatGPT.

1. Spin the wheel: Users spin a virtual wheel to win prizes, discounts or special offers.
2. Progress bar/goal tracker: A visual tracker that motivates users to complete tasks by showing progress toward a goal.
3. Scratch cards: Users 'scratch' a virtual card to reveal random rewards or bonuses.
4. Daily streak challenges: Encourage users to engage daily to maintain streaks and unlock cumulative rewards.
5. Badge and achievement system: Users earn virtual badges or trophies for completing specific tasks or milestones.
6. As a follow-up we can then use machine learning and content creation AI tools to further flesh out the one or two chosen ideas we're most interested in.

FIGURE 12.4 Gamification format ideas

1. **Spin the wheel**: Users spin a virtual wheel to win prizes, discounts or special offers.
2. **Progress bar/goal tracker**: A visual tracker that motivates users to complete tasks by showing progress toward a goal.
3. **Scratch cards**: Users 'scratch' a virtual card to reveal random rewards or bonuses.
4. **Daily streak challenges**: Encourage users to engage daily to maintain streaks and unlock cumulative rewards.
5. **Badge and achievement system**: Users earn virtual badges or trophies for completing specific tasks or milestones.
6. **Leaderboards**: Create a competitive element by ranking users based on points or performance.
7. **Mystery boxes**: Offer virtual boxes containing random rewards or surprises to incentivize engagement.
8. **Quiz challenges**: Users answer questions or solve puzzles to earn rewards or unlock achievements.
9. **Adventure/story-based quests**: Gamify tasks through a narrative where users complete quests to advance.
10. **Referral challenges**: Reward users for referring friends or sharing content, with milestones for additional perks.
11. **Time-limited challenges**: Users complete a task or series of tasks within a set time frame to earn exclusive rewards.
12. **Virtual currency/economy**: Users earn virtual coins or points through actions, which they can redeem for rewards.
13. **Spin-to-progress games**: Users spin wheels or engage in similar mechanics to move along a game board or virtual map.
14. **Lucky draws**: Users are automatically entered into a raffle or lottery after completing certain tasks.
15. **Social sharing challenges**: Users earn rewards for sharing achievements, products or tasks on social media platforms.

REAL-WORLD EXAMPLE

H2O.ai – Epsilon's marketing ROI boost

Epsilon is a global leader in data-driven marketing solutions, providing comprehensive marketing services, including targeted email campaigns, direct mail and advanced analytics. The company works with major brands across various industries, helping them engage their audiences more effectively and drive better results from their marketing investments.

Epsilon faced a challenge when its clients sought better returns from direct mail marketing campaigns. Despite running successful campaigns, the company struggled to maximize the ROI for its clients, particularly when it came to identifying the most responsive and profitable audience segments. Traditional targeting methods were not sophisticated enough to accurately predict consumer behaviour, resulting in suboptimal response rates and wasted marketing spend. As a result, Epsilon needed a solution to help their clients more effectively identify high-potential customers and refine their targeting strategies.

To overcome these challenges, Epsilon partnered with H2O.ai and integrated their advanced machine learning platform into their marketing analytics. By using H2O.ai's predictive analytics capabilities, Epsilon was able to develop more accurate audience segmentation models. These machine learning algorithms enabled the company to better understand and predict which consumers were most likely to respond to specific direct mail offers. This shift allowed Epsilon to create highly targeted marketing strategies based on data-driven insights, rather than relying on broad, general assumptions.

By leveraging advanced predictive analytics, Epsilon was able to increase response rates for direct mail campaigns by 3–5 per cent. For one large client, a brand selling gifts to both B2B and B2C customers, this shift resulted in an impressive 110 per cent increase in direct mail response rates, leading to an additional $9 million in revenue from a single campaign. This success demonstrated the value of using machine learning to optimize audience targeting, ultimately leading to improved customer engagement and significantly higher marketing ROI.

References

1. OpenAI (2016) OpenAI Gym beta, 27 April, openai.com/index/openai-gym-beta/ (archived at https://perma.cc/FFD4-EASA)
2. Grant, S (2024) How onboarding optimises user retention, 19 April, www.wyzowl.com/onboarding-user-retention/ (archived at https://perma.cc/YMR8-X5VN)

Further reading

Hubspot.com (2024) How to use AI for business development and startup growth, www.hubspot.com/startups/ai-business-development (archived at https://perma.cc/KY6T-UKEX)

Optimove (2014) Customer churn prediction, prevention & analysis, Optimove, www.optimove.com/resources/learning-center/customer-churn-prediction-and-prevention (archived at https://perma.cc/55UD-GK5B)

Rensburg, IV (2024) Intent data: what it is, how it's collected and 7 ways to use it, Cognism, www.cognism.com/blog/intent-data (archived at https://perma.cc/KSJ3-8N97)

Sivek, SC (2022) Why you need to predict customer lifetime value, Pecan AI, www.pecan.ai/blog/why-predict-customer-lifetime-value/ (archived at https://perma.cc/3L2D-LMVA)

Sivek, SC (2023) How and why to calculate and predict customer churn, Pecan AI, www.pecan.ai/blog/how-why-churn-analysis-prediction/ (archived at https://perma.cc/SF82-JPNE)

PART FIVE

AI management and planning

13

Data and privacy

What you will learn from this chapter

Understanding of the following:

- understand types of data
- learn about challenges in data collection
- how to comply with data privacy legislation
- data privacy considerations in using AI tools

Introduction

In this chapter we'll be looking into the area of data, its usage and discuss data privacy in relation to AI; before going further, let's explain data privacy.

Data privacy refers to privacy regarding information; under data privacy we are particularly interested in principles and laws which dictate how we should collect, store, use and share information. In digital and AI-based marketing in particular, we're more interested in personal and sensitive data such as names, email addresses and phone numbers.

Types of data

To discuss data privacy, we should first understand the different types of data which we may be directly or indirectly using in the area of marketing and AI-based marketing.

Examples of types of data can be categorized as internal, external, personal, account-level and sector data; we can also sort marketing data into opinion-based data, behavioural data and account data. Let's take a look at these in a bit more detail.

Individual data

Individual data, sometimes called personal data, can be broken down further into the following types.

- Basic identifiers such as name, postal code, telephone number, email address and social network handles.
- Professional information such as job title, department, seniority level and company name provide context about the individual's role and influence within their organization. For example, targeting a marketing manager requires a different approach than targeting a CEO.
- Behavioural data: Tracking interactions with your website, downloads of resources, participation in webinars or responses to marketing emails provides valuable behavioural signals. This helps identify individual interests, pain points and purchase intent.

Account level data

In a B2B scenario, this includes pooling information about multiple stakeholders or decision-makers within a target account. For instance, understanding the perspectives of different roles (i.e. procurement officers, technical evaluators and executive decision-makers) can help tailor a marketing or sales strategy that resonates across the buying unit.

Purchase data

Transaction data would include number of products or service purchased, frequency of purchase, trends in purchase and seasonality patterns. In the software space, you would also benefit from understanding subscription types, frequency and breadth of subscription. This data can be found in company records and is easier to analyse if captured via a CRM application such as Salesforce.com or Microsoft Dynamix, etc.

Digital behavioural data

This could be online activity specific to the account or individual, website visits, product views, online registrations and social network activity. Behavioural online data can be captured by identifying customers through cookie ID or IP address, but, of course, there's always the option to create a separate customer website and provide password and ID numbers; this way the customer activity can be easier tracked and managed. Behavioural data can be used to help improve content on the site or to understand which areas or pages are viewed and for how long or even the basic information as to whether customers use the online areas. Behavioural data can be identified at an account level or individual level.

Data collection

AI-based data collection is the use of AI and or machine learning to gather raw information from a variety of sources. We can look at data collection in terms of techniques and formats.

Data collection methods

- Web scraping and crawling: Many AI tools use the technique known as web scraping and crawling techniques; this technique allows tools to gather large amounts of data from the internet. Web scraping can systematically browse websites and draw relevant information from those sites; other web-scraping features involve using APIs to access structured data from online platforms.
- Purchase of datasets: some AI tools leverage data which has been purchased in pre-packaged datasets from third-party providers. Such datasets can be curated datasets specific to certain domains or tasks, and annotated image and video datasets for computer vision.
- Crowdsourcing is a method where data is collected from a large group of people, typically through the internet, to provide insights about companies or individuals. AI tools leverage crowdsourced data to gain valuable information about B2B customers, including organizational structures, decision-makers, behaviours and preferences. This approach is particularly effective for collecting large volumes of diverse and dynamic data that would be challenging to gather through traditional methods.
- Other AI systems use automated data generation and generate synthetic data to augment their training sets using features such as generative adversarial networks (GANs) to create artificial data samples.
- Using surveys and user feedback: Surveys and user tests gather targeted information by presenting specific queries to individuals or groups. This method helps collect qualitative data, which is subjective and non-numerical.

TABLE 13.1 Data collection by area

Objective	Recommended method(s)	Tools to consider
Lead generation	Intent data monitoring, web scraping	Bombora, ZoomInfo, Diffbot
Customer segmentation	Machine learning models, behavioural analytics	H2O.ai, Amplitude, Google Analytics
Content personalization	NLP, chatbots	OpenAI, Drift, HubSpot
Trend and competitor analysis	Social media analytics, web scraping	Talkwalker, Scrapy, Brandwatch
Real-time insights	IoT and sensor analysis, behavioural analytics	Azure IoT Central, Mixpanel

- Collecting sensor data: In Internet of Things (IoT) applications, sensors collect real-time data from various devices or systems. These sensors capture environmental, behavioural or operational data.
- Collection of formats: AI tools and data collection can also refer to different content formats such as text, images and video snapshots.

CROWDSOURCING AND ITS USES FOR DATA COLLECTION

B2B marketers can make use of crowdsourcing to collect data by looking at different types of platforms; for example, one can use a CDP platform like ZoomInfo which uses crowdsourcing by leveraging contributions from its user base, as well as data mining and AI, to provide detailed company and contact information. Kickfire also uses crowdsourcing to collect intent data with IP intelligence to track companies visiting a website and determine their interests. Another area of crowdsourcing is OpenStreetMap (for geospatial data), which uses crowdsourced geographic data from contributors worldwide and can be used by businesses to identify office locations or logistics hubs. B2B marketers can use this data to target companies in specific geographic clusters.

AI DATA COLLECTION SELECTION IN PRACTICE

In order to come up with the most suitable data collection method we first can have an idea of the best one according to different areas of B2B marketing from Table 13.1. Let's say we want to go into a bit more detail for lead generation. We might use the following process for the earlier stages in this process of defining lead generation goals, assessing required data types and evaluating data.

Step 1: Define specific lead generation goals

Identify what type of leads you need:

- High-intent leads: Accounts actively researching solutions.
- Segmented leads: Leads categorized by industry, size or geography.
- Engaged leads: Contacts who interact with your website, emails or content.
- Determine your lead sources:
  - Inbound: Website visits, social media or event registrations.
  - Outbound: Cold outreach, third-party data or referrals.

Step 2: Assess the data types required

- For contact data such as names, emails and phone numbers. We might use external data companies like ZoomInfo or web scraping tools (e.g. Diffbot).
- For behavioural data such as page views, content downloads or ad clicks we might use behavioural analytics tools like Mixpanel or Google Analytics.
- For intent data such as keywords searched, content consumed or company-level signals we might use intent monitoring platforms like Bombora or 6sense.

Step 3: Evaluate data sources

In the third step we evaluate and consider different sources where internal sources are CRM systems, website analytics or existing email lists and for this we can use predictive analytics or machine learning tools (e.g. Salesforce Einstein). External sources are online directories, social media or third-party databases and for this we might use data enrichment platforms (e.g. Clearbit and Apollo.io).

Challenges in data collection

The previously mentioned AI-based methods for data collection probably make us think the process is simple and straightforward, but there are a number of challenges that companies need to deal with to ensure effective and ethical use of data. One significant challenge is data quality. It is essential that the data being collected is accurate, comprehensive and relevant to the intended analysis. However, data can often be inaccurate, outdated or even biased, which in turn impacts the reliability and effectiveness of AI tools.

Another important consideration is privacy and ethics. As companies collect data, they must adhere to privacy regulations, ensuring that personal and organizational information is handled with care and respect. Data collection should not infringe upon the privacy of individuals or companies, and ethical guidelines must be followed throughout the process. This includes obtaining consent from data subjects and ensuring that the collected data is used solely for legitimate purposes. Ethical considerations extend to the transparency of AI processes, where businesses must be clear about how data is being used and how decisions are made based on that data.

The volume and variety of data present another challenge. The sheer amount of data generated from various sources can overwhelm systems, making it difficult to store, process and analyse. Large datasets often come in different formats and from diverse sources, further complicating the process. Techniques like data reduction, which involves filtering out irrelevant or redundant data, and feature engineering, which focuses on selecting the most relevant data attributes, can help manage and process these large datasets more effectively.

First- and third-party data

First-party data is that data which is collected directly by organizations from individuals or organizations. First-party data can be collected through a company's direct interactions from visitors and customers (i.e. through the company's own platforms) as well as a company's own software and services (e.g. marketing automation platforms, CRM, Google Analytics and other platforms).

Examples of where first-party data is collected are via website platforms, social media sites, email marketing data, surveys and polls. More can be found in Figure 13.1.

Advantages of first-party data over third-party data

There are a number of advantages in collecting first-party data over third-party data. As first-party data is collected directly from users' interactions

FIGURE 13.1 First party data sources

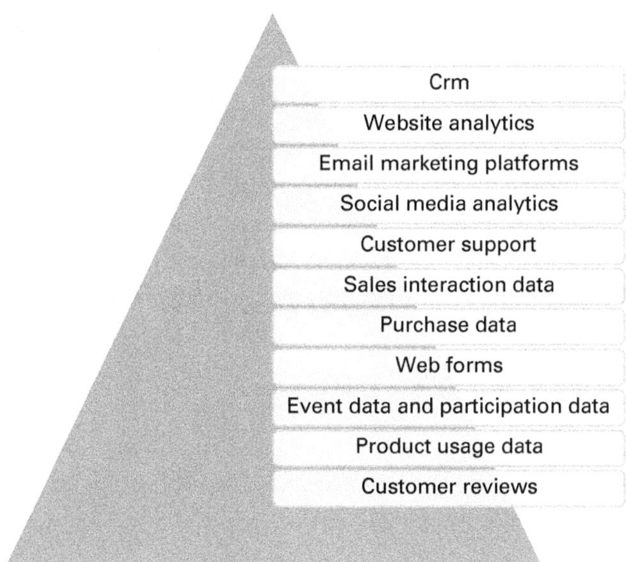

within the app, it is highly accurate and trustworthy. In contrast, third-party data can be less reliable as it's sourced from external providers and may not always be up-to-date or reflective of specific user behaviours.

First-party data provides real-time insights into user behaviour and interactions whereas third-party data may have a delay in report. Real-time insights can also respond quickly to changing trends and adapt their strategies in near real time.

Third-party data: challenges and considerations

Third-party data refers to data collected by external sources or organizations that are not directly involved in the interaction between the marketer and the customer. This data is often aggregated from various platforms and sources such as public records, social media profiles, data brokers and other commercial data providers. The advantage of third-party data is its ability to provide a broader perspective on potential customers, including insights about their industry, purchasing behaviours and organizational structure. AI tools have greatly enhanced the efficiency of collecting and processing third-party data by automating the extraction, aggregation and analysis of information from disparate sources.

However, the use of third-party data has been significantly impacted by evolving privacy regulations and changing industry norms. One of the key challenges is data privacy and compliance. Regulations like the General Data Protection Regulation (GDPR) in the EU and the California Consumer Privacy Act (CCPA) (Cloudflare) have set stricter rules around the collection, storage and usage of personal data. These laws require businesses to obtain explicit consent from individuals for their data to be used and shared. For B2B marketers, this means that relying on third-party data sources without proper consent can result in legal ramifications, fines and reputational damage. Furthermore, with many platforms and organizations tightening their data-sharing practices, obtaining comprehensive and reliable third-party data has become more difficult.

To overcome these challenges, marketers are increasingly turning to privacy-compliant AI tools that ensure data is collected and processed in accordance with privacy laws. AI tools can help by anonymizing customer data, allowing businesses to analyse patterns and trends without violating individual privacy rights.

Data privacy regulations and AI

Data privacy regulations such as GDPR increasingly influence B2B marketing; and though the GDPR doesn't explicitly mention AI, it does contain provisions which are relevant to AI technologies. Principles within the GDPR legislation address purpose limitation and data minimization, which are relevant to the data-intensive nature of AI, and also address principles such as balancing AI capabilities with data protection.

Similarly, in the US the California Consumer Privacy Act (CCPA) and its subsequent amendment, the California Privacy Rights Act (CPRA), impact B2B marketers using AI by imposing strict requirements regarding data transparency.

Aside of existing and amended privacy acts around the world there are some emerging AI-specific regulations in development.

EU AI Act

EU AI Act: The European Union is taking the lead with the proposed AI Act, which aims to regulate AI systems based on their risk level. It was proposed by the European Commission in 2021 and is expected to be one of the first legal frameworks worldwide to regulate AI across all sectors. The AI Act categorizes AI systems based on their risk level, ranging from minimal to high risk, and implements different requirements for each category. For example, high-risk AI applications such as those used in healthcare, law enforcement and hiring processes are subject to strict obligations for transparency, accountability and human oversight.[1]

The AI Act is especially significant because it introduces provisions for transparency and explainability in AI algorithms, aiming to prevent discrimination, bias and harm. Companies using AI systems in these high-risk sectors must also implement regular assessments and audits to ensure that their AI applications remain compliant. Furthermore, the regulation seeks to ensure that AI systems are used in a way that is ethical and respects fundamental rights, establishing legal frameworks for responsible innovation.

US state laws

While the United States has not yet enacted a comprehensive federal AI law, there is a growing trend at the state level to introduce AI-specific legislation, particularly around data privacy and AI's role in decision-making processes. Several US states are proposing or have already passed laws to address AI technology and its potential risks to privacy and fairness.

Challenges of data protection in AI-powered marketing tools

AI tools process a vast volume of data which can include personal data. Sometimes AI tools don't make it clear about how they process and use data, which can lead to inadvertently sharing personal information or providing unwanted access to data. The consequences can go beyond being uncomfortable with this data being disclosed and companies may cross lines in terms of legal aspects. Not being careful in using personal data in AI tools can in worst cases lead to financial implications.

Although the GDPR act doesn't specifically stipulate AI, it affects AI as GDPR is about protecting personal data of individuals in the EU; it acts for companies to enforce a governance and discipline in how they handle personal data and request that consent is clearly and freely given. In the event of a data breach, companies must report it to the relevant data protection authority within 72 hours of becoming aware of it, unless the breach is unlikely to pose a risk to the rights and freedoms of individuals. Because AI systems process personal data for a variety of reasons, the GDPR impacts how AI functions.

Considerations regarding data when using AI tools

Organizations and their employees need to ensure that any collected data and processing of data is complying with data protection laws; examples would include GDPR. Of course where data is collected across multiple geographies then the laws governing those geographies need to be adhered to.

In most cases the practices that govern data collection tend to align with each other and all focus on the same thing, i.e. protecting individuals' data and their privacy. Let's look at a few situations.

- Companies leveraging third-party AI tools: Where possible and necessary, companies behind AI tools should obtain consent of individuals or organizations in using and processing data. Consent should be freely given, informed, specific and unambiguous. Organizations using AI tools should also take suitable security measure to ensure confidentiality, integrity and availability of data; this may include data encryption, access controls, data backup and other security measures.
- Companies who develop own AI tools: Those developing their own AI tools or building own AI tools based on AI engines should provide clear and open information about how their AI systems process data and how this may affect the privacy of individuals. This can be done through privacy policies, terms of service or other sources of information.

Aside of the above situations companies and B2B marketing departments using customer data should conduct data protection impact assessments to identify and evaluate potential privacy risks associated with their AI systems.

What about marketers working in small business who use AI tools?

In this case, when using AI tools or other third-party services marketers should check that these tools comply with relevant data protection laws; most reputable AI tools will publish policies regarding data privacy, data usage and protection so one should simply find the page or area of the website where this is mentioned. Where there is no mention of compliance with data protection regulations then this should be seen as a red flag.

IN PRACTICE: CHECKING DATA COLLECTION AND PRIVACY

Using ZoomInfo

ZoomInfo is a popular AI-powered data intelligence tool used by marketers to gather business data, including contact details, company information and industry insights. To ensure data protection compliance when using ZoomInfo, marketers should look for specific sections that outline their data collection methods and legal compliance practices.

Steps to check compliance:

1 Navigate to the ZoomInfo website (www.zoominfo.com).
2 Scroll down to the bottom of the page and look for a link to the privacy policy or legal section, typically located in the footer.
3 Once in the privacy policy section, find the paragraph or section that addresses data collection methods. Here, ZoomInfo should outline how it gathers data (such as from publicly available sources, user-generated data or partners) and how it ensures compliance with GDPR and other privacy laws.
4 Specifically, look for references to GDPR compliance (if operating in Europe), the CCPA (for California-based consumers) and any other local regulations ZoomInfo may comply with, as well as how data is stored, processed and shared.
5 For example, ZoomInfo's privacy policy provides a dedicated section on GDPR compliance, detailing the lawful basis for processing personal data, data subject rights and how users can opt-out of having their data collected. If the privacy policy lacks such details or does not clearly address data protection, this could be a red flag.

PUT INTO PRACTICE: CHECKLIST FOR DATA PRIVACY IN GENERAL

Practically there are some things which B2B marketers can do to ensure they are complying with data privacy; here are some areas and examples.

Verify the tool's privacy policy and compliance

Before using any AI tool, marketers should thoroughly review its privacy policy and terms of service to ensure alignment with legal requirements. Check for certifications such as ISO 27001 or explicit GDPR compliance statements. For example, when working with Oppwiser, a marketer should confirm how the platform manages client data and whether it processes information in compliant regions, such as hosting data within the EU for European clients.

Minimize data collection and sharing

Marketers should adopt a data minimization approach, sharing only the information necessary for the AI tool to perform its functions. Avoid uploading sensitive or confidential data unless strictly required. For instance, when using ChatGPT to draft marketing emails, anonymize client information by using placeholders (e.g. 'Company X') instead of real names or sensitive details to maintain confidentiality and reduce risk.

Set up internal controls and access restrictions

Marketers should restrict access to AI tools and the data they process to authorized personnel only. Regular audits can ensure that sensitive data is protected and accessed responsibly. For example, when multiple team members use ChatGPT in a collaborative setting, creating team accounts with defined access levels and monitoring usage logs can help maintain data security and compliance.

See Table 13.2 for more scenarios and actions to ensure compliance.

Risks of data breaches or unauthorized access to AI tools

Data breaches within AI tools pose significant risks due to the vast amounts of data these systems process and store. It should also be understood that online, digital tools also face risks of data breaches, so AI is not alone in this; and over the course of the past two decades, we've seen some examples of such breaches in the public domain.

Main risks of AI and data breaches

AI technologies frequently deal with large datasets including personal, account, and even financial and proprietary data.

Aside of unauthorized access to sensitive information, there are risks of privacy violation; AI tools, especially those used for marketing, advertising or surveillance, can impact privacy in different ways.

- Data leakage: AI systems can inadvertently expose private information.
- Profiling: AI-powered profiling technology could invade user privacy on a scale beyond traditional methods.

There are also risks of AI systems being compromised through data poisoning, which is when malicious actors could inject harmful data into training datasets, altering the AI's behaviour and outputs.

PUT INTO PRACTICE: RISK MANAGEMENT – GRID/AUDIT – TOOLS FRAMEWORK

Please refer to Table 13.2. Here is a simple overview and table one could use to evaluate areas of data usage, management and types of risk, and mitigation strategy, and action one could take.

TABLE 13.2 Risk and mitigation

Risk type	Likelihood (high/ medium/ low)	Impact (high/ medium/ low)	Mitigation strategy	Examples
Data privacy breach	Medium	High	Ensure tools comply with GDPR/CCPA. Review privacy policies.	Anonymize data before sharing with tools like ChatGPT.
Data leakage	High	High	Use encrypted channels and secure APIs. Restrict access to sensitive data.	Avoid using unsecured networks for Factor.ai APIs.
Data misuse	Low	High	Limit data-sharing permissions. Vet AI vendors thoroughly.	Avoid uploading sensitive customer data to Oppwiser.
Unintended outputs	Medium	Medium	Validate AI outputs before use. Establish QA processes.	Review summaries from AI tools for accuracy.

AI risks vs non-AI

There are always some risks of cyber-attacks for any digital interaction; here are some of the differences for AI tools in terms of cyber security risks.

AI systems tend to use large amounts of data and often that includes sensitive personal information; but not always. This concentration of data makes AI tools particularly attractive targets for cybercriminals.

Many AI models, especially deep learning systems, are complex and often described as 'black boxes'. This lack of transparency makes it challenging to identify vulnerabilities, track data flow and detect security breaches. The unclear nature of AI systems can lead to undetected breaches or make it difficult to assess the full extent of a breach once discovered.

Academic researchers, government departments and leading AI organizations are actively investigating effective approaches to tackle these challenges by implementing robust encryption methods and secure communication protocols to mitigate the risk of data breaches.

What contributes to level of risk?

For a B2B marketer using an AI tool, the level of risk of a cyber security attack can vary depending on several factors. These factors can be listed as follows:

- the type of data processed by the AI tool
- the security measures in place
- the visibility and attractiveness of the company as a target
- the general threat landscape in the industry

Hence smaller businesses are probably already covered by simply taking out a subscription of a reputable cyber security software. It's important to note that not all cyber-attacks are of the same severity level. The severity can range from minor data leaks to major breaches that compromise sensitive information or disrupt business operations.

MINIMIZING CYBER SECURITY ATTACKS

B2B marketers using AI tools can take several steps to minimize and reduce the threat of cyber-attacks:

1. Implement cyber security tools which can also detect AI cyber security threats: AI-enhanced security tools can identify 99 per cent of security threats and reduce response time to cyber threats by 70 per cent.
2. Threat detection and prevention: AI can predict 86 per cent of cyber security breaches using machine learning algorithms. Implementing AI-powered threat detection can help identify 85 per cent of malware threats missed by traditional antivirus programs.
3. Choose reputable third-party tools; one can use online professional review sites which provide reviews of third-party tools.
4. Don't upload or input any sensitive information from your company.

Transparency AI-driven marketing practices

Transparency in AI refers to the clarity and openness with which AI systems, their decisions and their underlying processes are communicated to stakeholders. It means ensuring that all parties involved whether they are developers, businesses, users or customers can understand how AI systems are functioning, what data is being used and how outcomes are being determined. This involves explaining the logic behind AI decisions in a way that is accessible and comprehensible to non-experts as well, ensuring that the decision-making process is not a 'black box'.

Explainability

Explainable AI (XAI) is critical in B2B contexts, where decision-making often requires transparency and trust. XAI refers to an AI system's ability to offer clear, understandable explanations for its recommendations and actions. For instance, when a B2B company uses AI to analyse customer data or automate product recommendations, XAI can provide insights like:

- 'This recommendation is based on your company's purchasing history and preferences.'
- 'We suggest this service based on your previous positive feedback on similar solutions.'

Providing transparent explanations allows businesses to understand how the AI arrived at its decisions. These fosters trust and confidence in AI-driven tools, helping to build stronger relationships with clients. Additionally, explainable AI aligns with broader trends in responsible and trustworthy AI, ensuring that companies are operating with accountability and clarity in their use of advanced technology.

Levels of AI transparency

There are four main levels of AI transparency. See Figure 13.2 for a summary of the main areas of AI transparency.

Algorithmic transparency and its role in B2B marketing

Algorithmic transparency refers to explaining the underlying logic, processes and algorithms that drive AI systems. For B2B marketers, understanding and communicating how AI works is critical, as clients increasingly expect transparency around automated decision-making. In 2022, Gartner reported that 75 per cent of B2B companies were either using or planning to use AI-powered marketing tools. This makes transparency essential for maintaining client trust especially when leveraging advanced algorithms such as machine learning (ML) models, decision trees or neural networks.[2]

For example, a B2B firm using AI to segment customers or generate leads can benefit from algorithmic transparency by explaining how the AI identifies potential leads. A system based on machine learning might segment customers based on historical behaviour and purchase patterns, while a decision tree could identify leads through a series of if-then scenarios based on data.

Interaction transparency in client communications

Interaction transparency focuses on how businesses communicate AI-driven recommendations or insights to clients. B2B companies can enhance transparency by designing user-friendly interfaces that explain the AI's actions in real-time.

Social transparency and ethical AI usage in B2B

Social transparency goes beyond explaining algorithms and interactions; it addresses the ethical and societal implications of AI, such as bias, fairness and privacy. In a B2B context, where sensitive client data is often processed, ensuring AI systems are ethically sound is vital.

B2B marketers can demonstrate social transparency by openly addressing how their AI systems mitigate biases and safeguard client data. For instance, if a company uses AI to predict client behaviour, it must ensure that the models don't unfairly prioritize certain industries or regions due to biased data.

Data transparency in B2B marketing and AI

Data transparency refers to the practice of clearly and openly communicating how data is collected, processed, shared and used within a business context. For B2B marketers utilizing AI, data transparency is critical to building trust with clients and stakeholders.

FIGURE 13.2 Data transparency in AI

Algorithmic transparency
Providing insight into the algorithms and models behind AI decisions, explaining how they work, and revealing any assumptions or biases that may influence outcomes.
Data transparency
Openly sharing information about the data used to train AI systems, including its sources, quality and any limitations or biases that could affect the AI's outputs.
Data transparency in AI
Interaction transparency
Making it clear how users interact with AI systems, including how their inputs are used and how the AI responds to those input
Social transparency
Understanding the broader societal impact of AI systems, including their potential effects on social norms, inequalities and ethical considerations, and ensuring these impacts are communicated transparently

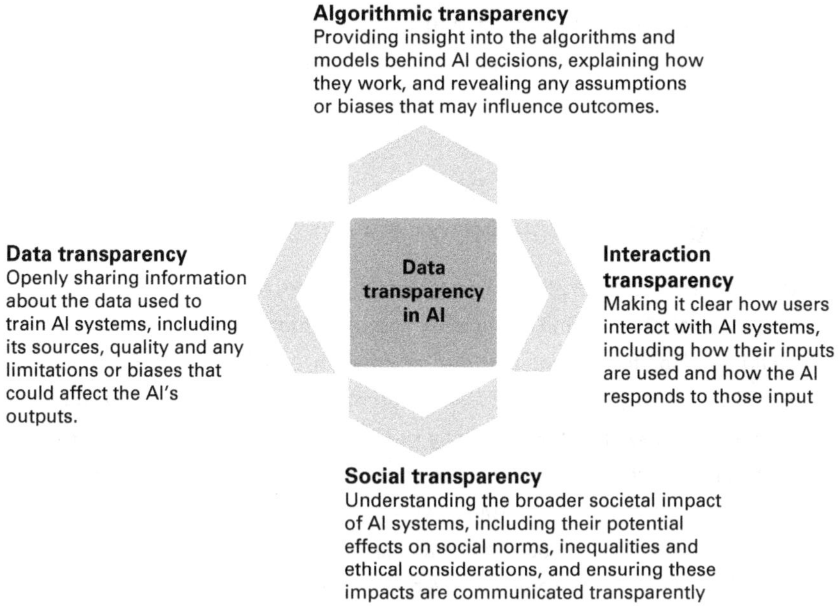

Consent and opt-in

Anonymization and pseudonymization techniques play an important role in ensuring privacy while using AI. Anonymization is about removing or altering personally identifiable information (PII) from data thus providing some protection to individuals whose data is being used. Pseudonymization is about substituting identifiable elements with artificial identifiers.

HubSpot in its CRM platform uses anonymization techniques to help B2B marketers analyse data without exposing PII. Anonymization involves removing or masking identifiable details, such as names, email addresses and company information, so that the data cannot be traced back to specific individuals or companies.

Data minimization

Data minimization refers to the practice of limiting the collection, processing and storage of personal data to the minimum necessary to achieve specific marketing objectives. This approach complies with data privacy regulations like GDPR which emphasizes that businesses use only the amount and type of data essential. For instance, if an AI model is used to predict the likelihood of a lead converting, the data collected should be strictly limited to what is necessary for that prediction, avoiding the collection of unrelated or excessive information.

PRACTICAL WAYS TO ADHERE TO DATA MINIMIZATION

Landing pages: When creating forms for landing pages (e.g. for downloading a white paper or ebook), limit the fields to essential information. For instance, instead of asking for detailed personal information, marketers can request just the name, company and email. If a phone number or job title isn't critical for the campaign, leave it out. Research by HubSpot shows that conversion rates drop by an average of 11 per cent when unnecessary form fields are added.

Webinar sign-ups: During webinar registration, ask for only the necessary details, such as name, company name and email. Avoid requesting additional information like location, company revenue or personal interests unless it is vital for the specific purpose of the webinar. This reduces data collection burdens and ensures compliance with privacy laws.

Lead generation forms: On lead capture forms, consider using progressive profiling, which collects additional data over time rather than in one go. For example, the first interaction might capture just the email address, while subsequent interactions (e.g. downloading a second report) could prompt the user to fill in a job title or company size. This approach minimizes the amount of data collected upfront and reduces friction for potential leads.

Configure AI tools with data filters: When setting up AI marketing tools like HubSpot, ZoomInfo or Marketo, marketers should configure data input filters to ensure only the necessary data is shared with the AI. For example, if an AI tool is scoring leads, ensure it only receives job titles and company information, not personal data like social media activity or detailed purchasing history unless absolutely essential.

Limit data collection from external sources: If using third-party AI tools that automatically scrape or aggregate data from various sources (e.g. Leadspace), make sure you limit the sources and types of data it can access. For instance, you might restrict it to public company data and avoid collecting individual-level data unless there's a specific, consented use case.

Use AI tools with built-in data minimization features: Choose AI marketing tools that allow for customizable data collection settings. Some tools provide options to select which data points are required for different use cases, enabling marketers to comply with minimization by using only the relevant data for particular campaigns.

Training employees

Data privacy and data privacy awareness training refers to educational courses and programmes designed to educate employees about data privacy regulations, best practices, company privacy procedures and the importance of protecting sensitive information.

These training courses typically cover various topics like compliance training, security awareness training, the importance of training programmes, privacy-specific training content and training requirements. Organizations can mitigate the risks associated with data breaches and privacy violations by equipping employees with the knowledge and skills needed to handle data securely.

References

1 European Commission (2025) AI Act, digital-strategy.ec.europa.eu/en/policies/regulatory-framework-ai (archived at https://perma.cc/V4YJ-C9LA)

2 Gartner (2025) Gartner Says by 2030 that 75% of B2B Buyers Will Prefer Sales Experiences that Prioritize Human Interaction Over AI, www.gartner.com/en/newsroom/press-releases/2025-08-25-gartner-says-by-2030-that-75-percent-of-b2b-buyers-will-prefer-sales-experiences-that-prioritize-human-interaction-over-ai (archived at https://perma.cc/GXX5-P8U8)

Further reading

Baker, J (2024) The CMO's data privacy checklist for 2024, The Drum, www.thedrum.com/news/2024/01/26/the-cmo-s-data-privacy-checklist-2024 (archived at https://perma.cc/5F5B-H5SB)

Opeyemi, S (2021) Data collection tools (and web scraping!) explained, Scraping Robot, https://scrapingrobot.com/blog/data-collection-methods/ (archived at https://perma.cc/RA7F-8GH8)

Routledge.com (2024) AI and its implications for data privacy, Routledge, blog. routledge.com/science-and-technology/ai-and-its-implications-for-data-privacy/ (archived at https://perma.cc/V84J-S2ZH)

14

Ethics

What you will learn from this chapter

Understanding of the following:

- explore ethical concerns
- understand bias in relation to AI tools
- bias in AI
- learn about explainable AI
- understand marketing accountability

Introduction

When discussing ethics in artificial intelligence (AI), we refer to a framework of moral principles and responsible business practices that guide the development, deployment and use of AI technologies. Ethics in AI aims to ensure that these technologies are used responsibly, minimizing risks and potential negative consequences.

A key aspect of AI ethics is fairness, particularly addressing biases that may arise from the training data. These biases can lead to discriminatory outcomes, resulting in the unfair treatment of specific groups of people.

As with any technology ethics also comes down to how technology is used and not necessary the technology itself, i.e. AI is not ethical or non-ethical, but it is about who and how it is used. For example, recently in an AI workshop one delegate mentioned how an attendee was using an AI-based software to record event-based content live and use that content as their own for their own businesses; here the example is demonstrating the unethical behaviours rather than the ability of AI to perform the action.

Above all, companies should strive to find the balance between ethics as well as leveraging and maximizing the capabilities of AI tools and technologies. Companies, as they build and increasingly leverage AI, should invest efforts to ensure ethical guidelines are understood and rolled out, not just for marketing but all departments.

Ethical use of data

Using AI, companies and people can collect and use customer data much more easily; as such, we need to be even more cognizant of some rules of operating with AI. One way to address this is to be open and honest in communicating to customers regarding how AI is being used, e.g. a typical example would be to be honest about using AI chatbots instead of real people.

Ethics role in the use of AI

AI tools and algorithms within tools can make discriminatory suggestions or decisions; this is due to biases in the training data; an example might be AI-generated images depicting flawless people. In B2B this might be presenting images of purchase managers, or other roles showing bias in terms of race or gender.

Where surveillance technologies are used to collect personal data, this might infringe on individuals' privacy. As AI takes over tasks and automates tasks, this can impact jobs and social inequality by making certain occupations obsolete or disadvantaging low-skilled workers.

Bias and fairness in AI tools

AI tools can accentuate biases which already exist within the core data (the training data), but what are we talking about in terms of biases? In order to eliminate AI bias, one needs to drill into the datasets and machine learning algorithms to identify sources of bias which can be any of the following (Figure 14.1).

Training data bias

AI tools learn to make decisions based on training data. One approach to identifying bias is to use data samples of different groups overrepresented as well as unrepresented groups and then run tests to identify if the output from the prompt/input are similar for both types of groups.

One B2B example might be where segmentation is carried out to identify suitable opportunities and the historical data shows more success with large enterprise companies then future outputs from the AI tools may skew responses to larger companies and under prioritize smaller businesses.

Bias can also result from mislabelling the training data. For example, AI segmentation tools that use inconsistent labelling or exclude or over-represent certain characteristics related to firmographics could mean key information is overlooked which should be taken into consideration.

Algorithmic bias

Where data is flawed this may result in outcomes including errors or exaggerate flawed data. Algorithmic bias can also be caused by programming errors, such as a developer unfairly weighting factors in algorithm decision-making based on their own conscious or unconscious biases. In a B2B marketing context, consider an AI-powered customer segmentation tool used by a company to identify high-value prospects. If the training data for the algorithm over-represents companies in a particular industry or region, the AI may unfairly prioritize leads from those areas while neglecting potential high-value customers from other industries or regions. Furthermore, if a developer programs the system with a bias toward certain factors such as company size without adequately considering other relevant attributes like growth potential, the AI could generate recommendations that overlook smaller but rapidly growing businesses.

Cognitive bias

When information is processed by people and judgements are subsequently made, those aspects are understandably influenced by those people's experiences and preferences. As a result, biases may be built into AI systems.

One example in B2B marketing might be lead scoring, where historical data is used to predict leads which are more likely to convert. In this case a marketing team's belief regarding most valuable leads which is reflected in the training data would then be reflecting a cognitive bias of the marketing team. Subsequent outputs from the AI tool then reinforce this belief and filter out leads from smaller or emerging industries.

According to NIST (National Institute of Standards and Technology), this source of bias is more common than you might think. In its report *Towards*

FIGURE 14.1 Types of AI bias

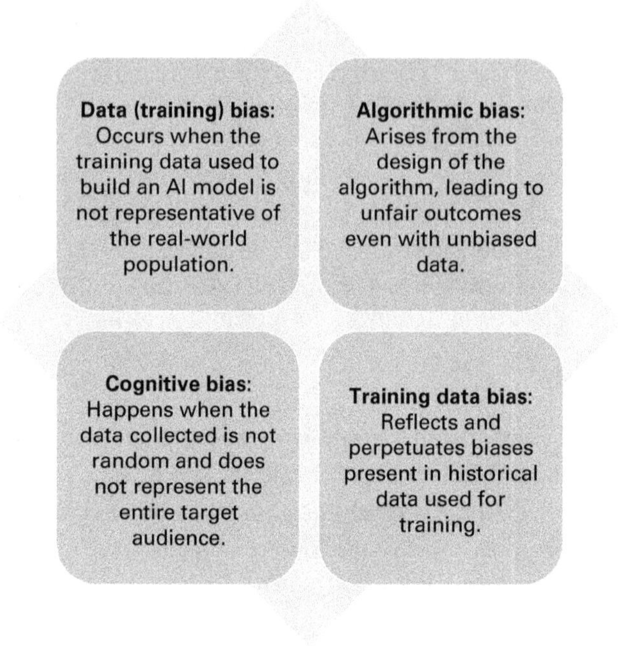

Data (training) bias: Occurs when the training data used to build an AI model is not representative of the real-world population.

Algorithmic bias: Arises from the design of the algorithm, leading to unfair outcomes even with unbiased data.

Cognitive bias: Happens when the data collected is not random and does not represent the entire target audience.

Training data bias: Reflects and perpetuates biases present in historical data used for training.

a Standard for Identifying and Managing Bias in Artificial Intelligence, NIST noted that 'human and systemic institutional and societal factors are significant sources of AI bias as well and are currently overlooked'.[1]

So exactly how does training data reflect bias?

One way training data can come to be cognitively biased is through labelling of data, e.g. with lead scoring models labels such as 'converted' or 'did not convert' are often used. If the marketing team's decisions about pursuing or nurturing leads were influenced by biases (e.g. prioritizing tech companies while neglecting other industries), then the training data will reflect those subjective preferences rather than an objective view of potential opportunities. For subsequent use of the data that bias is now built into the data, and AI will use that data for evaluating leads.

So, what are some solutions to such biases?

- Diverse and balanced datasets: Regularly review and diversify the datasets used for training AI models to ensure they reflect different customer segments, regions, industries and behaviours.

- Human oversight: Ensure that marketing teams periodically audit AI outputs to detect patterns of bias and apply human judgement to recalibrate AI recommendations when necessary.
- Bias-aware algorithm design: Use fairness-aware machine learning techniques that can detect and reduce biases during the training and decision-making process; examples are fairness dashboards from AI Fairness 360 and the Fairlearn toolkit from Microsoft can visually highlight biases in training data or model outputs.

PUT INTO PRACTICE: HOW TO ADDRESS BIAS

Here is a brief 10-point checklist for addressing bias when using AI tools.

1. **Ensure diverse data**: Use representative and diverse datasets to avoid over-representation of any group or demographic.
2. **Audit data sources regularly**: Continuously review data sources for balance, ensuring no group is systematically excluded.
3. **Test for algorithmic fairness**: Evaluate models for disparate impacts on different groups or outcomes and adjust algorithms accordingly.
4. **Avoid confirmation bias**: Challenge assumptions and test models with a variety of scenarios to reduce the risk of reinforcing preconceived notions.
5. **Eliminate historical bias**: Review historical data for outdated patterns and biases that may perpetuate discrimination in AI predictions.
6. **Implement transparent features**: Ensure that all features used in the model are justifiable and non-discriminatory.
7. **Validate model outputs**: Regularly check outputs for unintended bias and ensure fairness in decision-making.
8. **Involve diverse teams**: Include people from various backgrounds and perspectives in the development and evaluation process.
9. **Monitor user interactions**: Track how users interact with AI models and make adjustments to ensure inclusive and fair treatment for all.
10. **Conduct post-deployment audits**: After deployment, perform ongoing audits and monitoring to detect and correct biases that emerge in real-world use.

How to make AI ethical

Ethical AI marketing or ethical use of AI in B2B marketing encompasses aspects such as non-bias, fairness, transparency and others. In terms of fairness, this in itself is a complex area as fairness can be subjective. So, considering now the broader view of ethical AI beyond just bias the following are some other ways one can ensure that the use of AI is as ethical as possible also encompassing the elements of fairness and transparency.

1. Performing a preliminary review of data

A preliminary review of data is essential for identifying patterns, trends and outliers that may influence the model's performance. By analysing the data early in the process, teams can understand key attributes, their distributions and relationships. For example, a marketing team analysing B2B leads might review historical data to determine whether company size or region strongly correlates with conversion rates.

2. Data cleansing to remove biases or inaccuracies

Data cleansing is the process of refining the dataset by addressing errors, inconsistencies and biases that may compromise the integrity of the machine learning model. This step involves removing duplicate entries, filling in missing values and filtering out biased data points that could skew results. For instance, if data used for a lead scoring model overrepresents large enterprises, cleansing might involve rebalancing the dataset to include a more diverse range of company sizes. Effective data cleansing ensures that the dataset is representative of the target population and reduces the risk of perpetuating biases from historical or flawed data.

3. Making algorithms more transparent

When algorithms are designed to be interpretable, stakeholders can better understand how decisions are made and pinpoint areas where unfairness or unintended consequences might occur. For example, transparency can involve documenting the decision-making process of an AI model, providing insights into how it weighs various features, or using explainability tools like SHAP to interpret predictions.

4. Regularization

Regularization is a technique used in machine learning to add constraints to a model, preventing it from overfitting or relying too heavily on certain features that may introduce bias. For instance, in a B2B lead scoring model, regularization can minimize the impact of overly weighted features, like company size, if it skews predictions toward enterprises while ignoring smaller firms. This ensures the model makes balanced decisions based on a broader and more equitable range of features, improving fairness and generalizability.

5. Fairness metrics

Fairness metrics are quantitative measures used to evaluate the fairness of datasets and machine learning workflows. Common fairness metrics include demographic parity, which ensures outcomes are distributed equally across groups; equalized odds, which requires error rates to be consistent; and equal opportunity, which ensures equal true positive rates for all groups. For example, in a hiring algorithm, fairness metrics might measure whether candidates from all backgrounds have equal chances of selection.

Responsible AI

Under responsible AI we talk about transparency and accountability. Transparency refers to the degree to which an AI system's algorithms and decision-making processes are understanding and easily explained to people. A transparent AI system is one that can clearly demonstrate how it arrived at its conclusions or recommendations, and that allows stakeholders to understand the reasons behind those decisions.

Accountability

Accountability refers to the responsibility of individuals and organizations for the actions and decisions made by the AI they create and/or use. So, what is accountability about in marketing; this is about having mechanisms in place for oversight and monitoring of AI usage to ensure AI process and systems are happening as intended?

Here we are referring to the following:

- Creating governance frameworks and policies for AI development and deployment.

- Establishing ethical guidelines and codes of conduct for data scientists and researchers.
- Implementing systems for monitoring and reporting on the performance and impact of AI technologies.
- Auditing and testing AI systems using techniques like fairness testing and bias detection.

Ensuring ethical AI

Explainable AI (XAI) models

Companies can use explainable AI models that allow marketers to understand and explain AI-driven decisions. In B2B marketing, this is especially important for areas such as lead scoring, personalized content and predictive analytics. One example in B2B marketing is to use XAI for account-based marketing (ABM) to explain why a particular account is receiving higher engagement or content recommendations.

Features supporting explainable AI include decision trees, linear regression models and rule-based systems.

Rule-based systems use predefined 'if-then' rules to make decisions. These rules are easy to understand because they are explicitly programmed. For example, a rule might state, 'If a company has more than 500 employees and has engaged with marketing emails at least five times, assign a lead score of 80.'

Linear regression is another feature supporting XAI which indicates the relationship between two variables by fitting a straight line to the data. The model assigns coefficients to each input feature, which indicates how much the feature contributes to the final prediction.

Another feature is decision tree which is inherently explainable because it mimics human decision-making processes. It works by splitting data into branches based on decision rules that are easy to understand. Each node in the tree represents a decision based on one attribute, and the final output is a clear decision path that can be traced back to the original data points.

One can find some of these and other XAI features in AI tools such as H20.ai and Google's Cloud AI platform.

TABLE 14.1 Explainable AI

Feature	Description	Example	Key Advantage for XAI
Rule-based systems	Use predefined 'if-then' rules to make decisions.	'If a company has more than 500 employees and engages with marketing emails at least 5 times, assign score 80'	Rules are explicitly programmed and easy to understand.
Linear regression	Models relationships between variables by fitting a straight line and assigning coefficients.	If 'engagement score' increases by 1 unit, 'lead conversion probability' increases by 0.05.	Explains the impact of each feature via coefficients.
Decision trees	Splits data into branches based on decision rules, mimicking human decision-making.	A decision tree could evaluate 'Engagement > 5' and 'Company Size > 500' to assign a lead score.	Produces a clear, interpretable decision path.

PRACTICAL TIP: IMPLEMENTING XAI IN PRACTICE

Here are some simple steps a B2B marketing team can go about implementing explainable AI tools and processes.

Step 1: This is about understanding the goal and defining the specific problem which needs solving, e.g. this might be improving lead scoring accuracy or enhancing personalization. For this goal we might need to ensure the dataset is clean, relevant and representative of the target audience.

Step 2: In this next step we might choose simple, interpretable models by starting with machine learning models such as decision trees, logistic regression or rule-based models.

An example might be to use a decision tree to rank leads based on key factors such as job title, company size and engagement levels.

Step 3: This step is about leveraging XAI tools and platforms. Here we might use existing AI tools and platforms that emphasize explainability such as:

- Google's What-If Tool: Helps visualize model behaviour.

- LIME (Local Interpretable Model-Agnostic Explanations): Breaks down predictions of complex models into understandable chunks.
- SHAP (SHapley Additive exPlanations): Provides detailed insights into which features influenced predictions and to what extent.

Following on from step 3 we might look at no-code platforms as these would be easier to use and apply; and then move to testing and observing how the XAI is working.

FIGURE 14.2 Implementing XAI in practice

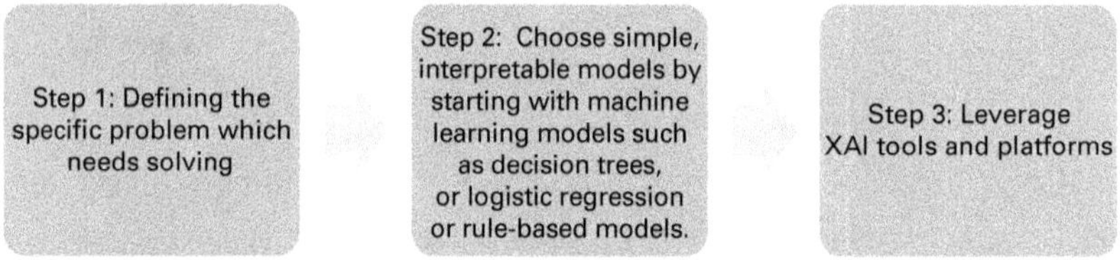

Step 1: Defining the specific problem which needs solving → Step 2: Choose simple, interpretable models by starting with machine learning models such as decision trees, or logistic regression or rule-based models. → Step 3: Leverage XAI tools and platforms

AI marketing accountability

Some of the questions to start asking might be.

- Who is responsible for AI-driven decisions in marketing?
- Who has legal and ethical accountability for AI errors?
- Which accountability frameworks do we need to establish?

Ensuring marketing accountability for AI should involve establishing a review process and some accountability and /or supervisory checks; such checks are there to correct biases or to ensure correct judgements are made.

Traditional top-down accountability models in organizations will encounter challenges with AI and may have a number of limitations. Accountability could be shared across multiple stakeholders although one downside of shared accountability is that no 'one' individual has full accountability.

Let's look at marketing and related marketing areas.

Situation – incorrect product information: Imagine an AI chatbot used by customer service which answers queries related to a product or related to how a product was communication.

Areas where things fall down in terms of AI accountability:

- No one person is held accountable.
- Customers aren't able to escalate issues where a faulty chatbot is in place or provided faulty information.

This leads to customers feeling their inquiry was not addressed and that their time was wasted.

Situation – inaccurate personalization in marketing campaigns: Consider a B2B company that relies on an AI tool to automate personalized email campaigns, recommending content and offers based on the prospect's browsing behaviour and past interactions. Imagine then if the AI misunderstands the data or uses flawed algorithms and then sends irrelevant or unsuitable information to the wrong people, e.g. it might suggest products or services that don't align with the customers' needs or it might address prospects with incorrect names or titles.

This situation would typically lead to frustrated prospects and subsequently a lack of trust from the prospect in the vendor. Who is accountable here? It is hard to pinpoint whether the error is due to faulty data input, an issue in the AI tool's algorithms or human error in configuring the campaign. This ambiguity makes it challenging to determine who is responsible for addressing the customer experience failure – data engineers, marketing teams or the AI vendor.

Situation – misleading lead scoring and qualification: Another example is where a company uses AI to score leads and assess and rank lead potential. If the AI model is trained on biased or incomplete data, it could misinterpret valuable leads as low-priority, causing sales teams to overlook important prospects.

As a result, potentially valuable customers might be lost or ignored. Again, it may be unclear whether the problem lies with the quality of the data, the model itself or the way sales teams interpret and act on the AI's predictions. This lack of transparency makes it difficult to determine who is responsible for fixing the issue – the data science team, the sales team or the marketing department that set the AI parameters.

Regulatory compliance and ethical standards

So how is ethics being addressed through regulations or laws? Here are some of the sub areas regarding ethics and legislation and regulations.

Addressing bias and ensuring fairness in AI

Addressing bias and ensuring fairness are central to AI ethics, and laws are increasingly being developed to prohibit discriminatory AI practices. An example can be found in civil rights laws (US and globally). In the US, existing anti-discrimination laws, such as the Civil Rights Act and the Americans with Disabilities Act, are being interpreted to address bias in AI systems.

Transparency and explainability in AI

Laws are also increasingly focusing on making AI systems transparent and explainable, ensuring that individuals understand how decisions affecting them are made. Under Right to Explanation (GDPR) individuals are granted the 'right to explanation', which means they have the right to understand how automated decisions are made, especially when these decisions significantly affect them. This regulation is crucial in AI ethics, as it ensures that individuals can challenge or seek clarification on decisions made by AI systems, such as credit scoring or hiring decisions. The transparency provided by the GDPR helps to ensure that individuals are not subjected to unjust automated decision-making.

Ethical guidelines and soft laws

In addition to binding laws, governments and international organizations have released ethical guidelines to influence the development of AI, helping ensure that AI technologies are used responsibly and ethically. The Organization for Economic Cooperation and Development (OECD) has developed a set of AI principles, which have been adopted by 42 countries.[2] These principles promote human-centred AI, accountability and transparency, with a focus on ensuring that AI technologies are developed and used in ways that benefit society. Although these guidelines are non-binding, they significantly influence national legislation and help shape the ethical standards that governments and companies follow in their AI development efforts.

Ethics Guidelines for Trustworthy AI (EU)

The European Commission's Ethics Guidelines for Trustworthy AI emphasize transparency, fairness and privacy, guiding the development of AI systems that respect fundamental human rights. These guidelines, while voluntary, have played a pivotal role in shaping mandatory legislation such as the EU AI Act. By encouraging developers to adhere to ethical principles, these guidelines promote responsible AI development and ensure that AI technologies serve the public good without causing harm or reinforcing societal inequalities.

AI misuse in B2B marketing

The following are main areas where AI can be potentially misused.

AI misuse 1: over-personalization and intrusive targeting

AI-driven personalization can potentially become invasive when it crosses boundaries of privacy. For instance, tracking a client's every action, even minor browsing habits or engagement times, can create discomfort if clients feel they're being monitored too closely. While such data can be used to deliver highly relevant and personalized content, it can also raise concerns about privacy and data security. A B2B marketing firm might track a company's web activity and start sending highly tailored recommendations, but if these are based on extensive data gathering, it could feel invasive, particularly if the client feels they are being 'watched' too closely. In practice, this issue might manifest when a B2B company uses AI to personalize emails or content at a hyper-individualized level, mentioning very specific actions the client has taken (e.g. 'We saw that you spent 45 minutes reviewing our product comparison chart last Tuesday').

AI misuse 2: over-automating client interactions

Many companies rely heavily on AI chatbots or automated response systems to handle client communications. While this is efficient, excessive automation without human involvement can lead to responses that miss context, appear insensitive or lack the nuance needed in complex B2B relationships. For example, imagine a client who has been negotiating a contract with a B2B supplier for several weeks. They ask the chatbot for clarification on a particular clause, but the bot gives a generic response based on previous data, missing the specific context of the negotiation. This lack of personalization can be frustrating, especially when the client needs to feel heard and understood in the negotiation process. Excessive automation can give the impression that the business values efficiency over genuine client relationships, leading to a decrease in satisfaction.

AI misuse 3: misleading predictive analytics

Predictive analytics play a crucial role in anticipating client needs, but their effectiveness is compromised when the underlying data or models are flawed. When marketers rely on these predictions without regularly validating their accuracy or making context-aware adjustments, their outreach efforts can become misdirected. The consequences of over-relying on inaccurate predictions include mismatched offers and poor timing, which can waste resources and frustrate clients. Ultimately, if customers receive irrelevant messages or offers, it can erode their trust in the brand, making them feel misunderstood or miscategorized.

AI misuse 4: spamming with automated outreach

While AI-driven marketing automation allows for high-frequency and personalized emails, its misuse can lead to overwhelming clients with excessive or irrelevant messaging. When companies overuse this capability, they risk creating a negative brand perception, with clients viewing the organization as spammy or overly aggressive. This bombardment of messages can prompt clients to unsubscribe or disengage from further communications, ultimately damaging the relationship and diminishing the effectiveness of future marketing efforts.

TABLE 14.2 AI misuse

B2B marketing scenario	Example of misuse	Potential consequences
1. Bias in lead scoring	AI model assigns higher lead scores based on biased data (e.g. favouring large companies or certain industries)	Discriminatory targeting, missed opportunities from smaller or diverse businesses, and unfair sales prioritization
2. Over-personalization of content	AI creates content that's too focused on personal data, like predicting too much about a customer's needs	Intrusive marketing, potential violation of privacy regulations (e.g. GDPR) and alienation of customers

(continued)

TABLE 14.2 (Continued)

B2B marketing scenario	Example of misuse	Potential consequences
3. Over-automation of customer interactions	Using AI chatbots for customer queries without proper human escalation options, leading to frustration	Poor customer experience, customer dissatisfaction and potential loss of business due to unresolved issues
4. Misuse of data for targeted ads	AI analyses personal or sensitive data improperly (e.g. using health data for marketing non-related products)	Privacy breaches, legal issues and damaged trust with customers
5. Misleading predictive analytics	AI tool falsely predicts that a lead is high-quality based on skewed data (e.g. overemphasis on certain behaviors)	Wasted resources on pursuing poor-quality leads, lowered sales conversion rates and frustrated sales teams

AI compliance best practices

B2B companies should ensure as best as possible they have compliance measures in place when using or creating AI marketing technologies. Here are some measures and best practices.

- Clear rules and guidelines for using AI: Companies should develop and communicate clear guidelines for using AI tools or using AI features of technologies. Guidelines might relate to how data is collected or how decisions are made as well as ethical aspects to take into consideration.
- AI system review: AI systems should be regularly reviewed to ensure they comply with legislation.
- Risk assessment and contingency: Risks related to AI should be identified, managed and then contingencies should be in place. For example, a risk assessment and simulation could be carried out relating to data usage, potential misuse and then this situation could be reverse engineered.

Ethical considerations for generative AI

In previous chapters we've looked at generative AI and its limitations, but we should also consider ethical implications regarding AI usage in creating content.

The ethical use of generative AI in content creation raises significant concerns, particularly regarding content authenticity. Generative AI models, such as GPT or image generators, can produce highly realistic text, images and videos that blur the line between artificial and authentic creations. This capability introduces risks of misleading content, where audiences may struggle to differentiate between AI-generated material and genuine human-created works. For instance, a study by Pew Research in 2023 revealed that 61 per cent of Americans were concerned about AI's potential to generate false information.[3] Misleading AI-generated content, like deepfakes or fabricated news articles, can manipulate public opinion, sow distrust and even incite harmful actions, underscoring the need for transparency in labelling and attribution. The ethical imperative here is clear: creators and platforms must implement robust measures to ensure audiences are informed about the origin of content, thus preserving trust and minimizing deception.

Another area of concern is the unregulated use of 'grabbed' content, where AI models often generate new material based on vast datasets scraped from the internet without proper consent or acknowledgment of original creators. This practice raises questions about intellectual property rights, plagiarism and compensation for the original work. For example, high-profile cases, such as those involving artists suing AI companies for training models on copyrighted art, highlight the tension between technological advancement and ethical usage. Without safeguards, generative AI could commodify creative labour, eroding its value and violating creators' rights. To address these issues, organizations must adopt policies ensuring that datasets are ethically sourced, properly credited and used within clear legal frameworks. Such steps would not only protect original creators but also bolster the credibility and accountability of AI-generated content.

REAL-WORLD EXAMPLE

Understanding ethical data use and model building at CACI UK

CACI UK is a leading provider of data-driven solutions, specializing in analytics, technology and consulting services. The company supports organizations across multiple industries in leveraging data to drive informed decision-making. With a strong commitment to ethical considerations, CACI UK prioritizes responsible data use, particularly in the areas of AI and machine learning.

Interpreting legislation related to data use and model building presents significant challenges, particularly for B2B organizations operating in highly regulated environments. Broad legal guidelines often lack the specificity required for direct application, necessitating careful analysis and strategic policy development.

To that end the CACI UK spent a lot of time ensuring they give enough depth of explanation for how and why data is being used in their model-building process, using the ethical concept of 'harm' in order to do that. AI is in use in the machine learning sense rather than generative AI. However, this is a common activity when identifying 'next best action' or targeting cohorts, and because it has been around for a long time, hasn't really been ethically challenged.

CACI UK adheres to seven core ethical pillars (see Figure 14.3), with particular emphasis on diversity and fairness, and societal and environmental well-being. These areas pose unique challenges, as interpretations vary across stakeholders within the B2B ecosystem.

Applying the concept of harm

To ensure alignment with ethical standards, CACI UK begins by identifying potential harm categories (see Table 14.3) that end consumers might experience as a result of data modelling. Each model is then assessed against these harm categories to proactively address ethical concerns before deployment.

For example, in one model, CACI UK developed a set of descriptors ('attributes') about individuals and mapped them to specific potential harms. This structured

FIGURE 14.3 Ethical principles

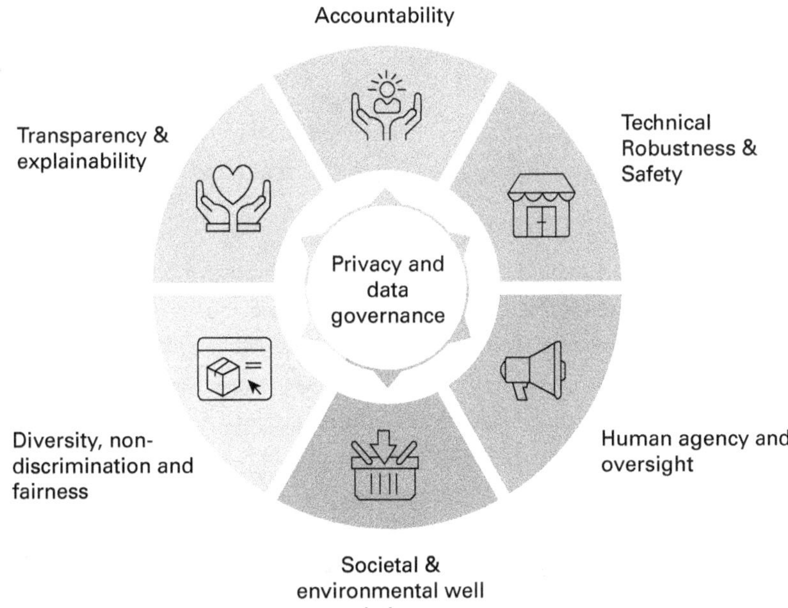

TABLE 14.3 Concept of harm

Ethical framework	Example of misuse	Harm version
Human rights	Dignity	Make incorrect assumptions
Human rights	Privacy	Not protect my personal data
Human rights society/community	Discrimination Participation in society	Not fairly represent Make me feel excluded
Society/community	Gainful employment	Take jobs away
Society/community	Impact on health and well-being	Make me anxious about using it
Society/community	Access to truth	Allow disinformation to spread
Society/community	Government intervention	Give too much power to the state
Resource allocation	Access to services and products	Make interacting with brands complicated
Resource allocation	Access to information and decision making	Make it hard to understand how companies operate
Environmental	Impact on the planet	Have a negative impact on the planet
Environmental	Impact on local environment	Have a negative impact on my local community

approach enabled the implementation of mitigation strategies, ensuring responsible data usage while maintaining model accuracy and effectiveness.

Enhancing model fairness and transparency

CACI UK not only incorporated harm-based evaluations into its modelling process but also additional fairness metrics. In one use case, the company examined gender fairness in relation to model accuracy, providing clients with greater transparency into the model's performance. This enables businesses to make informed decisions regarding the application and reliability of AI-driven insights.

Additionally, CACI UK has enhanced its focus on input data provenance, working to identify and mitigate biases before they impact model outcomes. By addressing biases at the source, they also help organizations build trust in AI-powered solutions while ensuring compliance with ethical best practices.

References

1 Henderson, S (2022) There's more to AI bias than biased data, NIST report highlights, NIST, www.nist.gov/news-events/news/2022/03/theres-more-ai-bias-biased-data-nist-report-highlights (archived at https://perma.cc/HR7X-G8BD)

2 OECD (n.d.) AI principles, www.oecd.org/en/topics/sub-issues/ai-principles

3 Rainee, L. et al, (2022) How Americans think about artificial intelligence, 17 March, www.pewresearch.org/internet/2022/03/17/how-americans-think-about-artificial-intelligence/ (archived at https://perma.cc/AQK9-G2FM)

Further reading

Clark, E (2024) The ethical dilemma of AI in marketing: A slippery slope, Forbes, www.forbes.com/sites/elijahclark/2024/03/14/the-ethical-dilemma-of-ai-in-marketing-a-slippery-slope/ (archived at https://perma.cc/J766-D844)

Clark, S (2024) AI in marketing: Ethical dilemmas explored, CMSWire, www.cmswire.com/digital-experience/ai-and-ethics-navigating-the-new-frontier/ (archived at https://perma.cc/2MVC-YHXS)

IBM (2023) Shedding light on AI bias with real world examples, IBM, www.ibm.com/think/topics/shedding-light-on-ai-bias-with-real-world-examples (archived at https://perma.cc/82TY-MA34)

Manyika, J et al (2019) What do we do about the biases in AI?, 25 October, hbr.org/2019/10/what-do-we-do-about-the-biases-in-ai (archived at https://perma.cc/63QD-7CMR)

15

AI-powered analytics

What you will gain from this chapter

Understanding of the following:

- understanding of marketing analytics areas
- how AI can benefit marketing performance management
- understanding AI for real-time analysis
- how to use AI for forecasting and attribution

The evolution of marketing analytics

Data accessibility and new technologies have been pivotal in transforming the marketing analytics space. Previously, if one wanted to measure marketing performance this would have been done more manually through customer surveys or through capturing sales information. Marketing analytics was more reactive in nature which meant companies would use information and react to what has happened.

Then around 20–30 years ago, something changed; digital channels and digital technologies started to enter the space of marketing analytics through web analytics and other digital platform analytics. Website metrics helped companies understand more about digital behaviours through metrics such as impressions, click-through rates and more. Digital metrics then expanded to accommodate search engine marketing metrics and email marketing metrics.

In the early 2010s we saw the advent of big data, which meant companies could digest and crunch large amounts of data as well as combine types of data.[1] In the late 2010s we've seen AI become more integrated into marketing analytics platforms as well as AI standalone platforms allowing marketers to do so much more. With AI we are now able to analyse not only large datasets but amalgamate different datasets to uncover trends and patterns which was not possible before. Such techniques have given rise to predictive analytics to be able to better understand historical performance and to predict future results. (See Figure 15.1.)

AI-powered analytics technologies also continuously learn from data and new data and so evolve according; through continuously learning they are able to update insights on a continuous basis. Using AI for marketing analytics is not just about better analytics but about automating analytical tasks and routines.

Types of AI tools for marketing performance analysis

So, in this book we've already been looking into a number of tools where AI tools can help with understanding and managing marketing performance. The main areas we can see AI benefit marketing performance analysis are as follows:

- Predictive analytics and performance measurement tools: These tools analyse large datasets to evaluate the effectiveness of marketing campaigns and predict future performance. By identifying patterns and trends in consumer behaviour, they enable marketers to make data-driven decisions, adjust strategies in real time and allocate resources more effectively for future campaigns.
- AI-driven A/B testing and optimization tools: These tools facilitate the testing of different marketing campaign versions. An example is Optimizely, which uses AI to run A/B tests on different marketing content (webpages, ads) and optimize based on user interactions. AI enhances this process by automatically adjusting tests, identifying significant trends quicker and improving conversion rates through real-time adjustments to content and design.
- ROI and attribution tools: These tools evaluate the ROI of marketing campaigns by attributing sales and conversions to specific marketing channels. By using AI to analyse the customer journey across touchpoints, these tools help marketers understand which channels and activities generate the most value, allowing them to refine their strategies and improve budget allocation for higher returns.

FIGURE 15.1 Evolution of marketing analytics

The birth of marketing metrics (early 20th century)
Rise of direct marketing and tracking
Emergence of media mix modelling (MMM)
The digital revolution and web analytics (1990s)
Growth of customer relationship management (CRM) systems (1990s–2000s)
Rise of attribution modelling (2000s)
Social media analytics (2005–2015)
Predictive analytics and machine learning (2010s)
Real-time marketing dashboards (2010s)
AI-powered marketing analytics (2020s)

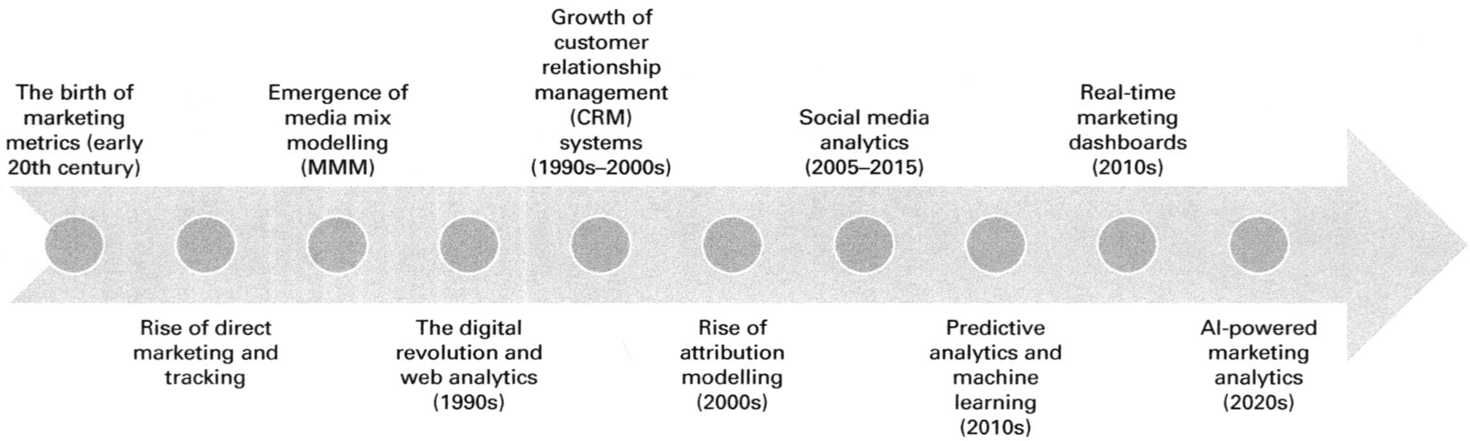

- Ad performance and targeting tools: These tools optimize paid marketing campaigns and assess their effectiveness through AI-driven targeting and performance metrics. By analysing vast amounts of data, these tools predict the most relevant audiences for each ad, optimize bidding strategies and adjust campaigns dynamically to maximize ad performance and conversion rates, ensuring that advertising budgets are spent efficiently.

Real-time data analysis

AI tools allow organizations to deal with data inputs and data streams in real time. This means analytics can be more rapid but also provide insights and information in the moment, which facilitates organizations to respond in the moment to such data and insights if they need to.

Lead scoring

A digital marketing campaign that drives traffic to its website and captures leads through webinars, content downloads and contact forms will benefit from real-time data analysis, particularly if the company receives a lot of leads daily; understanding in the moment how some leads are more valuable than others or have a greater urgency than others, will be invaluable for proper routeing and follow-up.

Real-time campaign performance optimization

Let's consider a B2B company running an integrated marketing campaign across multiple channels (Google Ads, LinkedIn, email, etc.) with the goal of generating leads for a new product launch. With AI tools they can track performance metrics (such as click-through rates, conversions and engagement) in real-time across channels. If a campaign underperforms on a particular channel (e.g. LinkedIn), real-time data allows marketers to adjust the ad spend or creatives immediately to optimize performance. AI can automatically suggest which channels are driving the highest ROI and recommend reallocating budgets to those channels. This can be seen in Figure 15.2.

Optimizing account-based marketing (ABM) targeting

Where a B2B company is running an ABM campaign, targeting a specific set of high-value accounts with personalized ads and email campaigns, the goal

FIGURE 15.2 AI for real-time campaign performance optimization

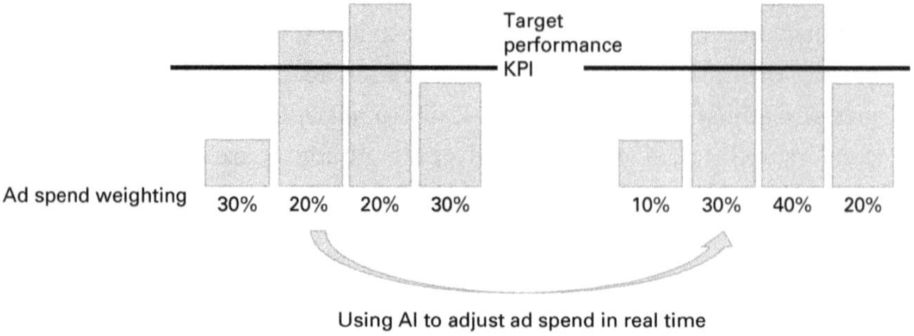

Target performance KPI

Ad spend weighting	30%	20%	20%	30%		10%	30%	40%	20%

Using AI to adjust ad spend in real time

might be to engage decision-makers and key influencers in these organizations. AI tools can track account engagement in real time, such as when a decision-maker from a target account interacts with a specific ad, email or website content. Based on real-time behaviour, AI can adjust ad targeting, sending follow-up content or trigger personalized emails to key account stakeholders. If a target account shows increased engagement (multiple stakeholders interacting with content), AI can notify sales teams immediately to act on the hot opportunity. This immediate engagement increases the likelihood of converting high-value accounts by capitalizing on timely interest.

Identifying and responding to market shifts

Consider the situation where a B2B software company is monitoring trends and market shifts during the launch of a new SaaS product. They are targeting prospects across different regions and industries and need to adapt quickly to changing market demands. AI tools track customer sentiment, competitor behaviour and industry trends in real time by analysing social media, news articles and online forums. If there's a sudden shift in customer needs or industry priorities (e.g. a new regulation affecting purchasing decisions), AI can alert marketers to adjust messaging or develop new campaigns to address these shifts.

AI for forecasting marketing results

AI tools can improve marketing performance in the area of forecasting outcomes or results; for example, in the area of demand planning. AI tools can be used to forecast demand based on latest promotions or offers and subsequently use that information to optimize inventory management or other resources. Such dynamic forecasting also helps businesses segment their customers, products and markets more effectively.

PLC management

AI can forecast when a product may reach maturity or decline, helping marketers adjust promotional efforts or plan for product updates or replacements.

AI tools can be instrumental in identifying the B2B product life-cycle stages (introduction, growth, maturity and decline) by analysing large datasets and uncovering insights from customer behaviours, sales trends and market dynamics. (See Figure 15.3.)

Customer sentiment and feedback analysis (AI-powered text analytics and NLP) tools like MonkeyLearn and Lexalytics can analyse customer feedback, reviews and social media mentions, to assess how customers perceive the product at different stages. Positive feedback during the introduction or early growth stage can signal increasing market acceptance, while negative sentiment during the maturity or decline stages could indicate product saturation or dissatisfaction.

Tools like Salesforce Einstein or Pega for tracking sales and revenue trends can analyse sales data to identify trends and forecast future revenue, tracking metrics like sales velocity, growth rate and customer acquisition cost (CAC). For instance, during the growth phase, you'd expect rapid sales increases and decreasing CAC as word-of-mouth and customer referrals grow. If the sales trend starts to plateau, it could indicate the maturity phase.

Market share and competitive analysis tools like Crayon and Kompyte gather and analyse data on competitors, allowing businesses to track their position in the market relative to other products. During the growth stage, a product will typically see increasing market share as competitors are less established. However, as the product enters maturity, competitors might have caught up or new entrants could dilute market share.

Product usage and feature adoption tools like Pendo and Mixpanel can provide insights regarding customers usage of product's features, which could also indicate where the product is in its life cycle. During the growth phase, new features may see high adoption rates as customers explore and utilize them. In the maturity phase, this could slow down as the product becomes a 'staple' in the market. Declining usage or feature adoption in the decline phase often means customers are moving toward competitors or alternative solutions.

FIGURE 15.3 AI tools and PLC identification

Customer sentiment and feedback analysis	Sales and revenue trends	Market share and competitive analysis tools	Product usage and feature adoption tools
e.g. MonkeyLearn and Lexalytics	**e.g. Salesforce Einstainor Pega**	**e.g. Crayon, Kompyte**	**e.g. Pendo and Mixpanel**
• Positive feedback during the introduction or early growth stage can signal increasing market acceptance. • Nuringthe maturity or decline stages could indicate product saturation or dissatisfaction.	• During the growth phase, rapid sales increases and decreasing CAC as word-of-mouth and customer referrals grow. • Sales trend starts to plateau, could indicate the maturity phase.	• During the growth stage, a product will typically see increasing market share as competitors are less established. • As product enters maturity, competitors might have caught up or new entrants could dilute market share.	• During the growth phase, new features may see high adoption rates as customers explore and utilize them. • In the maturity phase, this could slow down as the product becomes a 'staple' in the market. • Declining usage or feature adoption in the decline phase

Product planning: product feature prioritization

AI tools play a crucial role in identifying product feature usage and prioritization by analysing customer feedback, usage data and market trends, helping businesses make informed decisions about which features to develop or enhance. One such tool is Anaplan, which uses AI-driven predictive analytics and machine learning to forecast customer preferences and trends. It leverages historical data, customer feedback and market behaviour to generate insights into which features are most likely to resonate with users, enabling product teams to prioritize them in the roadmap.

Marketing process optimization

AI forecasting can improve marketing processes, making them more efficient and responsive to market conditions. AI can predict bottlenecks in marketing processes, such as campaign execution or lead nurturing workflows, enabling teams to optimize resources. AI can predict how marketing teams can optimize workflows to ensure campaigns are delivered on time and within budget. Examples of AI tools include Pardot and Marketo.

Price forecasting

AI forecasting tools can analyse market data, customer behaviour and competitive pricing to optimize pricing strategies. This is critical in maximizing revenue and ensuring competitiveness. AI tools can forecast demand fluctuations and adjust prices in real time, helping companies respond to market conditions, seasonality and competitor pricing.

Price sensitivity analysis: AI can forecast how changes in pricing might affect customer demand, helping marketers understand which price points will maximize sales while maintaining profitability. Examples of AI-enabled tools include Dynamic Yield, Revionics and Pricefx.

Post-marketing campaign optimization and AI

We've already covered a lot of aspects where performance can be optimized, e.g. through AI features in advertising tools and channel attribution tools; though there are other key areas where AI can improve marketing productivity and operations.

AI-powered platforms, such as Adobe Experience Cloud and Salesforce Marketing Cloud, use machine learning to tailor content and experiences to individual users. By analysing user behaviour and preferences, AI can dynamically adjust email content, web pages and advertisements to suit each customers' needs. This leads to higher engagement rates, improved conversion rates and a better return on investment (ROI) for marketers.

A/B testing, a common method for comparing the performance of different versions of marketing assets, has also been transformed by AI. Traditionally, A/B testing required marketers to set up experiments manually, compare two variations (such as different email subject lines or website layouts) and analyse the results. AI-powered A/B testing platforms, like Optimizely and VWO, automate this process by running multiple tests simultaneously, analysing performance in real-time and recommending the best-performing variation based on data. This allows for faster decision-making and more granular insights into what works best for a particular audience. See Table 15.1 for a view on the main A/B testing areas in using AI.

AI can conduct multivariate testing, which involves testing multiple variables at once rather than just two variations. This can lead to deeper insights into how different elements of a campaign interact with each other. For example, Optimizely uses AI to run multivariate tests on website elements, helping

TABLE 15.1 A/B testing areas

Area	Websites	Emails	Social media
1. Headlines	Test page titles and headlines	Test subject lines	Test post captions or headlines
2. Call to action (CTA)	Test CTA text ('Buy Now' vs 'Learn More')	Test CTA buttons (e.g. 'Subscribe' vs 'Join Us')	Test CTA text in posts or ads
3. Layout	Test different page layouts	Test email design formats (e.g. single vs multi-column)	Test ad layout (carousel vs single image)
4. Images	Test hero images or product visuals	Test header images or embedded visuals	Test image types (illustrations vs photos)
5. Navigation	Test menu structure or links	Test placement of links in email body	Test link placement in posts or bios
6. Copy length	Test short vs long product descriptions	Test concise vs detailed email body	Test long captions vs short captions
7. Forms	Test form field length (e.g. 3 fields vs 6 fields)	Test embedded forms vs linked forms	Test sign-up links in posts or forms on platforms
8. Timing	Test time-to-load speed impact	Test send times (morning vs evening)	Test posting times (weekday vs weekend)

businesses identify the combination of headlines, images and call-to-action buttons that drive the highest conversion rates. By continuously learning from these tests, AI can also automate future optimizations, making ongoing improvements without the need for manual intervention.

Marketing budget management and tracking

For a B2B marketing team, effective budget management and tracking is essential for maximizing ROI and ensuring that resources are allocated efficiently across various initiatives. Marketing budget management refers to the identification, summarizing, monitoring and optimizing of marketing budgets.

Proper management helps marketing teams focus their investments on strategies that drive the highest returns, while ensuring alignment with business goals. Below are the key areas within marketing budget management that help ensure efficient spending and optimal outcomes.

Campaign budgeting and allocation

Campaign budgeting and allocation is a key part of effective marketing budget management. This process involves setting budgets for individual campaigns and distributing resources across various marketing channels. These channels may include paid search, social media, email marketing, etc. Proper allocation ensures that each campaign receives the right level of funding based on its objectives, audience and potential impact. By adjusting budget allocations according to campaign performance, marketers can optimize resource use and improve overall ROI.

Media spend tracking

Media spend tracking is essential for monitoring how marketing dollars are spent across various advertising platforms. Marketers must track ad spending across channels such as paid search, social media and display ads to ensure that campaigns are running within their budget. By consistently reviewing ad performance, marketers can adjust bids, targeting and creative to maximize the efficiency of their media spend. This helps prevent overspending and ensures that the investment is driving results in terms of impressions, clicks, conversions and, ultimately, revenue.

Tracking lead generation costs and customer acquisition costs (CAC)

Tracking lead generation costs and CAC is vital to understanding how effective marketing campaigns are in driving qualified leads and generating sales. CAC refers to the total cost incurred to acquire a customer, including marketing and sales expenses. By closely monitoring CAC and lead-generation costs, marketing teams can assess the cost-effectiveness of different channels and tactics. This insight enables them to allocate resources more effectively, optimize campaigns and focus on channels that deliver the best return on investment. Please see Figure 15.4 for visual breakdown of the category of costs.

FIGURE 15.4 CAC costs

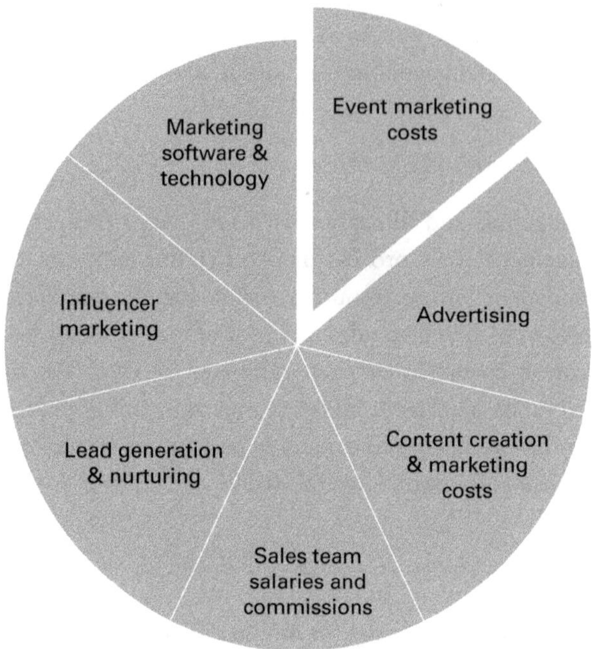

Tracking marketing automation and technology costs

Marketing automation and technology costs are an important aspect of budget management, particularly for B2B companies that rely on platforms such as Marketo, HubSpot and Pardot. These software tools help streamline marketing processes like lead nurturing, email campaigns and customer segmentation. However, their costs, including software licensing and ongoing maintenance, need to be carefully managed. Tracking these costs ensures that marketing teams are investing in the right technology solutions that drive efficiency and help scale marketing efforts while staying within budget.

Event marketing and sponsorships

Event marketing and sponsorships often represent significant expenditures for B2B marketing teams. These activities can include attending or sponsoring industry conferences, setting up booths and covering travel expenses. While these events provide valuable networking opportunities and brand exposure, they can also be costly. By closely monitoring event-related costs, marketers can evaluate the ROI of participating in or sponsoring events, ensuring that the benefits (such as lead generation and brand recognition) outweigh the expenses.

Reporting and analytics

Reporting and analytics play a critical role in managing and tracking marketing expenditures and performance. Tools like Datorama, Google Analytics and Tableau provide real-time dashboards and insights, allowing marketing teams to assess campaign ROI, track spending and make data-driven adjustments. With these tools, teams can evaluate the effectiveness of their marketing strategies, identify areas for improvement and optimize their budgets in real time. Regular reporting and analysis help ensure that every dollar spent contributes to business goals and maximizes marketing outcomes.

AI tools: how they help marketing budget management

Several areas of marketing budget management (MBM) can be significantly improved through the use of AI tools, enhancing both efficiency and effectiveness across B2B marketing initiatives.

First, campaign budgeting and allocation can benefit from AI-powered tools like Allocadia and HubSpot, which offer predictive budgeting features. These tools analyse historical campaign performance and suggest optimized budget allocations for future campaigns. AI-driven forecasting ensures that resources are directed to the most promising channels, reducing the risk of overspending or underfunding high-potential campaigns.

In the area of media spend, tracking tools such as Google Ads Smart Bidding and LinkedIn Campaign Manager use machine learning algorithms to adjust bids in real time. These AI systems continuously optimize paid media investments by predicting which ad placements are likely to yield the best results based on historical performance, audience behaviour and current market conditions. By automating bid adjustments and budget reallocation, these tools maximize return on ad spend (ROAS) and prevent wasted media spend.

Under lead generation and CAC management, AI tools like Salesforce Einstein and Marketo leverage predictive analytics to prioritize high-quality leads. AI helps identify patterns in customer behaviour and engagement, enabling marketers to focus their budgets on leads that are most likely to convert.

With regard to content marketing and SEO, AI tools such as MarketMuse and Moz optimize the content creation and distribution process. By using AI to analyse SEO trends and predict content performance, these platforms help marketers allocate their content marketing budget more effectively.

Finally, AI enhances reporting and analytics through tools like Datorama and Google Analytics. These platforms use AI to generate real-time insights and recommendations for budget adjustments based on campaign performance. With AI-driven dashboards and multi-touch attribution, marketers can quickly identify which campaigns and channels are delivering the best ROI, allowing for more agile and data-driven budget management.

Challenges in using AI for performance analysis

There are a number of challenges which marketers may face when using AI tools in measuring marketing performance; one of those is data privacy, which we covered in earlier chapters.

Data integration challenges

Particularly in the area of pre purchase in B2B marketing there are numerous data sources which may need to be merged to provide an accurate picture of marketing. AI tools require high-quality, well-integrated data from various sources to yield accurate insights, but many companies struggle with fragmented and inconsistent data. Examples of diverse sources, include social media, marketing automation platforms, CRM systems and websites. Without a unified data framework, the AI tools can produce inaccurate insights, affecting decision-making.

Data accuracy

AI models rely on high-quality, precise data to deliver accurate insights that inform decision-making. When the data fed into AI systems is incomplete, outdated, inconsistent or inaccurate, it can lead to misleading conclusions, incorrect optimizations and ineffective strategies. One challenge arises when using AI to optimize campaign performance. Many B2B marketers rely on AI tools to analyse large volumes of campaign data across multiple channels (email, paid search, social media, etc.) to optimize ad spend and increase ROI. AI models analyse key performance indicators (KPIs) such as click-through rates, conversion rates and cost-per-lead to make real-time adjustments.

Data interpretation

AI models may sometimes act as black boxes providing challenges for interpreting exact reasons behind data. For example, if an AI tool suggests that a particular demographic is likely to churn, but can't explain why, marketers may be hesitant to implement retention strategies targeting that demographic. A survey by IBM found that 60 per cent of businesses consider lack of transparency a major barrier to AI adoption, highlighting the need for interpretable AI models in marketing applications.[2]

Implementation resourcing challenges

Deploying and maintaining AI tools for marketing performance measurement can be expensive and resource intensive, also at times dependent on the skills of personnel. Many companies, especially small and medium enterprises, will find it difficult to justify such resources.

AI for social media marketing performance

Let's take a look more specifically at measuring social media marketing performance in B2B and how AI tools and AI features can help.

Sentiment analysis in brand monitoring

Sentiment analysis leverages natural language processing (NLP) to track sentiment across brand mentions. This feature helps B2B companies understand customer emotions and opinions in real time. It helps detect potential issues quickly, allowing for proactive reputation management.

Predictive analytics of social media interactions

Predictive analytics can also be used for social media behaviours and interactions; this feature can be used to identify leads with high purchase intent. For example, an AI-powered lead scoring tool can help prioritize leads based on their engagement with B2B content on LinkedIn.

Social media content performance prediction

AI can be used to likely engagement for content before it's published, allowing B2B marketers to make data-driven content choices based on predicted content engagement. An example of a tool with this feature is **BuzzSumo,** which analyses past content performance, enabling a tech company to determine the most engaging formats for LinkedIn articles or Twitter threads.

Social indicators for churn prediction

AI predictive models included in tools such as Salesforce Einstein can analyse social engagement to identify at-risk accounts. Social signals which may point to an at-risk account might be a decreased engagement levels such as a significant drop in likes, shares, comments or clicks on social media content from an account. For example, if a customer's engagement with your brand's LinkedIn posts drops noticeably, this could indicate dissatisfaction or shifting priorities. Other signals might be a drop in content engagement. For example, if a customer shifts their engagement from in-depth, product-related posts to general content or starts ignoring your brand's posts, it might signal that they're losing interest in the specific value propositions of your brand.

Social media ROI attribution

Google Analytics 360 leverages AI-driven multi-touch attribution, helping a B2B brand measure the ROI of their LinkedIn and Twitter campaigns.

AI-powered dashboards

AI-powered marketing dashboards use AI to streamline data collection, processing and visualization, giving marketers immediate access to real-time insights for data-driven decision-making. This capability is especially valuable in B2B contexts, where data volumes are high and decision timelines can directly impact complex sales cycles. Unlike traditional dashboards, AI-powered dashboards continuously learn and adapt from incoming data, enhancing accuracy and delivering predictive insights that guide marketers toward strategic opportunities.

Streamlining data collection and analysis

Tools like Tableau and Power BI, when integrated with AI, are invaluable in processing large datasets and identifying key trends, anomalies and patterns that might otherwise go unnoticed. These platforms generate sophisticated visualizations that highlight crucial insights, allowing B2B marketers to spot shifts in customer preferences, emerging demands or potential market expansions swiftly. For example, an AI-powered tableau dashboard could alert a B2B marketer to a growing trend in a particular geographical area, signalling an opportunity to target new markets. The market for AI grew beyond $184 billion in 2024, a considerable jump of nearly $50 billion compared to 2023. This staggering growth is expected to continue with the market racing past $826 billion in 2030.[3]

AI-driven visualization features: simplifying complex data

AI-driven visualization features, such as heat maps, trend forecasting graphs and custom charts, make interpreting vast amounts of data much simpler for marketers. These tools reduce cognitive load and allow for a greater focus on strategic planning rather than manual data crunching. For example, Salesforce Einstein Analytics leverages AI to produce intuitive dashboards that offer predictive insights, such as forecasting customer behaviour based on previous interactions. In a B2B scenario, this could help identify which industries are most likely to convert based on historical patterns. These advanced visualizations enable B2B marketers to prioritize opportunities, fine-tune targeting strategies and make more informed decisions about where to allocate resources effectively.

Unlocking predictive insights to optimize marketing strategies

One of the key benefits of AI in B2B marketing is its ability to detect patterns in large datasets, offering insights that human analysts may overlook. With tools like Google Data Studio, enhanced by AI, data can be pulled from various marketing platforms such as Google Ads, social media and CRM systems. This integration provides a comprehensive performance overview and highlights actionable insights, such as customer behaviour trends, engagement rates and conversion metrics. By utilizing these predictive insights, B2B marketers can refine their strategies to enhance customer acquisition, retention and overall marketing effectiveness.

ROI and attribution tools

Measuring the return on investment (ROI) for AI projects presents several challenges. One of the primary difficulties is the complexity and uncertainty surrounding AI technologies. As AI applications continue to evolve rapidly, it becomes challenging to establish consistent and long-term ROI metrics.

Another obstacle is the integration of AI solutions with existing IT infrastructure. The process of incorporating AI into established systems often incurs additional costs and complexities, which can significantly impact the overall ROI. These integration challenges need to be considered when evaluating the potential returns of AI investments.

Furthermore, AI projects typically do not yield immediate financial returns. The benefits of AI often accumulate gradually over time as the system learns and improves. This requires organizations to adopt a long-term perspective when assessing ROI, as the full value of AI may not be realized in the short term.

Additionally, AI projects can provide intangible and qualitative benefits that are harder to measure in financial terms. While tangible outcomes such as increased efficiency or cost savings are easier to quantify, improvements in areas like customer satisfaction or enhanced decision-making capabilities are more abstract. These intangible benefits can be just as valuable but are often overlooked when calculating ROI.

Attribution modelling and AI

AI-driven attribution modelling in B2B marketing focuses on analysing the influence of various marketing touchpoints across a customer's journey to determine their impact on conversions and revenue. One of the key features of AI attribution modelling is its ability to process large datasets and track multiple touchpoints across different marketing channels. Unlike traditional models, AI-driven models can account for both direct and indirect influences, enabling a more nuanced understanding of how different interactions contribute to the overall outcome. AI models continuously evolve by learning from new data, enhancing their accuracy in predicting which touchpoints are most influential in driving revenue.

Additionally, AI attribution models can incorporate factors such as the timing and frequency of touchpoints, which can play a crucial role in the buying decision. This level of sophistication helps marketers create more effective strategies that take into account the long and complex B2B buyer journey.

How AI can support better attribution modelling

AI can significantly improve attribution modelling by providing deeper insights and more accurate predictions. One of the primary ways AI supports better attribution is through machine learning algorithms that analyse historical data and identify patterns in customer behaviour. These algorithms can assign weighted values to different touchpoints, reflecting their true impact on conversion rates. This enables marketers to understand the relative importance of each touchpoint in a multi-channel campaign and avoid oversimplified models that might overlook crucial interactions.

AI can also help marketers optimize their attribution models by adapting to new data over time. As AI continuously learns from incoming data, it can refine its understanding of customer behaviour and provide real-time insights into what is driving conversions. This dynamic approach allows for more responsive and agile marketing strategies, which is especially beneficial in B2B marketing where buyer journeys are often lengthy and complex. Additionally, AI-powered attribution tools can also integrate with other data sources, such as CRM systems, website analytics and social media platforms, to provide a more comprehensive view of the customer journey.

Key AI tools for B2B attribution modelling

Several AI-powered tools can enhance B2B marketing attribution modelling by offering advanced features tailored to the complexities of B2B sales cycles. Dreamdata is one such tool that provides a unified approach to attribution by connecting different marketing platforms, CRM systems and sales data to give a holistic view of the customer journey. Dreamdata uses AI to track how each marketing touchpoint influences the buyer's decision, offering valuable insights that help B2B marketers allocate resources efficiently and optimize ROI.

Another valuable tool is Windsor.ai, which integrates with various marketing and sales platforms to provide attribution insights across multiple channels. Windsor.ai uses AI to analyse data from various sources and provides marketers with a more granular understanding of which touchpoints are driving conversions. It also offers predictive analytics, helping marketers forecast future trends based on historical performance. These insights allow B2B marketers to make data-driven decisions, adjust strategies on the fly and ultimately improve marketing effectiveness.

References

1 Jackson-Barnes, S (2023) The evolution of big data? 11 January, www.orientsoftware.com/blog/big-data-evolution/ (archived at https://perma.cc/Q86L-RNKT)

2 Statista (n.d.) Artificial intelligence (AI) market size worldwide from 2020 to 2031, www.statista.com/forecasts/1474143/global-ai-market-size (archived at https://perma.cc/PG37-SU6E)

3 Zoominfo (2023) 65+ Statistics about artificial intelligence, 22 December, pipeline.zoominfo.com/sales/statistics-about-artificial-intelligence (archived at https://perma.cc/78NZ-JFEL)

Further reading

Sivek, SC (2023) Maximizing your marketing budget with AI and machine learning, Pecan AI, www.pecan.ai/blog/maximizing-marketing-budget-ai-machine-learning/ (archived at https://perma.cc/Z47T-EH75)

Sivek, SC (2023) The 7 steps to achieving AI-driven marketing optimization, Pecan AI, www.pecan.ai/blog/marketing-optimization-steps-ai/ (archived at https://perma.cc/TK7E-SR6J)

16

Marketing operations and AI

> What you will learn from this chapter
>
> Understanding of the following:
>
> - understand how AI can improve marketing team collaboration
> - AI and project management and campaign management
> - how AI can improve marketing productivity
> - knowledge sharing improving through AI

Introduction

Up to now we've been discussing AI and how it supports different areas of marketing but, of course, AI tools can go a long way to help other areas of marketing. AI can significantly improve marketing productivity and marketing effectiveness.

For the purposes of this chapter, we'll include these aspects under the umbrella of marketing operations which include marketing team collaboration, marketing team productivity, marketing process management and marketing planning.

Marketing collaboration

Engagement and idea storming

AI tools can be used to generate ideas and improve engagement within marketing teams.

We've talked earlier in this book about ideation related to content creation, although idea generation and the use of AI can also be used in other ways.

Product development and concept testing: AI tools can analyse consumer preferences, feedback and market gaps to suggest new product ideas or improvements to existing products. By processing large datasets, AI can identify unmet needs and emerging trends, helping teams brainstorm innovative product features or entirely new offerings. For example, AI tools can also analyse social media and review data to suggest product features that would enhance customer satisfaction, like introducing eco-friendly packaging.

Examples of AI tools for marketing ideation include the following:

- Crimson Hexagon (now part of Brandwatch) which can be used to analyse the voice of the customer and emerging trends for product ideation.
- Zappi can be used to test new product concepts and optimize them using consumer feedback data.

IN PRACTICE: COLLABORATION FOR IDEA GENERATION AND PROBLEM SOLVING

Take the example of a challenge of creating engaging campaign themes for niche industries.

Example problem: A B2B marketing team is tasked with developing a campaign for a highly technical industry (e.g. manufacturing automation) but struggles to generate creative and compelling themes that resonate with their audience.

AI tool – Notion AI/ features to use: Brainstorming templates and AI-generated idea prompts.

Solution: The team uses Notion AI's brainstorming features to generate content ideas based on keywords like 'manufacturing automation', 'ROI' and 'efficiency.'

AI suggests themes such as 'The Future of Smart Factories', 'Driving Efficiency with Predictive Maintenance' or 'ROI in Automation Investments'.

These ideas can then be shared collaboratively in a centralized workspace for team discussion and refinement.

Marketing team meetings

AI tools can also be used to improve meetings themselves; not only through scheduling or identifying availability for team members to meet up but within meetings. AI tools can be used for transcribing audio to text. AI transcription tools like otter.ai and Fireflies can save time and effort and improve the effectiveness of the meeting itself.

Below are some examples where transcription can be used in marketing.

1 Meeting summaries: AI transcription tools can automatically generate summaries of marketing meetings, allowing users to review and access information more easily.
2 Convert to other content formats: As well as being used within marketing team meetings these transcription tools can also be used to improve and simplify other marketing areas; for example, an AI transcription tool can convert podcasts, interviews, webinars or speeches into text, enabling marketers or content creators to repurpose the spoken material into blog posts, social media snippets or articles.
3 Converting service and sales calls: AI transcription tools can also be used in the area of customer interactions by capturing and converting service and sales calls. Through this automated capture this makes it easier to review interactions, identify key take-aways and any issues and optimize areas of marketing, e.g. FAQ documents.
4 Support deaf and hard of hearing at work: Transcription tools make audio and video content more accessible to diverse audience. For example, transcripts can be used to share with people who are deaf or are hard of hearing; in this way AI can also be seen as a great tool to improve diversity and inclusivity.

See Figure 16.1 for use cases of AI transcription tools in B2B marketing.

Project and workflow management

Marketing collaboration covers activities such as managing and sharing schedules; facilitating sharing of notes; organizing project teams. For such tasks one can use AI-based project management tools such as Wrike, Trello and Asana, which automate various project management tasks; these tools can help identify and remove bottlenecks as well as remove any risks which impact project schedules.

Some tools have more specific features for workflow management such as Asana, which includes an AI feature for assessing group members' availability for assigning tasks to ensure overall workloads are smoothed out.

FIGURE 16.1 Use cases for transcription tools

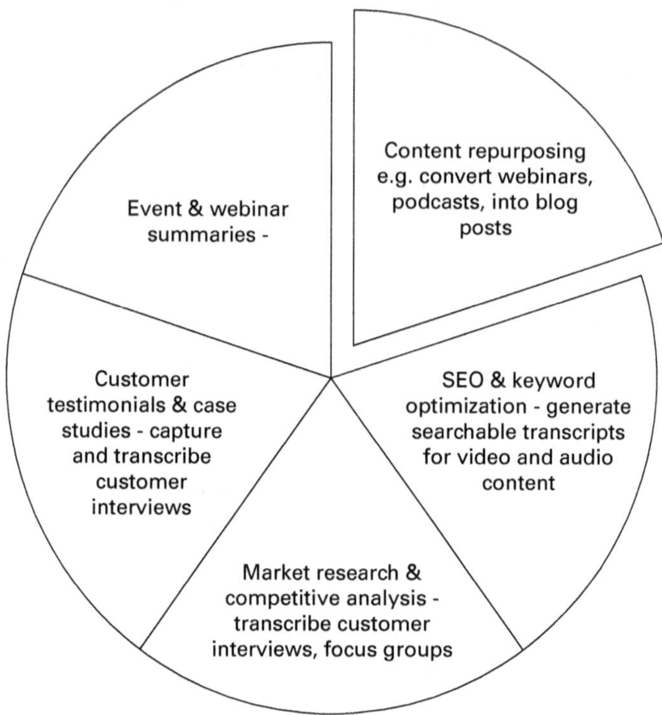

AI-powered project management tools can help predict project timelines and allocate resources. These systems can dynamically adjust project plans based on real-time data, ensuring that the implementation phase is as smooth and efficient as possible.

AI-powered chatbots can also be employed to handle routine customer inquiries, allowing team members to spend more time on delivering a personalized and meaningful service.

Microsoft Team Copilot

Microsoft Team Copilot is a new AI NLP/ML tool from Microsoft which can integrate with the Microsoft Teams platform. Copilot brings an AI-driven approach to enhance the productivity and efficiency of teams in various aspects of their daily operations. Below is a breakdown of how Microsoft Team Copilot can be leveraged in B2B marketing.

Project/campaign management

Microsoft Team Copilot can assist in project and campaign management by tracking progress, coordinating tasks and facilitating communication across team members. For example, in a B2B marketing campaign, Copilot could automatically generate reminders, update timelines and even suggest action items based on ongoing project status.

Meetings: automatic summaries and action items

Another feature of Copilot is its ability to summarize meetings and highlight key takeaways. Copilot can capture meeting notes, provide summaries and identify action items in real time. For instance, during a weekly B2B marketing meeting discussing client acquisition strategies, Copilot can automatically generate a brief summary of key discussions, highlight the next steps for different team members and even assign deadlines to tasks discussed.

Document sharing and collaboration

Microsoft Team Copilot also significantly enhances document sharing and collaboration, particularly important for B2B marketing teams working on documents such as campaign briefs, proposals or presentations.

Optimizing documents for clarity and professionalism

Copilot also serves as an AI-powered tool to optimize documents for grammar, tone and clarity. For B2B marketing teams working on high-stakes documents like proposals, emails to potential clients or marketing presentations, Copilot can suggest improvements to make the content more polished and professional. For instance, if a marketing and sales team are jointly preparing a proposal for a large B2B customer, Copilot could analyse the draft, providing feedback on areas where the language could be made more concise, persuasive or aligned with the client's needs.

Knowledge sharing

AI is transforming how businesses share, analyse and act upon knowledge. Due to its ability to process large data and to do this quickly, it can enable teams to collaborate more effectively, make data-driven decisions and stay ahead in competitive markets. Knowledge sharing, particularly in B2B marketing, has become more streamlined and impactful with AI-powered tools like Yammer, Scribe and Guru, which aid in monitoring competitors, analysing campaigns and fostering product innovation. Let's look at three areas of knowledge sharing.

Competitor knowledge sharing

AI tools excel at monitoring competitor activities, such as product launches, pricing changes and promotional strategies, on an ongoing basis. These insights are then automatically shared with marketing teams, enabling swift adjustments to strategies. For instance, an AI-driven competitive intelligence tool like Crayon can track competitor website changes, ad placements and social media activities in real time. In B2B marketing, such tools empower businesses to fine-tune their positioning by staying one step ahead in understanding competitor tactics.

Campaign knowledge sharing

AI tools can automate this marketing campaign process, producing detailed performance reports and key actionable takeaways. For example, tools like HubSpot and Marketo utilize AI to track ad engagement, click-through rates and ROI metrics. These tools also provide recommendations for refining ad creatives and suggest optimal campaign strategies. A case in point: a B2B SaaS company might use AI to identify that LinkedIn ads targeting a specific demographic outperform others, prompting budget reallocation.

Product innovation knowledge sharing

AI can extract, analyse and share customer feedback insights effectively. Sentiment analysis tools, such as Qualtrics or Medallia, capture customer complaints, suggestions and trends, providing product teams with actionable insights. For example, a B2B software provider might discover through AI analysis that users frequently complain about a particular dashboard feature. This insight, shared seamlessly with the product development team, can lead to targeted improvements or entirely new features. According to McKinsey, companies that integrate AI into their product development processes experience a 20–30 per cent reduction in time-to-market, emphasizing the role of AI in streamlining innovation.[1]

NOTION EXAMPLE

Notion is an AI-driven platform designed to simplify workflows, knowledge sharing and team collaboration, making it particularly valuable for smaller businesses that need an all-in-one solution. By combining notes, tasks and databases, Notion provides a centralized space to organize, manage and share knowledge effectively. For B2B marketing teams, its adaptability supports key areas such as content management, client documentation, sales enablement, project management and event planning.

Content repository for centralized knowledge

Notion's database functionality serves as an excellent tool for creating a centralized content repository. B2B marketing teams can use it to store and organize essential materials such as case studies, competitor research, industry reports and client data. By creating dedicated pages or databases, teams can categorize and tag materials for easy retrieval. For example, a B2B team might create a database with separate views for 'Competitor Analysis,' 'Customer Case Studies' and 'Marketing Campaign Reports'. These views could include filters or properties such as client industry, campaign type or publication date, ensuring that insights are readily accessible when planning future strategies.

Client relationship documentation

Notion's notetaking and database capabilities make it ideal for documenting client interactions, which is critical for account-based marketing (ABM) in the B2B space. Marketing teams can create individual pages for each client within a database, logging meeting notes, feedback and next steps. Using Notion's timeline or calendar views, teams can track the progression of conversations and personalize follow-ups effectively. For instance, if a B2B marketer is managing a relationship with a high-value client, they could record specific feedback on past campaigns, outline key decision-maker preferences and note deadlines for deliverables – all in one accessible location.

Sales and marketing playbooks

B2B marketing teams often rely on structured playbooks to ensure consistency in messaging and strategy across different segments. Notion is an excellent platform for creating and maintaining these playbooks. Teams can use interconnected databases and templates to organize best practices, messaging frameworks and outreach strategies. For example, a sales playbook might include a section on value propositions for various industries, a database of email templates for prospecting and a step-by-step guide for nurturing leads. With Notion's real-time collaboration features, these playbooks can be continuously updated as the market evolves or as new insights emerge from campaigns.

Client onboarding and project management

Notion's project management features, such as kanban boards, timeline views and pre-built templates, make it an effective tool for client onboarding and project tracking. Marketing teams can use these features to outline client expectations, timelines, deliverables and workflows, ensuring transparency and alignment from the start. For instance, when onboarding a new B2B client, the marketing team can create a Notion page that includes a project timeline with milestones, a database of deliverables and a space for client feedback. This page can be shared with the client, fostering collaboration and keeping all stakeholders on the same page.

Event planning and lead tracking

For B2B marketing events such as webinars, trade shows and conferences, Notion provides a centralized platform to manage logistics, track invite lists and document follow-up strategies. Using its table and database features, teams can create detailed event plans that include timelines, budgets and assigned responsibilities. For example, a team organizing a webinar can use Notion to track registration numbers, manage speaker schedules and document post-event strategies for nurturing leads. By linking event plans to a lead-tracking database, teams can ensure seamless follow-up, making it easier to convert attendees into prospects or clients.

PUT INTO PRACTICE: CHOOSING THE RIGHT AI-BASED KNOWLEDGE MANAGEMENT TOOL

The following are some steps one could follow in selecting an AI-based knowledge management tool.

Step 1: Evaluate your organization's needs

Understanding specific requirements is the first step. Different organizations have unique needs based on their size, industry and type of knowledge being managed. For example, a large enterprise may need to handle a vast volume of documents, while a small startup might focus more on collaboration and innovation.

Step 2: AI KM feature assessment

A robust AI knowledge management (KM) tool should offer essential features such as seamless integration with existing systems and advanced search capabilities. These tools allow companies to efficiently capture and manage large volumes of data.

Step 3: Review ease of roll-out and adoption

It's crucial to choose a knowledge management solution that is user-friendly and has a short learning curve (Rimol, 2021). AI-powered tools should provide intuitive navigation and clear workflows to encourage widespread use. Guru is an AI-powered knowledge management tool that is designed to be easy to use, integrating directly into everyday workflows with features like browser extensions and Slack integration to ensure high user adoption.

FIGURE 16.2 Choosing the right AI based knowledge management tool

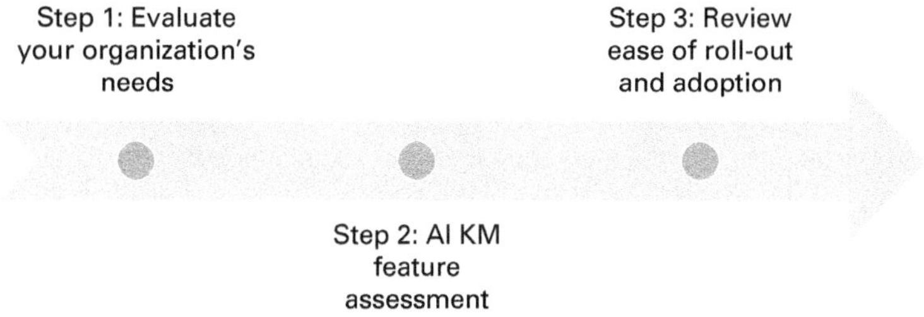

Limitations or considerations

While AI tools are great for adding value and go a long way in improving marketing productivity they are not without limitations; for example, AI systems often struggle to grasp the nuanced context behind the data they analyse. They may misinterpret subtleties in customer sentiment or market trends, leading to oversimplified conclusions. For instance, an AI tool monitoring competitors might flag a new product launch as a significant threat without recognizing that the product targets a different customer segment altogether. This lack of contextual understanding underscores the necessity of human oversight to interpret AI-generated insights correctly.

Other limitations might be inability to integrate AI tools into existing systems and workflows. Many organizations, particularly small and medium-sized enterprises, lack the infrastructure or technical expertise to implement AI solutions effectively. Additionally, employees may struggle to adapt to these technologies, limiting their use.

Finally, through using AI, marketing teams may become over reliant on the automation capability of AI tools. While AI excels at generating insights, it cannot replicate the strategic decision-making and creativity that human marketers bring to the table. In B2B marketing, for instance, a nuanced understanding of interpersonal relationships and buyer motivations often goes beyond what AI tools can analyse, emphasizing the importance of maintaining a balance between AI automation and human involvement.

IN PRACTICE: CONFLUENCE

Atlassian Confluence is an invaluable tool for marketing teams looking to streamline workflows, organize information and foster effective collaboration. Here are some scenarios that demonstrate how Confluence can be applied in real-world marketing situations.

Scenario 1: Note taking

Let's take the scenario of a marketing manager taking quick, disorganized notes during a brainstorming session for a product launch campaign. The notes, though full of valuable ideas, lack structure, making it difficult for the team to act on them. Using Confluence, the manager can upload the raw notes, and Confluence's AI-powered features will automatically organize the content into clear headers, bullet points and sections. Key points such as campaign goals, target audiences and action items can be identified and categorized, with tasks and follow-ups assigned to specific team members. For instance, a jumbled note like 'Talked about influencers... need someone to research. Maybe Rachel? Also discussed launch timing... late Feb seems good. Budget TBD' is transformed into a clean, actionable summary:

- Campaign platform: TikTok Influencers, with
- Action item: Rachel to research suitable influencers.
- Launch timing: Late February; and
- Budget: Pending discussion with finance.

Scenario 2: Repository for content

Another scenario is with a content marketing team struggling with scattered resources, such as SEO best practices, brand tone guidelines and social media strategies, spread across emails, Slack messages and spreadsheets. Confluence serves as a centralized repository where all this information can be stored, updated and accessed by the team. The team could create a 'Content Marketing Hub' with dedicated pages for resources like SEO Best Practices, outlining checklists for meta descriptions and linking strategies, and a Brand Tone and Style Guide, detailing voice, tone and approved vocabulary. Confluence's AI ensures that all team members access the latest version of these documents and flags outdated materials for archiving. Furthermore, the centralized hub can be shared with other departments, such as product or design teams, ensuring cross-functional alignment and consistency.

Internal communication translation

AI translation tools are increasingly useful for translating internal marketing communication within global organizations. These tools can facilitate smoother communication between teams that speak different languages, ensuring that marketing strategies, updates and materials are consistent (Table 16.1).

Microsoft Teams, when paired with its AI Translator, provides real-time translation during video meetings. This feature allows marketing teams from different regions to collaborate effectively by ensuring all participants understand key points in their native languages. Another tool is the Google Cloud Translation API, which enables instant translation of global marketing campaign briefs into multiple languages, maintaining the context and intent of the original content.

For internal newsletters targeting multilingual teams, DeepL Translator is an example of a tool which accurately converts newsletters into various languages, ensuring key updates and company news are effectively communicated worldwide. Such an AI-enabled translation tool can support marketing teams in translating detailed product launch plans, including specifications and promotional materials, enabling regional teams to receive accurate translations for local execution.

Additionally, for daily internal communication, one can use Google Translate or Microsoft Translator, allowing marketing teams to seamlessly collaborate across regions.

Internal communication improvement

AI tools can significantly enhance the tone and sentiment of internal marketing communication, ensuring that messages resonate effectively with employees. By utilizing natural language processing (NLP) and machine learning, these tools can analyse and optimize the tone of communication, helping organizations foster a positive work environment and improve employee engagement.

One use is in internal newsletters. Before sending out newsletters, companies can use tone optimization tools such as Grammarly to ensure that the

TABLE 16.1 AI translation

<table>
<tr><th>Internal communication scenario</th><th>AI translation feature</th><th>AI tool</th></tr>
<tr><td>Marketing strategy meetings across global teams</td><td>Real-time translation during video meetings</td><td rowspan="5">Microsoft Teams with AI Translator
Google Cloud Translation API
DeepL Translator
Amazon Translate
Slack with Gengo Translation Plugin</td></tr>
<tr><td>Translating global marketing campaign briefs</td><td>Automatic document translation in multiple languages</td></tr>
<tr><td>Internal marketing newsletters for multilingual teams</td><td>AI-based translation for emails and newsletters</td></tr>
<tr><td>Translating product launch plans</td><td>Instant translation of complex documents such as product descriptions</td></tr>
<tr><td>Cross-region marketing collaboration tools</td><td>AI-powered translation integrated into team collaboration platforms</td></tr>
</table>

language used is engaging and aligns with company culture.[2] This ensures that the content is relatable to employees, thereby enhancing its effectiveness and encouraging higher engagement levels.

> PUT INTO PRACTICE
>
> Grammarly's tone detection feature provides real-time feedback on the tone of your content, ensuring it matches your company's communication style. Whether your tone is formal, casual, friendly or authoritative, Grammarly analyses your writing and offers suggestions to maintain consistency.
>
> How one uses the tone detection features:
>
> 1 Draft your content, such as emails, blog posts or proposals, in Grammarly.
> 2 Grammarly will indicate whether your tone is confident, neutral or formal based on your word choices.
> 3 Adjust tone to reflect your company's voice by following Grammarly's suggestions.

Analysing meeting summaries and notes is another valuable use case. After meetings, organizations can employ tools like MonkeyLearn to analyse meeting notes for sentiment. This analysis provides insights into the overall mood expressed during discussions, helping identify any underlying issues or sentiments that may need to be addressed, thus improving team dynamics and communication.

When drafting important company announcements, AI tools can play a crucial role in tone optimization. By assessing and adjusting the tone of the messages, organizations can ensure that their communications are motivating and supportive, rather than neutral or negative. This can enhance employee morale and foster a sense of community within the organization. With internal marketing announcements of communication one can use tools like ProWritingAid to ensure the tone is positive and encouraging; this tone optimization in turn can create a more positive experience for internal teams or between teams.

In addition to these use cases, AI tools can also be applied in various other internal marketing communication scenarios. For instance, during crisis communication, sentiment analysis can help gauge employee reactions and adjust messaging to be more reassuring and supportive. In onboarding processes, AI can optimize the tone of communication to ensure new employees feel welcomed and integrated into the company culture.

Task review through visual aids

AI tools with visualization capabilities are invaluable for marketers aiming to visually organize, track, and manage activities and projects. These tools enable teams to create dynamic visual representations of tasks, timelines and progress, improving coordination and productivity in B2B marketing scenarios.

Visualizing schedules and timelines

One can create collaborative to-do lists, Kanban boards and timelines with the help of AI for task management and reminders. AI also suggests project structures and content outlines, helping teams map and prioritize tasks based on urgency or dependencies. An example of a tool and scenario is Taskade where it can be used to manage a product launch, with different team members visualizing and tracking tasks across content creation, social media scheduling and press outreach.

Figure 16.3 shows different types of visuals which can be supported by visualizing tools.

Trello with Butler (AI-powered automation)

Trello's AI-powered Butler feature allows marketers to automate repetitive tasks, create visual project boards and organize tasks by priority or due date. An example scenario where this could be used is a B2B marketing team at a logistics company that uses Trello to manage a lead-generation campaign with automated reminders for each stage of the buyer journey, triggered when leads move through different phases in the sales pipeline.

Automated data visualization with AI

AI-powered data visualization is transforming how B2B marketers analyse, interpret and act on data. These tools enhance decision-making and drive targeted strategies. Below, we can explore different areas and tools of AI-enabled data visualization.

Unifying data to create comprehensive view

Google's Looker Studio generates cloud-based data visualizations, consolidating information from CRM, email campaigns and social media analytics

FIGURE 16.3 Visualization of information

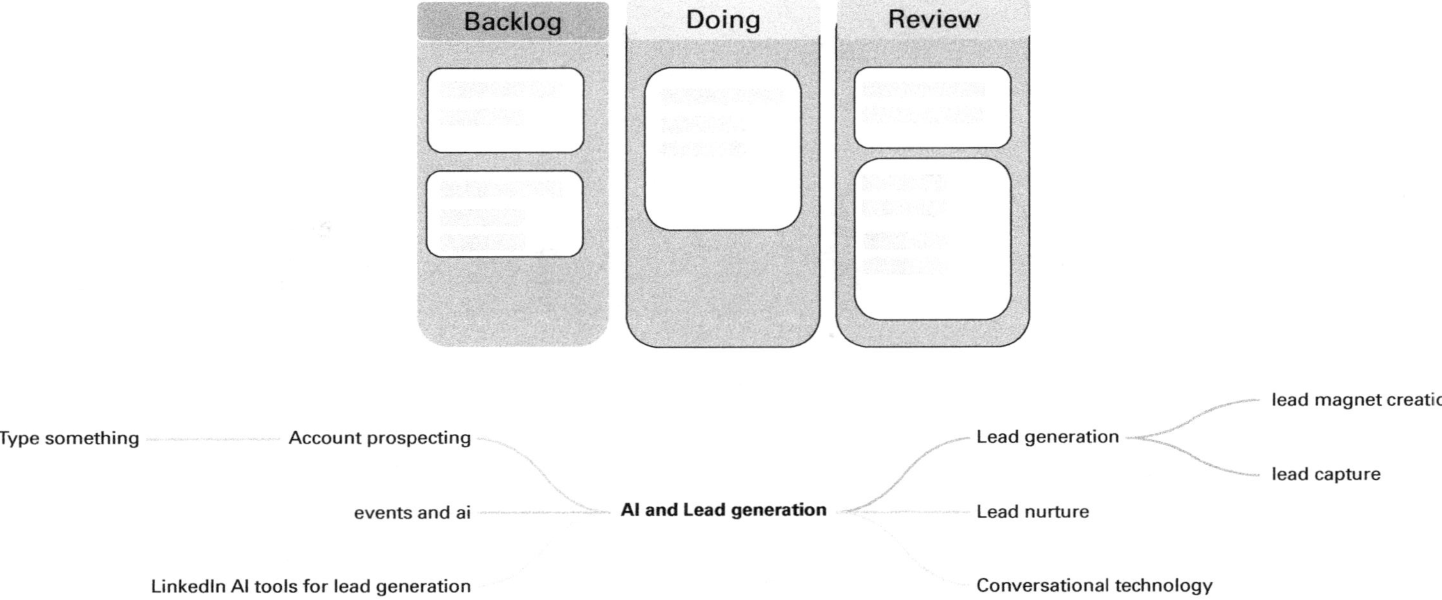

into a unified dashboard. This could be useful in the example of a B2B financial services firm needing to target high-net-worth clients; here they may use Looker Studio to visualize campaign metrics across platforms and to identify yields of personalized email campaigns.

No-code automation for quick insights

Akkio allows users to upload datasets and specify goals, providing automated visualizations without needing a data science team. This could be interesting in the case of a B2B manufacturing company that wants to upload regional sales data to Akkio, to highlight sales performance by region or market, and they can then subsequently use such information to tailor campaigns to focus on high-growth areas.

Quick queries and insights, e.g. AnswerRocket

By using the platform's natural language querying capability, the team asked, 'Which product categories had the highest growth last quarter?' AnswerRocket quickly analysed their sales data and provided a visual representation of the top-performing categories. This insight allowed the provider to focus their marketing campaigns on high-growth product segments, ensuring better resource allocation and improved ROI. The use of AnswerRocket not only saved time but also empowered the team to make informed decisions without requiring advanced data analytics expertise.

When choosing an AI data visualization tool, factors like ease of use, data source integration, customization options and collaboration features are essential. For B2B marketers, these tools' ability to combine multiple data sources, automate visualizations and facilitate cross-functional collaboration are key to making informed decisions quickly.

AI-driven data visualization is unique because it can process and analyse vast data volumes at high speed, identifying trends and anomalies with a depth not possible in traditional visualization tools. By integrating machine learning these platforms can automatically choose the best visualization forms, such as graphs or heat maps, based on data type and trends.

Proofreading with AI

AI-powered tools are also now being used more in the area of proofreading and copywriting, enabling marketers to produce polished, error-free content quickly and efficiently. The following are some examples and situations where copywriting and proofreading are used in B2B marketing.

In proofreading, tools like Grammarly and Trinka simplify error detection while improving tone and clarity. Grammarly's advanced AI identifies complex grammar issues, enhances readability and ensures a professional tone across diverse materials. For example, a B2B SaaS company can use Grammarly to refine its website copy, making technical jargon more accessible to potential customers.

Trinka, on the other hand, is tailored for technical and formal writing, making it an excellent choice for industries such as technology, healthcare and finance. A B2B healthcare firm could use Trinka to proofread research content, ensuring precision and adherence to industry standards. Both tools empower marketers to produce polished and professional materials with minimal effort.

These AI tools are indispensable for maintaining efficiency and consistency in B2B marketing. They help ensure a cohesive brand voice across platforms, languages and markets while automating labour-intensive tasks like proofreading and translation. For example, a B2B logistics firm managing a multilingual ad campaign could use Grammarly for copy refinement, Smartcat for translation and Jasper AI for creative ideation. This integrated approach ensures high-quality, localized messaging while saving time and resources.

REAL-WORLD EXAMPLE

Tokenizz use of Fireflies

Tokenizz, a blockchain company specializing in asset tokenization, faced significant challenges in managing its global marketing team. Operating across various languages and time zones, the team encountered barriers in communication, inefficiencies in capturing and leveraging customer feedback and difficulties in tracking action items effectively. These obstacles hampered collaboration, reduced productivity and limited the ability to create targeted marketing strategies.

To address these issues, Tokenizz adopted Fireflies.ai, an AI-driven meeting assistant that transcribes, summarizes and analyses conversations. Fireflies' multilingual transcription capabilities allowed the team to overcome language barriers by accurately documenting and summarizing discussions in 69+ languages. This ensured clarity and cohesion across diverse team members. Additionally, the tool's automated action tracking feature helped streamline workflows by assigning and monitoring tasks, which improved accountability within the team. Fireflies also enabled Tokenizz to repurpose customer feedback into marketing materials, including testimonials and soundbites, enhancing campaign personalization and effectiveness. Furthermore, its integration with CRM systems eliminated the need for manual data entry, ensuring meeting insights were readily available for strategic decision-making.

The implementation of Fireflies.ai led to noticeable improvements. Collaboration across regions became more seamless, reducing delays and enhancing workflow efficiency. The team's ability to derive actionable insights from customer discussions improved campaign success rates by aligning strategies with customer expectations. Automation saved time, allowing the team to focus on creative and strategic priorities. Lastly, Fireflies' analytics capabilities provided valuable data for refining marketing approaches, fostering a culture of continuous improvement and data-driven decision-making.

Overall, Fireflies.ai transformed Tokenizz's marketing operations by addressing key challenges and enabling the team to achieve higher levels of efficiency and effectiveness. This case demonstrates how leveraging AI tools can optimize business workflows and deliver measurable results.

References

1 Oca, A, Panikkar, R, Sampat, C and Brown, T (2024) Harnessing the power of AI in distribution operations, McKinsey & Company, www.mckinsey.com/industries/industrials-and-electronics/our-insights/distribution-blog/harnessing-the-power-of-ai-in-distribution-operations (archived at https://perma.cc/9UXZ-CCL3)

2 Grammarly (n.d.) Tone detector by Grammarly, www.grammarly.com/tone (archived at https://perma.cc/5KQ8-LPHQ)

Further reading

blog.hubspot.com (n.d.) I tried 10 AI project management tools to see if they're worth it (results & recommendations), https://blog.hubspot.com/marketing/ai-project-management (archived at https://perma.cc/9QPU-4BDQ)

Jarrahi, MH, Askay, D, Eshraghi, A and Smith, P (2022) Artificial intelligence and knowledge management: A partnership between human and AI, *Business Horizons*, 66(1), 87–99. doi:https://doi.org/10.1016/j.bushor.2022.03.002 (archived at https://perma.cc/V5Y7-LT4E)

Knowmax (2021) AI knowledge management for effortless customer support knowmax.ai/blog/ai-knowledge-management/ (archived at https://perma.cc/34J9-QPM9)

Neha Motaiah (2025). Revolutionizing project management: How AI powers smarter workflows, proqsmart.com/blog/revolutionizing-project-management-how-ai-powers-smarter-workflows/ (archived at https://perma.cc/F2HN-4CTJ)

17

Technology planning

> What you will gain from this chapter
>
> Understanding of the following:
>
> - setting objectives
> - how to prioritize use cases
> - understand how to research AI technology
> - learn about securing buy-in for roll-out
> - what to consider when rolling-out AI solutions

Introduction

In this chapter, we'll delve into the essential process of planning for AI technologies in the context of B2B marketing. This involves understanding how to approach AI adoption strategically, categorizing tools based on specific marketing needs and ultimately selecting the right tools for your business objectives.

As highlighted throughout this book, the landscape of AI-powered marketing tools is both vast and rapidly expanding. These AI tools include tools for content creation, data analysis, personalization, customer engagement, lead generation and much more. This number includes tools for content creation, data analysis, personalization, customer engagement, lead generation and much more.

For B2B marketers, this abundance can be both a blessing and a challenge. While the options allow for specialization and customization, the sheer variety can make it difficult to identify the tools that align with your organization's goals. A systematic framework for planning, categorizing and selecting AI tools is essential to cut through the noise and make informed decisions.

The process

To select the right AI tools for B2B marketing we can use the following process, as shown in Figure 17.1.

Step 1: Objectives, use case and prioritization.

Step 2: Assess current in-house marketing technologies.

Step 4: Test and integrate AI tool.

Step 5: Secure buy-in for roll-out.

Step 6: Roll-out and scale

We'll now go into detail on each of these steps.

Step 1: Objectives, use case and prioritization

As part of this step, we'll look at the key areas of objective identification, use cases and prioritization.

Objective identification

One way to identify objectives for AI technologies is to understand current marketing challenges or pain points; we can call these starting points. Below we can see starting points based on AI's impact or starting points based on goals and objectives.

FIGURE 17.1 Selecting technology

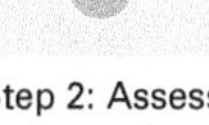
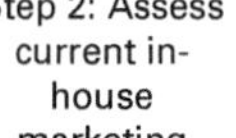
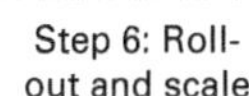

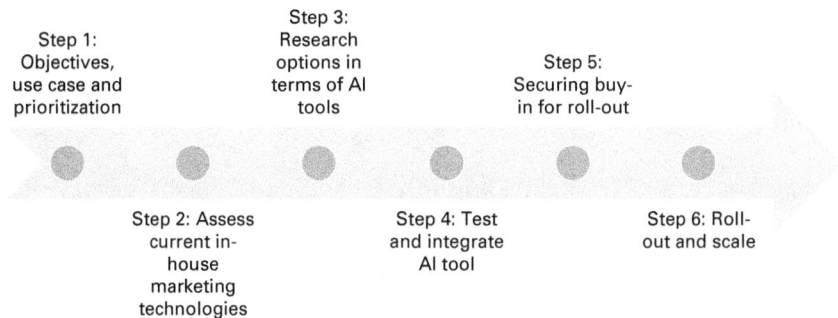

1. MAIN BENEFITS AND IMPACTS AS A BASIS FOR AI TECHNOLOGY PLANNING

One can start by identifying the key areas where AI can make a significant impact. This could be enhancing customer engagement, improving campaign ROI or streamlining operations.

In considering the main impact we can look at where the main challenges and pain points are; for example, data overload might be a pain point which makes insights and interpretation challenging. Marketers often have access to massive amounts of data from various sources (CRM, website analytics, email campaigns, etc.), but extracting actionable insights from this data can be overwhelming and complex. Other pain points are in the need to create content or optimizing but where there are bottlenecks in physically and practically doing this.

2. GOALS AND OBJECTIVES AS A BASIS

We can also use the starting point of main AI goals and objectives to identify AI tools and technologies; for example, for lead generation, AI systems such as lead scoring tools and predictive analytics focus on identifying high-quality leads by analysing customer behaviour and intent.

Prioritizing use cases

As we've seen from the above there are a lot of possible use cases in marketing so it may be challenging to prioritize the use case; one way to prioritize use cases is by ranking goals or objectives for the business or marketing, but that approach may be a bit broad.

See below two possible methods which may serve better for prioritizing AI use cases.

1. BUSINESS VALUE VS FEASIBILITY MATRIX

This simple framework helps prioritize use cases based on their business impact and technical feasibility (see Figure 17.2):

Business value	Feasibility
High	Easy to implement
Low	Hard to implement

- **High value, high feasibility:** Prioritize these use cases first. They provide immediate business value and are technically easy to implement.
- **High value, low feasibility:** These should be considered for future projects. High impact, but require significant time, resources or data.

FIGURE 17.2 Business value vs feasibility matrix

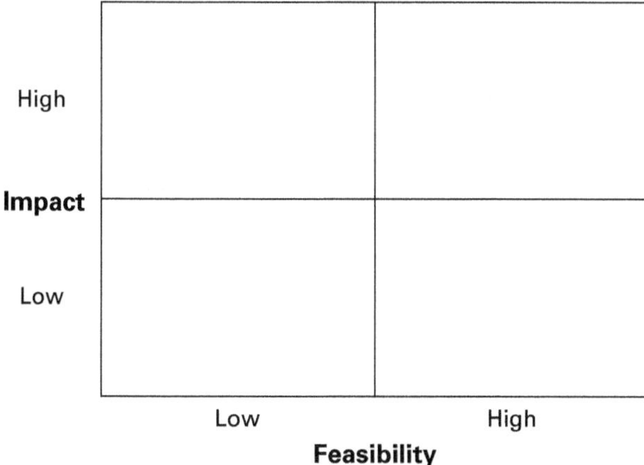

- **Low value, high feasibility:** These can be implemented if resources allow, but they won't deliver significant business outcomes.
- **Low value, low feasibility:** De-prioritize or discard these use cases as they will not provide enough value to justify the effort.

2. ICE SCORING METHOD (IMPACT, CONFIDENCE, EASE)

The **ICE score** is used to evaluate AI use cases based on three dimensions: **Impact, Confidence** and **Ease.** Each dimension is scored on a scale (e.g. 1–10), and the total score is used to rank and prioritize use cases (see Table 17.1).

- **Impact:** How much value will this AI use case generate for the business?
- **Confidence:** How confident are you that this use case will be successful based on available data and resources?
- **Ease:** How easy is it to implement the use case in terms of technical complexity, cost and time?

TABLE 17.1 ICE score

Use case	Impact (1–10)	Confidence (1–10)	Ease (1–10)	ICE score
Predictive lead scoring	9	8	7	24
Chatbots for lead engagement	7	9	6	22
Content creation automation	8	7	9	24

PUT INTO PRACTICE: ICE

One example is where a B2B marketing department is considering AI-powered content creation tools like Jasper AI, they might rate its Impact as high due to the potential for generating personalized, high-quality copy at scale. Confidence could also score well based on the tool's proven effectiveness in optimizing ad copy and email campaigns, while Ease might vary depending on the team's familiarity with generative AI.

Similarly, applying ICE scoring to AI-driven analytics platforms such as Tableau or Sisense could involve evaluating their ability to centralize and visualize complex data from multiple sources. A B2B marketing team might assign high Impact scores for these tools if they enable better campaign performance analysis and more informed decision-making. Confidence could hinge on user feedback or the tools' reputations in the market, while Ease might reflect considerations like integration requirements with existing CRM systems. By leveraging ICE scoring, B2B marketers can strategically prioritize AI technologies that align with their goals, balancing potential benefits with practical implementation challenges.

In Table 17.1 you can find a summary of scores for different B2B marketing contexts in terms of technology evaluation.

Step 2: Assess current in-house technologies

In this stage of the process we need to do two things; understand what is available already and what the gaps we have are in terms of technology needs. We'll use the above prioritization to work through the main use cases and areas of AI.

Revisit prioritized AI use cases

We probably want to start by revisiting AI use cases from the Introduction to ensure they align closely with overarching business goals (e.g. improving lead generation, increasing customer retention). One method we can use is a balanced scorecard to understand how AI use cases connect with the top business objectives.

Audit

After this we should put together an inventory of existing technologies and tools; this might include CRM tools, marketing automation technology, content management systems, content creation technologies and data analytics platforms.

Assess current capabilities against AI use cases

Before trying out and then buying AI tools one should review current technologies in terms of their capabilities in conducting or fulfilling tasks. It may be the case that features and functionalities are underused, e.g. where a CRM or marketing automation software is only used in terms of 20 per cent of its possibilities or features can be unlocked to perform better certain tasks. This step should be done for each AI use case.

For this area one could use capability mapping to evaluate whether current tools support the AI-driven processes needed for each use case (e.g. automated lead scoring, customer segmentation, personalization).

Identify technology gaps

Identify where the current technology falls short in enabling AI use cases. Such gaps may exist in data availability, system integration, automation capabilities or AI-readiness.

Gaps might be as follows (see Figure 17.3):

- Data gaps: Is there sufficient data (quality and volume) to train AI models?
- Automation gaps: Are existing systems capable of supporting automation (e.g. real-time decision-making)?
- Integration gaps: Can AI tools integrate with the current systems (APIs, data compatibility)?
- Scalability gaps: Are existing tools scalable enough to handle AI workloads?

FIGURE 17.3 Technology gap check

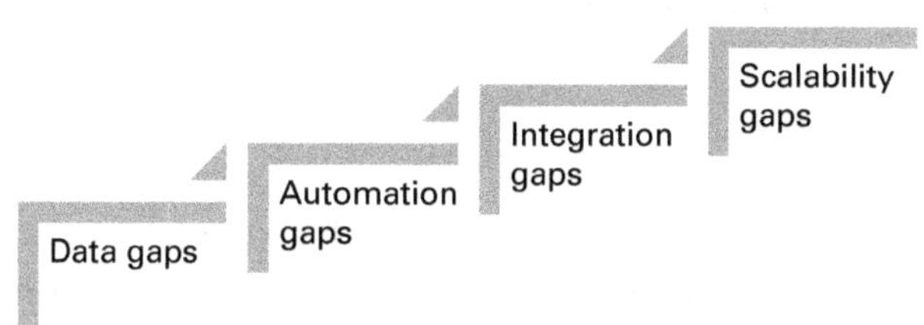

THIS STEP IS ABOUT THE ACTUAL GAP ANALYSIS.

To carry this out one could use a simple table like Table 17.2 to highlight use cases, current tool and capability gap. This is a gap analysis matrix.

TABLE 17.2 Capability gap table

AI use case	Current Tool	Capability	Gap
Predictive lead scoring	CRM (e.g. Salesforce)	Partial (basic scoring)	Lack of AI-driven scoring
Personalized email campaigns	Email marketing tool	Full	No gap
Churn prediction	Customer support tool	None	Requires AI-based churn models

Some examples of where existing technology is not fully used which may overlap with AI tools are as follows:

1 Customer relationship management (CRM) systems: Many businesses utilize CRM systems primarily for contact management and sales tracking, yet they often overlook advanced features like predictive analytics, lead scoring and automated follow-ups. This underutilization frequently occurs due to a number of factors, e.g. unaware of features, lack of training.
2 Marketing automation platforms: Many businesses are unaware of or fail to use powerful features such as A/B testing, advanced segmentation and dynamic content creation.

Step 3: Research AI tools

Step 3 is about researching AI technologies; for B2B marketers there are a variety of options for exploring and evaluating AI marketing tools. Here are examples of such online resources:

Online websites and directories

Online websites and directories serve as invaluable resources for marketers seeking to evaluate, compare and select the right tools for their needs. These platforms provide features such as user-generated reviews, detailed product comparisons and filtering options to help businesses make informed decisions. Below, we explore the key features and functions of leading websites and directories and highlight how they can support marketers.

1. G2 CROWD: COMPREHENSIVE SOFTWARE REVIEWS AND COMPARISONS

G2 Crowd is a robust platform that offers user-generated reviews and comparisons for a wide range of software tools, including AI marketing solutions. Its standout feature is its ability to rank tools based on authentic user feedback, allowing marketers to see how various tools perform in real-world applications. Marketers can filter tools by industry, feature set and customer ratings to find solutions tailored to their needs.

2. CAPTERRA: DETAILED INFORMATION AND FILTERING CAPABILITIES

Capterra is another popular directory that excels in offering detailed product descriptions, feature breakdowns and user reviews. One of its key features is the ability to filter tools based on specific criteria, such as pricing, deployment type (cloud-based or on-premises) and user ratings.

3. TRUSTPILOT: REVIEWS BEYOND SOFTWARE

While Trustpilot is primarily known as a review site for businesses, it also hosts reviews for software tools, including marketing solutions. The platform's emphasis on transparency makes it a reliable source for understanding user experiences. Marketers can browse reviews for tools they're considering and get a sense of customer satisfaction, ease of use and support quality.

Other online websites and directories include Software Advice and GetApp.

Community forums and social platforms for insights

In addition to websites and directories, community forums and social platforms provide marketers with real-world insights and practical advice. These platforms are excellent for engaging with peers, asking questions and staying updated on industry trends. Examples include Reddit and Quora.

Common criteria for evaluating AI tools

We can use AI tools to evaluate or to come up with ideas to evaluate AI tools in addition to the review website and community forums mentioned earlier.

Let's use the example of AI-based lead scoring tools. A typical set of criteria might be ease of use, scalability, integration, accuracy and customization. We can see an example of how an evaluation table might look by asking ChatGPT to provide a table based on this criterion.

Step 4: Test and roll-out

The importance of testing AI technologies in B2B marketing

Before fully integrating AI technologies into B2B marketing workflows, rigorous testing is essential to ensure these tools align with business goals and deliver tangible benefits. Testing allows marketers to evaluate whether AI solutions such as predictive analytics platforms, generative AI for content creation or chatbot automation meet specific performance benchmarks.

Ensuring seamless integration with existing systems

A critical aspect of integrating AI technologies into B2B marketing workflows is ensuring compatibility with existing tools and platforms. AI solutions must integrate seamlessly with CRM systems, marketing automation software and data analytics platforms to avoid workflow disruptions. For instance, a B2B financial services firm implementing an AI-powered chatbot for lead qualification would need to ensure the tool syncs with its salesforce CRM to provide a unified view of customer interactions. Proper integration allows businesses to leverage AI-generated insights across departments, improving collaboration and decision-making.

We can use the above criteria to come up with a simple table and evaluate each on a low to high scale.

Step 5: Securing buy-in for roll-out

This step is about securing buy-buy in for rolling out the AI technology. One key question to consider is which stakeholders do we want to secure buy-in from and what does secure buy in mean in practice?

To identify stakeholders, we should look at stakeholders from a marketing perspective of using and implementing AI tools for marketing. We can categorize stakeholders by looking at two main areas.

- One: Their level of interest in using and rolling out AI. Which stakeholders would be interested in the use and roll-out of AI tools? There would be high interest from marketers, and there will be particular marketers that will be more interested depending on the type of AI tool. Outside of marketing there might be an interest from IT in terms of the technology stack which needs to be maintained and audited, and managed on an ongoing basis.
- Two: The other area to consider is power or influence. When we look at power we can look at different types of power, such as referent power, which is based on position in the organization, and information power which relates to knowledge of the technology. If we generally think of power as influence to help with the use and roll-out we can revert to referent power more so we're looking at those that can derail or stop efforts or positively help more.

Internal stakeholders

Internal stakeholders encompass a variety of teams and individuals, each bringing unique concerns and objectives to the table. Executive leadership, for example, focuses on the strategic alignment of the AI technology with the organization's overall goals and vision. The executive leadership team are particularly concerned with how the AI initiative will drive growth, improve efficiency or provide a competitive advantage. IT teams, on the other hand, are deeply involved in assessing the technical feasibility of the implementation, ensuring that the technology integrates smoothly into the existing infrastructure while meeting scalability and maintenance requirements. Sales teams may evaluate how the technology can help in automating lead generation, personalizing outreach or providing better insights into customer behaviour. Product teams, meanwhile, may look at the potential for AI to innovate the product roadmap or enable new functionalities that resonate with customer needs.

External stakeholders

External stakeholders include partners, clients and any third parties who may be impacted by the adoption of AI technology. For external partners, ease of integration is a top priority. They will want to ensure that the AI technology can seamlessly connect with their systems and processes without creating unnecessary friction or requiring significant reconfiguration on their end. Transparency around how the technology operates and how data is exchanged can alleviate concerns about disruption or incompatibility. For clients, data privacy is often a major concern, especially if the AI technology involves the collection, storage or analysis of sensitive customer information.

Group stakeholders by interest

Here we look at what is of particular interest per stakeholder grouping. For example, executives care about ROI, scalability and strategic advantage; marketing teams focus on efficiency, personalization and insights; sales teams need assurances about how the AI will improve client relationships. IT and compliance will prioritize data security and regulatory compliance.

PLOTTING THE POWER INTEREST GRID

Let's take the example of a marketing team wanting to secure the purchase of a CDP platform which incorporates all the latest AI features to support full database integration, as well as providing a richer set of insights for an account and its decision-making unit.

Stakeholders can be categorized into four quadrants based on their level of power and interest: high power, high interest; high power, low interest; low power, high interest; and low power, low interest. Below is a breakdown of potential stakeholders and their viewpoints for each category.

- High-power, high-interest stakeholders are those with significant influence and a vested interest in the success of the CDP implementation. Executive leadership, such as the chief marketing officer or chief data officer, is focused on how the platform aligns with the company's strategic goals, such as driving growth, improving customer experience and delivering measurable ROI.
- High-power, low-interest stakeholders are influential in the decision-making process but may not be directly involved in the platform's day-to-day usage. For example, the finance team, including the CFO, is primarily interested in the financial feasibility of the CDP. They focus on the cost structure, total cost of ownership (TCO) and projected ROI, rather than its technical or functional features.
- Low-power, high-interest stakeholders are those who may not have decision-making authority but are deeply interested in the CDP's impact on their daily workflows. Marketing analysts and campaign managers, for

instance, are enthusiastic about the potential of AI-powered features to improve segmentation, automate campaign execution and provide actionable customer insights.

- Low-power, low-interest stakeholders are individuals whose roles are less directly affected by the implementation of the CDP and who may not have much influence over the decision. For instance, customer support teams may benefit indirectly from the improved customer insights provided by the platform but are unlikely to have a strong opinion on the decision itself.

FIGURE 17.4 Stakeholder mapping

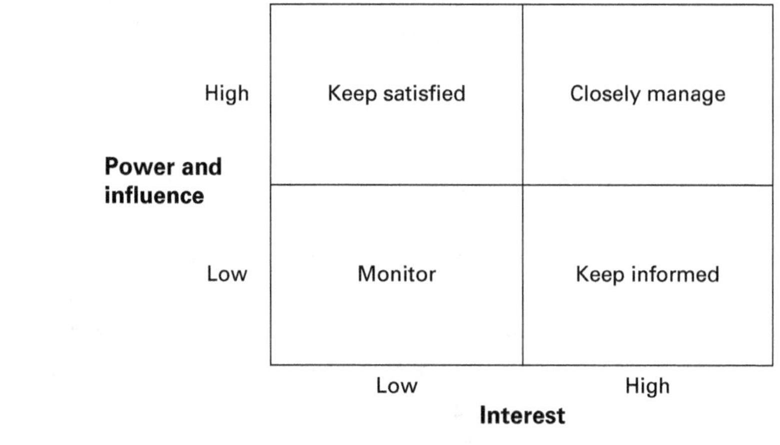

Communicating with stakeholders

So, we've plotted the stakeholders to understand where to start in terms of engaging stakeholders; we now need to communicate with them and present our arguments. One model we can use is known as ADKAR Change Management Model (Awareness, Desire, Knowledge, Ability, Reinforcement): The acronym is as follows:[1]

a. Awareness: Clearly explain why the AI is needed and what gaps it fills.
b. Desire: Show benefits for the organization and specific stakeholders to spark interest.
c. Knowledge: Share details of how the AI will work and how it impacts each team.

d. Ability: Provide training and resources to ensure smooth implementation.
e. Reinforcement: Implement tracking and feedback mechanisms to confirm successful adoption.

PUT INTO PRACTICE: APPLYING THE POWER INTEREST SCENARIO

The following shows how the power interest scenario might look for each element of ADKAR applied to high power, high interest stakeholders.

Awareness: For high-power, high-interest stakeholders like executive leadership, IT leaders and marketing leadership, the marketing team must clearly articulate the strategic importance of the CDP and how it aligns with broader business goals, such as improving marketing efficiency and driving customer insights.

Desire: High-power, high-interest stakeholders will desire the CDP if they see its potential to improve strategic decision-making and enhance customer relationships.

Knowledge: Knowledge involves equipping stakeholders with the information they need to understand how the CDP works and how it will be implemented. High-power, high-interest stakeholders need in-depth knowledge about the technical integration process, AI capabilities, security measures and how the CDP will contribute to long-term business goals.

Ability: Ability refers to the capability of stakeholders to implement the change effectively. High-power, high-interest stakeholders such as marketing leadership and IT teams will need to ensure that their teams are trained on the CDP's features and functionality.

Reinforcement: Reinforcement ensures that the change is sustained over time. For high-power, high-interest stakeholders, reinforcement may involve regular reporting on the CDP's performance, such as ROI metrics and customer insights, to show that it continues to meet business objectives.

Step 6: Roll-out

As part of rolling out AI tools and technologies we can look at the main areas of defining responsibilities and accountabilities, providing relevant training and support, monitoring early-stage use, ensuring we are looking at impact of AI tools and ensuring we communicate those results and ROI.

Defining responsibilities and accountabilities

Clearly defining who is responsible and accountable for each part of the rollout ensures clarity, reduces overlap and prevents bottlenecks. This clarity is especially important in AI projects, which often involve cross-functional collaboration between departments such as marketing, IT, compliance and data analytics.

Methods and frameworks

One method we could use is the RACI model which stands for Responsible, Accountable, Consulted, Informed (Learning Loop). This model is ideal for assigning roles, as it helps to define who will handle each aspect of the project, who holds decision-making authority and who needs to be consulted or informed.

PROCESS

The typical process for using this tool is as follows.

- **Step 1:** List all tasks associated with the AI rollout.
- **Step 2:** Assign each task to the appropriate person or team as per the RACI model.
- **Step 3:** Regularly review and update responsibilities to reflect changes in the project scope or team dynamics.

Training and support

Since AI adoption often involves a learning curve, ensuring adequate training and support is essential for effective and confident use of the tools. Training should be role-specific, focusing on how different functions (e.g. marketing, IT, sales) can leverage the AI to meet their unique needs. A mix of live training sessions, self-paced online modules and hands-on workshops enables flexibility and ensures users with different learning preferences and paces are accommodated. Enablers for this area might be providing online training, demos, having easy to use documentation.

PROCESS

- Step 1: Conduct a skills assessment to identify gaps and tailor the training programme accordingly.

- Step 2: Develop a comprehensive training plan that includes introductory sessions, role-specific modules and troubleshooting workshops.
- Step 3: Provide ongoing support through a help desk or dedicated IT support, and maintain resources like FAQs, user guides and video tutorials.

Monitoring early-stage use

Monitoring the AI tool during its initial stages allows the team to identify and address issues promptly. This phase is critical for gathering early feedback, understanding how the AI is being used and ensuring that it integrates well into existing workflows.

Approaches one could use in this monitoring stage might be identifying KPIs such as tool usage rates, user satisfaction scores and task completion times will provide a structured way to evaluate early-stage performance.

Assessing the impact of AI tools

Understanding the impact of the AI rollout goes beyond usage metrics; it should encompass both direct and indirect effects on business outcomes, operational efficiency and user satisfaction. This assessment should also look at whether the tool has achieved its intended objectives and aligned with broader strategic goals.

To assess impact, one could use the balanced scorecard framework which assesses impact across multiple dimensions – financial, customer, internal process and learning/growth – to provide a holistic view of the AI tool's effectiveness. See Figure 17.4, for example, regarding how to assess impact for two different AI tools.

Other ways to assess impact might be to conduct an ROI analysis and look at a before and after in terms of impact on the area of marketing or business which relates to the cost investment.

Budgeting for AI

When budgeting and drafting a financial business case for AI marketing tools, one should consider direct and indirect costs.

Direct costs of AI tool

For direct costs we can discuss the actual software and licensing costs themselves; but one should consider the following questions.

1. Does the company offer different options in terms of software pricing, if yes – would the cheaper version be enough?
2. Do higher-priced versions support more than the user – in which case does it work out cheaper to buy a group licence or company licence?
3. Does everyone need a licence or just one person or a few people?
4. Consider whether the tool allows for flexible scaling. If the initial rollout proves successful, it may require a higher-tier subscription or additional licenses for expanded use.

Indirect costs

Indirect costs may relate to integration, training, ongoing maintenance, data privacy reviews, etc. Incorporating AI tools into a broader tech ecosystem may require data integration services or additional software, which can involve specialized development resources or third-party vendor support. Integration costs vary depending on the complexity of existing systems and the compatibility of the AI tools.

Introducing AI tools may require training; though it probably should be said that any AI tool for marketing teams which require in-depth training might not be the right tool. We should expect that AI tools are intuitive and easy to use in most cases; however, there are exceptions, e.g. sophisticated generated AI, mid- to high-tier predictive analytics tools; in this case if the marketing team needs additional data scientists, AI specialists or engineers to manage and optimize the tools, salary and onboarding costs should be factored into the budget. Alternatively, the cost of upskilling existing team members through courses or certifications should be considered.

Reference

1 Olmstead, L (2019) ADKAR model: What is it and how to use it?, 21 November, whatfix.com/blog/adkar-model-what-is-it-and-how-to-use-it/ (archived at https://perma.cc/7A56-GG73)

Further reading

LinkedIn (n.d.) Evaluating AI in marketing: The four metrics that matter in assessing impact, www.linkedin.com/pulse/evaluating-ai-marketing-four-metrics-matter-assessing-natalie-lambert/ (archived at https://perma.cc/62CW-FDXM)

INDEX

Note: Page numbers in *italics* refer to figures or tables.

More from Kogan Page

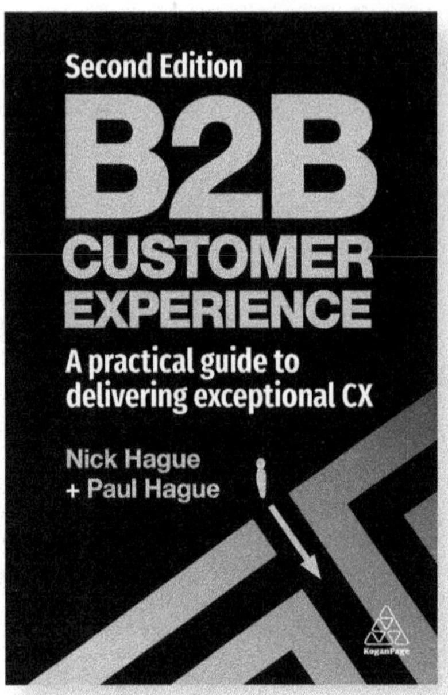

ISBN: 9781398608511

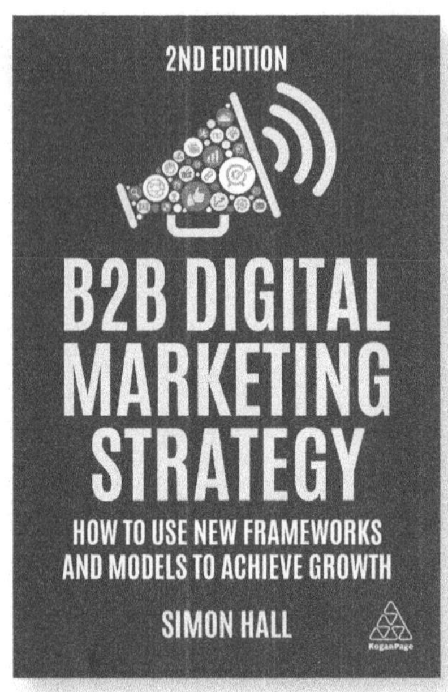

ISBN: 9781398610170

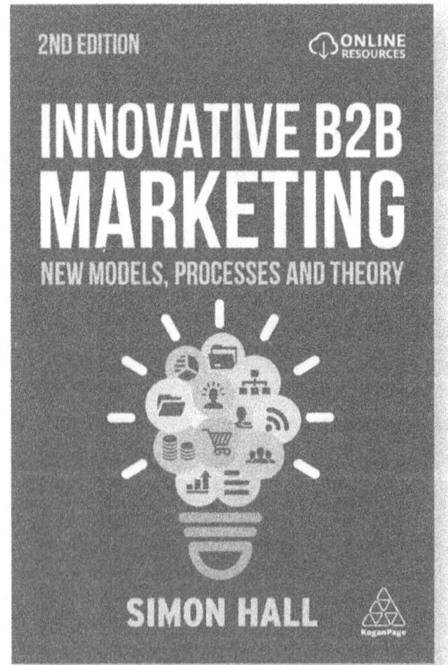

ISBN: 9781398604766

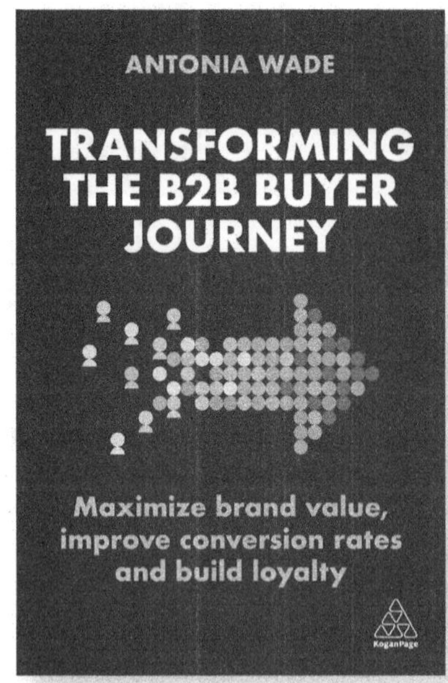

ISBN: 9781398606807